THE STRATEGIC DEVELOPMENT
OF CREDIT UNIONS

THE STRATEGIC DEVELOPMENT OF CREDIT UNIONS

Charles Ferguson and Donal McKillop

John Wiley & Sons
Chichester • New York • Weinheim • Brisbane • Singapore • Toronto

Baffins Lane, Chichester,
West Sussex PO19 1UD, England
National   01243 779777
International (+44) 1243 779777
e-mail (for orders and customer service enquiries): cs-books@wiley.co.uk
Visit our Home Page on http://www.wiley.co.uk
or http://www.wiley.com

Other Wiley Editorial Offices

John Wiley & Sons, Inc., 605 Third Avenue,
New York, NY 10158-0012, USA

VCH Verlagsgesellschaft MbH,
Pappellalee 3, D-69469, Weinheim, Germany

Jacaranda Wiley Ltd, 33 Park Road, Milton,
Queensland 4064, Australia

John Wiley & Sons (Asia) Pte Ltd, 2 Clementi Loop #02–01,
Jin Xing Distripark, Singapore 129809

John Wiley & Sons (Canada) Ltd, 22 Worcester Road,
Rexdale, Ontario M9W 1L1, Canada

Library of Congress Cataloging-in-Publication Data
Ferguson, Charles
    The strategic development of credit unions / Charles Ferguson and
    Donal McKillop.
        p.   cm.
    Includes bibliographical references and index.
    ISBN 0-471-96912-5
    1. Credit unions—History.   2. Credit unions—Great Britain.
    I. Ferguson, Charles, 1951- . II. Title.
    HG2035.M36   1997
    334'.22'09—dc21   96–40879
                                            CIP

British Library Cataloguing in Publication Data

A catalogue record for this book is available from the British Library

ISBN 0-471-96912-5

Typeset in 10/12 Times from the author's disks by MCS Ltd, Salisbury
Printed and bound in Great Britain by Biddles Ltd, Guildford and Kings Lynn
This book is printed on acid-free paper responsibly manufactured from sustainable forestation,
for which at least two trees are planted for each one used for paper production.

To our wives and children,
Joan, Michael, Kate, Conall and Jamie,
Janice, Ciara, Barry and Michael.

Contents

Foreword

Had I done nothing else in my life other than be involved, as I was, in the foundation of the Credit Union Movement in my city and country I would be a very happy person. It is the greatest, most widespread and successful co-operative movement in the history of my country and provides enormous benefits and social security to our members, most of whom are from working-class backgrounds. I certainly hope this book will lead to the continued growth and expansion of the Credit Union Movement and its benefits.

This book conveys far more that its title suggests, underlining social dimensions as well as the economic principles and models involved. Its appraisal of the different types of Credit Unions in different countries and economies make it not just a thorough study but a powerful testimony to a self-help movement inspired by hard-nosed idealism.

The examination, explanation and exploration contained in this book offer not just intellectual enlightenment but practical encouragement.

John Hume
Member of the Westminister Parliament
for Foyle and
Member of the European Parliament
for Northern Ireland
President Credit Union League
of Ireland 1964–1968

Preface

The original vision of credit unions developed by the nineteenth century founding fathers of the credit union movement has proved to be enduring and compelling. Established as a worldwide movement, credit unions are important social and economic institutions that have been in the vanguard of promoting co-operative, self-help principles. The distinctive philosophy of credit unions, and their purpose as enabling organisations that allow people to better control their financial destinies, marks them out from 'for-profit' organisations. In the late twentieth century, credit unions are in greater demand than ever, and their prospects going into the twenty-first century are assured, given the pressing need of communities and individuals, particularly those who are disadvantaged, to have access to savings and credit facilities.

Credit unions throughout the world share a core value system, although the historical and cultural contexts of particular countries will affect how they have developed. Economic context also plays a significant role; hence the credit union movement encompasses the sophisticated credit union industries in the United States, Canada and Australia, which enjoy both large membership and asset wealth, and infant industries in other parts of the world, such as Eastern Europe and Africa, where credit unions face developmental challenges. The dynamics of different environments and how credit unions respond and adapt, particularly in maintaining the relevance of their co-operative and democratic traditions to ever-changing social and economic needs, is an issue that makes credit unions interesting objects of study.

Credit unions, particularly those found in the more mature credit union industries, have reached a defining stage in their history as the forces of financial services deregulation and competition become stronger. The power of the credit union vision may be challenged because of this. However, credit unions have proved to be enduring in the past and represent a co-operative success story. In the future, their vision and values should ensure that they continue to be a success story.

Our text aims to be of value to members of the worldwide credit union movement, to students within this industry, and to others within the financial services sector interested in tracking recent developments. Much of the information and data contained in this text will also be of direct relevance to researchers in the field of credit union development. As far as possible, we have attempted to make this text user-friendly and suitable for a wide readership.

Needless to say, the opinions herein expressed and any errors are entirely our own.

Charles Ferguson
Donal McKillop

Acknowledgements

As part of the background work for this text, discussions were held with a selection of individuals from within the credit union movement. Particularly helpful were representatives from: the World Council of Credit Unions, Wisconsin; the Filene Research Institute, Madison, Wisconsin; the National Association of Federal Credit Unions, Washington; the Scottish League of Credit Unions; the Association of British Credit Unions; the National Federation of Credit Unions; the National Consumer Council; the Registry of Friendly Societies in both London and Belfast; plus a host of UK-based credit unions too numerous to mention.

The final version of this text benefited greatly from helpful comments by our colleagues. On this count, however, we owe a special debt of gratitude to Alex Sibbald at the Department of Management in the University of Otago, New Zealand.

Finally, for his invaluable research assistance, we owe much thanks to Gary O'Rourke.

1

Introduction

It has been described as the largest socioeconomic movement in the world, for it has nearly 600 million individual members. According to membership statistics of the International Co-operative Alliance (ICA), which actually understate the movement's size as they exclude non-affiliated organisations, there were 674,967 co-operative societies in the world in 1988, and more than 500,000 of them were in developing countries. They are active in every type of economy and in almost all sectors (Thordarson, 1990).

A defining feature of this enormous movement—besides its diversity—is its rate of change. As we approach the twenty-first century, co-operatives of all types throughout the world are undergoing a period of significant challenge brought about by dynamic and ever-changing economic and social environments. In keeping with other organisations seeking to survive and prosper, co-operative organisations are required constantly to adapt their values and operations to suit new demands. Therefore, co-operatives are, because of changing economic and social environments, in a constant state of development. Given the diversity of the co-operative movement, mapping this continual development is not that easy, since it will vary, not only between different kinds of co-operative, but also between different sectors and between different countries.

Co-operatives encompass a wide variety of species. There are, of course, almost endless variants of consumer co-operatives where people group together to buy goods and services, for example housing, healthcare, groceries and childcare. The other main types of co-operative found throughout the world might be classified simply as producer co-operatives, worker co-operatives and multi-stakeholder co-operatives. Producer co-operatives, as the name suggests, exist where groups of producers come together to market their goods and services, for example, farmers and craftspeople. Worker co-operatives, again, can be interpreted literally, in this case where the members own an enterprise that gives them employment. Where members form more than one type of co-operative and different types of co-operative overlap, this creates a multi-stakeholder co-operative. For example, members of producer co-operatives frequently also form consumer co-operatives to buy the materials they need for their work or to provide themselves with financial and other services.

It is important to understand credit union distinctiveness in terms of their co-operative credentials. The International Co-operative Alliance (ICA)—which represents the worldwide co-operative movement—identifies the character-istics of genuine co-operatives in terms of several attributes. Open membership and democratic control are considered defining features of a co-operative. Equally, limited return on share capital and profits belonging to members are also indispensable defining features. The role of education, so that members can exercise real control of their co-operative, is similarly essential to co-operative identity. Finally, commitment to co-operation between co-operatives at local, national and international levels is further seen as an essential ingredient of a true co-operative identity. Credit unions, the focus of this book, conform to the co-operative principles endorsed by the ICA and subscribe to the underlying values contained in these principles and fit the ICA's designa-tion of a co-operative organisation.

This book takes as its focus the credit union, which is one important and distinctive type of consumer co-operative. Members of a credit union group together to create an organisation dedicated to providing them access to a savings and loans facility. Diversity within the credit union movement is also significant, and the basis upon which members can group together in terms of a credit union common bond varies. With a wide geographical spread spanning all types of societies, diversity within the credit union movement is perhaps inevitable. The universal appeal of credit unions is, however, a major hallmark and, in the century or so that they have existed, their appeal to a wide variety of groups throughout the world has mushroomed. Worldwide, credit unions now have over 90 million members and the trend is that they should continue to grow. Without question, credit unions can be seen as a co-operative success story.

The origins of the credit union movement lie in the self-help ideals that blossomed in nineteenth-century Europe. It can be argued that, if anything, the need for a voluntary self-help organisation is, in fact, greater in the late twentieth century, and that we are now in the midst of an 'associational revolution', which is taking the form of a global growth in the 'third sector'. This 'third sector' is a massive array of self-governing, private organisations not dedicated to distributing profits to shareholders or directors, who pursue public purposes outside the formal apparatus of the state. The rise in this 'third sector' arises from a distinct set of social and technological changes, as well as a diminishing reliance on the role of governments to provide for all the needs of their citizens. In the developing countries especially, the significance of 'third-sector', grass-roots, voluntary organisations in helping to create sustainable development is of fundamental importance.

Mapping out the historical origins of the unique economic and social philosophy that has governed the growth of credit unions from the nineteenth century to the present day is an early objective in our consideration of the strategic development of credit unions. Key historical episodes from nineteenth-century Germany, Britain and other European countries provide an appreciation of the origins of the credit union movement. It should go without saying that consideration of the determining values that governed their establishment is very important to an understanding of present-day credit unions. Given the dominant position of US credit unions in the worldwide credit union movement, an historical appreciation is also given of the early twentieth-century development of credit unions in North America. At the risk of falling into a reductionist approach to history, the role of many of the key historical founding figures of the movement is highlighted and their role in helping to diffuse the credit union ideal to other parts of the world is acknowledged.

This historical appreciation is not, however, meant to be purely descriptive of key events. It is important to draw from this historical appreciation the fundamental and distinctive organisational features of credit unions. The fundamental attributes of 'co-operativeness' have already been alluded to, as these are an integral component of the distinctive organisational identity of credit unions. But, as already pointed out, credit unions are also unique financial institutions in that, as consumer co-operatives, they are generally limited to serving the market for consumer credit and saving. At the centre of all credit union identity lies the concept of a common bond, which is, in effect, the legitimisation of the relationship between members that allows them to join together in a member-controlled, self-help credit union. The existence of a common bond as the organisational basis of credit unions has been seen by many commentators as a strength of credit unions; equally it has also been seen as an Achilles' heel. Actual definitions of a common bond—and whether this is defined tightly or loosely—depends to a large extent on the nature of social, political, and economic environments, and also, crucially, on the particular legislation governing the operation of credit unions. The main types of common bond are community, occupational and associational. Particular credit union types therefore exist with characteristics that reflect the nature of their common bond.

If credit unions are essentially self-help savings and loans organisations dedicated to serving the needs of their members, then the actual economic operation of credit unions is an important area that deserves scrutiny. The historical concept of a credit union stresses the importance of co-operative values and the mutual economic interests of members. The assumption is that mutual self-help prevails over self-interest. Credit unions have, though, a potential for a degree of membership conflict, and it is possible for a credit union to be either saver- or borrower-biased. A credit union can also occupy a neutral stance between savers and borrowers, which is the ideal form of credit union economic behaviour. Debating this issue in the early part of the book adds to an appreciation of the distinctiveness of the organisational identity of credit unions. Much later, this issue of the potential for membership bias is revisited in the later in-depth investigation of the UK credit union industry. Here, actual behaviour of different credit union types is exhaustively tested through the detailed empirical examination of the incidence of membership bias that is found to exist.

A FRAMEWORK FOR ANALYSING CREDIT UNION INDUSTRIES

Although the focus of this book is on one subset of the co-operative movement, dealing with the worldwide credit union movement still remains an ambitious project. Credit unions are in a constant state of development, and the dynamic flux of their environments—particularly in the sophisticated financial services markets of the industrialised countries—plays a major role in their continued evolution, so that credit unions are not static phenomena. As one would expect, there is great diversity within the credit union movement worldwide, which is a reflection of the varied economic, historic and cultural contexts within which credit unions now operate. In terms of a framework for analysing the credit union movement worldwide, this book divides the movement into three distinct industry types; that is, mature, transition, and nascent industries. These industry types also carry an assumption about three distinct growth stages in the evolution of a credit union industry, although whether, in practice, all credit union industries would automatically follow such a unilinear development path is, of course, not guaranteed. Also, such a three-stage categorisation does not mean that any simple claim can be made about the homogeneity of particular industries, since there will be wide variations in the characteristics of particular credit unions; for example, in terms of asset size, operational practice and business philosophy. Our industry framework simply aims to add explanatory value to the discussion of the strategic development of credit unions and can be regarded as an 'ideal-type' model. The typology of mature, transition and nascent industries is explained in full detail in Chapter 2; although, in simple definitional terms, the evolutionary element of this typology is apparent in the words used to describe the different industry types. We use the credit union industries in the United States, Canada and Australia as examples of mature industries; the United Kingdom as the main example of a transition industry (although some emphasis is also placed on Ireland and New Zealand); and Central and Eastern Europe and Africa as examples of areas where nascent industries are to be found.

There is more than an implication in this book that the mature US and Canadian industries hold out a demonstration effect, particularly for transition industries. The deregulated and competitive financial services markets in North America have forced credit unions to be innovative and adaptive to match the financial sophistication of their mainstream financial services competitors.

Focusing mainly on the US industry, detailed attention is, therefore, devoted to determining precisely what are the defining attributes of this mature industry. Our analysis of the US industry considers major changes in the industry environment, particularly during the past few decades, to highlight the changing nature of US credit unions.

The perspective applied to the US industry suggests that credit unions in a mature industry are relatively more business orientated where, for instance, products and services are based on market rate structures and where emphasis is increasingly placed upon the economic viability and long-term sustainability of credit unions. The US industry has undergone restructuring during the past few decades in terms of a more concentrated industry structure, which involved a reduction in the number of credit unions yet a steady rise in membership. Enjoying the services of progressive trade organisations and well-developed central services in the form, for example, of corporate credit unions, the US credit union industry demonstrates a sophisticated industry support framework. Equally, there is an evident professionalisation in respect of the management and operation of credit unions, with less reliance upon volunteer aspects. A major hallmark in terms of its classification as a mature industry is the extent to which deregulation has impacted on the nature of the US industry. Here, the major effect has been on formulations of the common bond and the associated fields-of-membership concept, where both have undergone a loosening in their definition, which allows a more permissive interpretation of the activities and membership basis of credit unions. This explains the diversification of products and services that US credit unions have engaged in, and also helps to explain the sustained membership growth enjoyed by the US industry. A final deciding factor in classifying the US industry as a mature industry is the obvious one relating to asset size. As a $347 billion industry, it should be differentiated from the much smaller asset sized industries to be found in transition and nascent industries. We also place emphasis in our analysis of the US industry on the role of an economic determinism created by the growth in credit union assets, which, we believe, helps to create a momentum for a more business-orientated approach to credit union affairs.

Most of the emphasis in our consideration of transition credit union industries is placed upon the UK industry. A detailed case study of the UK credit union industry therefore forms a substantial part of the content of this book. For comparative purposes, reference is also made to New Zealand and Ireland as examples of transition credit union industries. The UK industry is a young, vibrant, and high-growth one, which we use as a test-bed for our assumptions about the development path implicit in our development typology. In other words, the UK industry provides a useful case study against which to test the notion that the US experience provides a broad demonstration for the future development of this transition industry. Additionally, the UK industry is a good test-bed for scrutinising the earlier findings of US research on such important issues as, for instance, economies of scale and membership bias. US research by far dominates the research work undertaken on credit unions, so that the level and amount of detailed empirical research conducted on the UK industry hopefully adds to the research base on credit unions by providing new material for an industry other than the United States, which can complement previous research work.

In the UK transition industry, shifts in the regulatory framework governing credit unions are beginning to emerge, with adjustments to the common bond being prominent in this reform process. Not only can a weakening of reliance on voluntarism be expected, but there is also a strong emphasis on growth and efficiency within the UK industry, plus a desire to see greater scope for product diversification. There is also an overwhelming need for the creation of central services and support mechanisms in the form of an identifiable credit union system in the United Kingdom, and its current absence is perhaps a hallmark of the status of the UK industry as a transition credit union industry. Whilst relative to nascent industries the asset base of the UK transition industry is large, there is still a huge gulf in its asset base when compared with the mature US and Canadian industries.

Our focus on mature and transition industries reflects a concern to examine the evolution and operation of credit unions in the context of well-established financial services markets. Earlier, the significance of co-operatives to the developing countries of the world was highlighted, and credit unions have a major role to play in helping to create sustainable development through the mobilisation of the power of self-help in such countries. Equally, the reform of centrally controlled economies in Central and Eastern Europe has brought into sharp relief the potential role of credit unions as significant instruments of economic and social change there. Serving the poorer and weaker sections of society, and a high commitment to traditional self-help ideals, is a strong feature of nascent industries. In this instance, emphasis is on winning recognition for credit unions and establishing an appropriate statutory framework, and the operation of credit unions in this context is in terms of a tight common bond with a single savings and loans product. Nascent industries often require sponsorship from the wider credit union movement in order to take root. The credit union movement, through the auspices of the World Council of Credit Unions (WOCCU) is active in promoting nascent credit union industries throughout the world, particularly in Africa, Asia, Central and South America, and Central and Eastern Europe. WOCCU is not, however, the only source of international assistance given by the credit union movement. Assistance is also given directly by individual credit union industries, often in collaboration with government programmes. Thus, Australia, Canada (both English- and French-speaking), France, Germany, Korea and the United States are all active in providing international assistance.

Since our perspective is such a broad one, it should be recognised that the framework for examining different credit union industries cannot mask the importance of variations in historically- and culturally-specific factors. When we deal with particular industries, such historical and cultural dimensions are, in fact, invariably discussed. Notwithstanding its obvious limitations, our typology of credit union industries can nevertheless serve as a useful vehicle for discussing such a large and diverse movement. In using a development typology, our intention is to make it easier for readers to appreciate the key dynamics operating within the credit union movement. Discussing the future strategic development of credit unions is an ongoing fact of life within the credit union movement, and the analysis contained in this book is meant to help inform that debate by providing, as far as possible, an objective appraisal of the operational dynamics involved in different credit union industries.

CONTENTS OVERVIEW

The rationale for this book, and the broad methodological approach taken, hopefully makes clear that, in considering segments of the credit union movement as industries, we are employing a perspective that emphasises not only historical and ideological aspects, but that also focuses upon hard economic performance data whenever possible. We are interested in the development of credit union industries as such and, in particular, have a special interest in the UK credit union industry.

An indication of the content of the early chapters of the book has, by default, already been given. Thus, the historical, ideological and developmental aspects of credit unions are important foundation issues dealt with in Chapter 2. Here, important definitional issues are examined and, as already indicated, the detail of our development typology is mapped out. The substance of Chapter 3 relates to an examination of the credit union industry in the United States in order to see how it matches the attributes of a mature industry determined by our typology. The Canadian industry also figures in this chapter but in much less depth, and is used mainly as a broad comparator to the US industry. Since we believe that the US industry holds out lessons for transition industries, we are anxious to determine what these lessons might be. How the US industry has adapted to a deregulated, competitive environment; how it has increased its membership base; how it has used new definitions of common bond and fields of membership; how its deposit insurance scheme works; how it is regulated; how its central support mechanisms work; how its trade organisations operate; and many more questions are relevant to credit union industries elsewhere, particularly transition industries heading increasingly into deregulated, competitive environments. In dealing with such questions, we do not adopt a didactic approach, but aim to provide an appraisal of the US industry, particularly over the past few decades, that is focused upon the key forces and events that have shaped this industry. In undertaking such an appraisal, we attempt to highlight major issues that are of universal interest to all credit unions.

Six chapters of this book, from Chapter 4 through to Chapter 10, are dedicated to an in-depth analysis of the UK credit union industry. Chapter 4 documents the legislative and structural framework within which UK credit unions operate. Salient trends within the industry are identified and the role and position of the various credit union trade bodies are examined. This chapter aims to provide a broad overview that serves as a backdrop to the more specialist treatment provided in subsequent chapters dealing with the UK industry. One point should be made with regard to the in-depth analysis of the UK industry contained in these chapters, and this relates to the statistical analysis that is utilised. The UK industry is of such a size that it is possible to have confidence in the statistical findings. By utilising data for 597 credit unions over the period 1991 to 1994, the analysis of the UK industry is founded upon, we believe, solid empirical evidence. Conducting such a rigorous case study of the US industry, given the size of this industry, would, of course, have been difficult, if not impossible, given the research resources this would have required.

The subject matter of Chapter 5 is targeted at considering the economic viability of, and the quality of the services on offer from, UK credit unions. The method employed in this chapter is to examine the income and expenditure accounts of three credit unions which are at different stages of development— one recently formed, the other 10 years in operation and the third over 30 years in existence. 'Economic viability' is a concept that does not have a universally agreed definition and, therefore, a wide range of measures are examined in respect of these credit unions. In terms of examining the quality of service that UK credit unions provide for their members, this is conducted in terms of price; in other words, the dividend and loan rates that are applied to members. Equally, emphasis is placed upon assessing the risk profile of these particular credit unions and a number of financial ratios are utilised for this part of the analysis. This chapter empirically tests the hypothesis that, as credit unions become more economically viable, they are in a position to offer a better quality service in a lower risk environment. Given its subject matter, this chapter offers insights into the strengths and weaknesses of the UK industry.

The purpose of Chapter 6 is to examine the UK industry in terms of its operational efficiency, which entails testing for economies of scale in particular. While the industry in aggregate is considered, the position of subgroupings of credit unions according to trade organisation affiliation is also analysed. This trade grouping perspective is important, given the differences that exist towards growth between, on the one hand, the National Federation of Credit Unions (NFCU), and, on the other, the Association of British Credit

Unions (ABCUL) and the Irish League of Credit Unions (ILCU). The primary focus of the NFCU is on community development, self-help and small units. While the NFCU encourages its credit unions to become economically viable, it nevertheless prefers them not to exceed a few hundred members. Expansion, where it occurs, should be in the development of new credit unions. ABCUL and the ILCU, in contrast, are in favour of individual credit unions achieving significant critical mass, which is supposed to result in the generation of business efficiency and scale economies. For a sizeable component of the UK industry, growth and the achievement of scale efficiency is, therefore, an issue of considerable importance.

The issue of economies of scale can be considered of more importance to credit unions than to other forms of financial institution. There is some existing US evidence that the potential for conflict between borrowers and savers may be exacerbated as the credit union increases in size. Given the unique nature of credit unions, testing for the existence or otherwise of membership bias in the UK industry is a matter fully explored in Chapter 7. In particular, this chapter considers whether the regulatory environment leads to a biased allocation of the benefits of membership, and an estimation is made of the likely effect of regulatory changes on the issue of membership bias.

Chapter 8 takes as its focus growth and development within community- and employer-based credit unions. Community credit unions dominate the UK industry, and this chapter examines, in particular, the future potential for growth through an increase in employer-based credit unions. In keeping with the approach adopted elsewhere, both community- and employer-based credit unions are subjected to hard comparative economic analysis in terms of their key performance measures. Again, a case study methodology is employed in this chapter, where two recently formed credit unions, one community-based and the other employer-based, are studied in terms of the factors instrumental in their growth. In particular, the initiatives that they have pursued to promote themselves, and the obstacles that they have faced in their formative period, are examined. The prospects of both of these types of credit union are then assessed in the light of anticipated legislative changes and the shift in the United Kingdom towards a more permissive concept of the common bond.

The analysis made of the UK industry in earlier chapters supports the case for an upward revision of the deposit and borrowing ceilings and a liberalisation of the common bond. Such changes would, in all probability, entail moves towards greater product diversification. In these circumstances, where the UK industry is seeking enhanced flexibility and freedoms, with obvious implications for its risk profile, the absence of a depositor/shareholder protection scheme is a matter of some concern. Chapter 9, therefore, examines the design of an optimal deposit insurance mechanism for the UK industry. The potential for moral hazard, where the existence of a deposit insurance scheme might induce greater risk-taking, is examined against the backdrop of US experience where a Federal Deposit Insurance Scheme has been in existence since 1970. This chapter arrives at some detailed suggestions concerning the shape of a deposit insurance scheme for the UK industry, and how it might be implemented.

The purpose of the remaining chapter on the UK industry, Chapter 10, is to synthesise the previous chapters by offering a commentary on the future prospects of the UK industry. The vision for the future of the UK industry is an optimistic one. The economic climate in the United Kingdom, coupled with recent changes in the composition of the financial services sector, offer conditions that are advantageous for significant and pronounced expansion by UK credit unions. The demutualisation of UK building societies, in particular, offers credit unions the opportunity of filling the gap left by the demise of mutual building societies. This chapter also revisits the question of regulatory reform and the implications of various regulatory changes on the future shape of the UK industry. Similarly, consideration is also given to the need to strengthen the industry's own support mechanisms, which are offered by the various trade organisations.

The position of credit unions in developing countries and in the former Soviet bloc countries forms the basis of Chapter 11. The nascent credit union industries found in these countries are qualitatively different from the industries previously examined, and this chapter explores the main attributes of such nascent industries. The platform for the discussion of nascent industries takes the form of case studies relating to the Ukraine and Poland. Consideration is also given to the issues of establishing a credit union industry in Africa, with selective reference being made to particular countries. As previously indicated, the role of the wider credit union movement in providing assistance is a crucial aspect, and this chapter considers in detail the approach taken by WOCCU with discussion of its model credit union development guidelines. This chapter also reinforces the *caveat* stated earlier that historical and cultural factors make any unilinear development for credit unions in nascent industries far from automatic.

Drawing together the strands of the previous chapters in the final chapter, Chapter 12, leads to reflection upon the meaning of strategic development. Rightly, the discussion dwells on the central importance of values in determining the future strategic direction of particular credit union industries. This chapter attempts to highlight key debates surrounding credit union values that arise as a result of the wide-ranging appraisal of the different industry types considered. The issue of conflicting values is also omnipresent, and this is mapped against possible scenarios, depending upon which values prevail, for the future of particular credit union industries. The intention in this chapter is to be reflective and to help to stimulate debate.

An objective of this book is to make research on credit unions accessible to as wide an audience as possible. An appreciation of the distinctive philosophy of credit unions is hopefully more likely as a result of locating credit union industries in a context of change and evolution. No one can be certain what the future holds for the credit union movement, but perhaps the material contained in this book will allow a clearer understanding, particularly for those new to credit unions, of the forces at work in particular types of credit union industry.

2

The Historical, Ideological and Developmental Aspects of Credit Unions

INTRODUCTION

Credit unions are co-operative financial institutions that have successfully established themselves throughout the world. In excess of 95 million people in 90 nations now belong to a credit union and, in aggregate terms, the assets of credit unions worldwide are calculated at $418.5 billion (World Council of Credit Unions, 1995). As self-help, democratic institutions, credit unions have demonstrated the efficacy of co-operative principles to the management of their financial affairs for millions of people. The major strength of credit unions lies in the fact that their basic philosophy and objectives have such a universal appeal to a diverse range of people, who see benefit in achieving greater self-sufficiency in the running of their financial affairs. The growth of credit unions during this century can be deemed a success story for mutual principles of economic co-operation.

The future strategic development of credit unions is, however, problematic. Credit unions face a rapidly changing environment in the late twentieth century, where fundamental debate about their purpose and function is thriving. The future role of credit unions is a prominent issue for credit union officers, activists and members, and the broad purpose of this book is to inform the ongoing debate concerning the strategic development of the credit union movement. The credit union movement has traditionally been driven by a strong value system that has determined its operational objectives. Defining and clarifying values is, of course, a prerequisite for any future strategic development process. Thus, the mission of credit unions can never be static and must be subject to refinement, and adjust to new demands and opportunities. Mapping out some of the major demands and opportunities that exist for the credit union movement is an important aspect of the coverage of this book.

In the context of a worldwide movement, it is the case that the strategic development of credit unions does not entirely conform to a single, universal blueprint. Nevertheless, an important aim of this book is to examine the credit union movement in the light of a development typology that might better explain the dynamics of growth and change. Classifying credit unions within such a development typology yields a useful framework for locating the issue of strategic change within the movement worldwide. A development typology is, therefore, a useful heuristic device that allows for an interpretation to be made of what is, in reality, a complex subject.

However, before proceeding further to consider a development typology of credit union industries, it first seems sensible to look at its historical roots. Although a strong emphasis is placed on 'economic determinism' in our later analysis of the strategic development of credit unions, historical dimensions, and the importance of country-specific factors, cannot be ignored. Consequently, the historical origins of the unique economic and social philosophy that has governed the growth of credit unions from the nineteenth century to the present day, needs to be examined. Most organisations are, to an extent, the product of their history and this, as will be shown, is especially the case with credit unions.

Historical material on co-operative initiatives is drawn from nineteenth-century Germany, Britain and other European countries, and the historical development of credit unions in North America is also sketched out. Initially, some consideration needs to be given to definitional issues, and an attempt is made to provide an overview of the unique organisational features and operational principles traditionally associated with credit unions. The opportunity is also taken later in this chapter to reflect upon the effect of a more business-orientated approach to transforming these organisational principles.

DEFINING CO-OPERATIVE ORGANISATIONS

That co-operative ventures such as credit unions have a distinct economic and social philosophy is perhaps an obvious point, although defining the essence of this is not that straightforward. For example, there is no unitary definition of the word co-operative and it can, therefore, mean different things in different contexts. In everyday usage it may mean simply 'working together' or 'ready to help'. When used as a technical term it often has a very precise meaning, where it comprises the legal definition of a particular kind of business organisation. But even when used as the description of a business organisation, the explanatory value of the word is diminished by the sheer range of organisations that can lay claim to the title of co-operative.

One particularly useful definition of co-operative, which manages to highlight the common element in all co-operative enterprises, is provided by Mladentaz (1933), cited in Digby (1960):

> [Co-operatives] are associations of persons, small producers or consumers, who have come together voluntarily to achieve some common purpose by a reciprocal exchange of services through a collective economic enterprise working at their common risk and with resources to which all contribute.

Essentially, co-operative ventures employ a particular rationale that distinguishes both the means and the ends of their business activities. The definition provided by Mladentaz (1933) captures this important defining feature of a co-operative. Credit unions are co-operative organisations based on thrift that are directed at fulfilling human and social needs. They stand in stark contrast to the more dominant form of organisation found in industrial societies that is based on speculative gain of a private or corporate kind.

The impetus for the development of credit unions as co-operative and mutual-aid organisations can be directly traced to the economic and social transformations that took place as a result of the rise of industrialised society. The increased depersonalisation of society, the loss of communal identification and the rise of egoistic economism threatened the traditional social and moral relationships of feudal society. Co-operation of all types can be looked upon as an attempt by farmers, craftsmen and other small producers both to improve their position in a non-feudal, modern industrialised society and also, at the same time, to regain social relations based on a community identity.

EUROPEAN HISTORICAL ROOTS OF CREDIT UNIONS

Coping with the profound economic and social changes created by the Industrial Revolution moved the search for new forms of co-operative enterprise beyond the more ancient forms. Europe in the nineteenth century proved to be fertile ground as various pioneers established their own variant of a co-operative business organisation. Throughout this period, co-operative initiatives were much in evidence and the origins of the modern credit union movement can be traced back to specific ninteenth-century initiatives in co-operative business organisation.

Whilst a number of historical co-operative ventures are recognised as having shaped credit unions as distinctive mutual aid societies, the origins of the modern credit union movement owes much to co-operative pioneers in Germany in the nineteenth century. In particular, two types of loan society emerged that are recognised as being the antecedent of modern-day credit unions; Schulze-Delitzsch, and Raiffeisen credit societies. In the former, the first of which was established in 1850, democratic control by depositors was an important principle and loans were approved by members not on the basis of collateral but rather on the basis of the character of the person borrowing. Loans were made for productive purposes only and members were bound to save on a regular basis in order to add to the capital of the society. An important tenet of such 'people's banks' was the supreme authority of the general meeting where the principle of 'one man, one vote' predominated. Members were encouraged to be active in the running of their societies and emphasis was placed upon educating members in respect of their responsibilities towards them.

Raiffeisen established his first society in 1849. Although Schulze-Delitzsch societies espoused the fundamental principle of self-help, the Raiffeisen model was founded more distinctly on the basis of Christian ethics as the motivation for forming a loan society. Schulze-Delitzsch societies, with their concern for the promotion of economic self-sufficiency, were motivated by more secular desires. The operating ethos of these organisations differed. Raiffeisen societies preferred to restrict membership to mainly urban workers and shopkeepers. Schulze-Delitszch principles stressed the importance of a membership drawn from a large and economically varied area, and attracted mainly members from the farming community. Significantly, Raiffeisen societies adopted a principle that profits were only distributed to investors after a reserve fund was established. Also, it was held that capital was unalienable and, if the society were ever to dissolve, then its capital would be distributed for the benefit of the poor.

Initially, Raiffeisen credit unions grew slowly, but by 1888 there were 425 societies in Germany served by the Rhein Agricultural Union Bank, which had been created by Raiffeisen in 1872 to act as a central banking institution and to oversee and control local societies. By 1882, there were over 3000 Schulze-Delitszch societies in Germany. The foundations of the modern credit union movement are to be found in these German co-operative initiatives where many of the distinctive features of credit union guiding and operating principles were first actively formulated. In other words, the particular rationale that distinguishes both the means and the ends of the business activities of what have come to be known as credit unions is clearly expressed in these nineteenth-century loan societies.

The diffusion of co-operative ideals from Germany to other parts of Europe played an important role in the further development of the credit union movement. In Italy, for instance, there was a direct transference of the ideals of Schulze-Delitszch via Luigi Luzzatti, an Italian scholar who promoted and formed co-operative 'people's banks' on the basis of the developments he had observed whilst in Germany. One fundamental departure from the German models of co-operative institutions was the adoption, by Luzatti's 'people's banks', of limited liability. As these banks increased in number and developed their operational methods, they became all-purpose banking institutions. By

1909, the People's Bank of Milan was one of the largest banking institutions in Italy and served as a model for numerous other banks. Rural banks for farmers were also established in Italy by Leone Wollemborg and by 1913 there were over 2000 such rural banks in existence.

Co-operative institutions flourished in other European countries. Austrians organised their first Schulze-Delitzsch society in 1858 and, by 1913, there were over 3500 Schulze-Delitszch societies. The first Raiffeisen society in Austria was founded in 1886, with the number increasing to nearly 8000 by 1912. At about the same time, experimentation with co-operative societies in France was occurring amongst farmers. Interestingly, Raiffeisen credit societies throughout Europe have evolved in modern times into mutual co-operative banking institutions. In Germany, the Raiffeisenbank and the Volksbank have been unified into one credit co-operative movement. The French rural credit co-operative system divided into Credit Agricole and Credit Mutuel, with a third provider of co-operative credit being the Banques Populaires. In the Netherlands and Belgium, only rural credit co-operative systems exist and these are known, respectively, as Robobank and Cera. In Italy, the Casse rurali ed artigiano directly developed from the German Raiffeisen model, and the Banche populari are the main providers of co-operative credit. It should be noted, therefore, that, by 1994, the rural credit co-operative movement in Europe accounted for about 20% of all bank deposits.

Much of the inspiration for co-operative ideals in the nineteenth century can also be traced to important developments in Great Britain, especially the experiments of Robert Owen at New Lanark and the Rochdale Pioneers formation of a co-operative store in 1884. Motivated by humanitarian concern for the excessive conditions created by the industrial revolution, Robert Owen established model factories at New Lanark where he established self-contained and virtually self-sufficient communities. By agreeing to limit their returns on invested capital and to use whatever profits that might accrue for the benefit of the entire community, the owners at New Lanark engaged in a social experiment that helped to propagate co-operative ideology. The fact that Owen was able to drastically reduce working hours and not employ child labour, yet still make a profit, astounded other mill owners; although it should be noted that the commercial basis for this experiment was founded on cotton at a time when the cotton industry was booming. New Lanark eventually failed but the influence of Owen's experiment proved to be widespread and enduring.

Of even more practical and lasting effect in propagating co-operative ideals was the establishment of the Rochdale Co-operative store in 1844. The group of workers who organised the Rochdale Society of Equitable Pioneers subscribed to shares, payable in small amounts weekly, in order to raise capital to buy goods at less than retail cost and sell them to their members at a saving. Members were paid 5% interest on their shares and were entitled to a proportionate division of the society's savings or surplus at the end of the year.

The Rochdale principles of co-operation included open membership to all; democratic control of the society, with each member having only one vote regardless of the number of shares owned; a limited interest on share capital; and the return to members of the co-operative's surplus in proportion to their patronage. The success of the Rochdale Pioneers subsequently again influenced the co-operative movement in other parts of the world by further defining the distinctive means–ends rationale of a co-operative business enterprise.

The particular characteristics of co-operative developments throughout the world have, of course, been governed by historically specific conditions. These early developments in Germany and Britain did, undoubtedly, have a key influence in shaping co-operative ideology. The co-operative ideals they enshrined spread throughout Europe and, subsequently, by a process of diffusion, to other parts of the world. Adapted to suit the requirements of local conditions and contexts, these early models of co-operative venture helped lay the foundations of what has become a worldwide credit union movement. It is interesting to note that in Britain credit co-operatives of the kind that developed in the rest of Europe failed to take hold; the major indigenous co-operative institutions in the twentieth century have been the Co-operative Bank and the Co-operative Wholesale and Retail Societies. Since weaker sections of society in Britain have been supported by a well-developed trade union movement, perhaps they became, to an extent, a substitute vehicle of self-help. It is the case that the consumer-based, and often rural, credit societies prevalent in Europe simply failed to develop. Britain did develop its own distinctive mutual societies in the form of building societies, although these specialist savings and loans societies were dedicated—at least prior to the 1986 Building Societies Act—almost exclusively to providing mortgages relating to house purchase.

NORTH AMERICAN HISTORICAL ROOTS OF CREDIT UNIONS

Today the credit union movement is at its strongest in North America. It is worth pursuing the historical theme to consider the development of credit unions in the early part of this century when the wave of European immigrants to North America helped diffuse further the principles and benefits of this form of organisation. In nineteenth-century Europe, co-operative loan societies mostly involved producers who were borrowing to buy tools or raw materials that would later produce saleable articles and earn their own cost and the interest on the loan. The development of credit unions in North America in the early twentieth century represents a shift from this tradition. Members were, for the most part, employees, and lending was for provident purposes only (Digby, 1960). Credit unions became a mechanism of anticipating savings and, thereafter, making those savings virtually compulsory by assigning them to the service of a loan. In common with loan societies in Europe, the credit unions established in North America sought to combat the evils of usury not only in the form of moneylenders, but also in a rising tide of credit trading such as hire purchase.

There had been a direct transference of Schulze–Delitszch societies to North America as early as 1864. German craftsmen organised in New York City an organisation known as the Arbeiter-Bund to provide a range of self-help services for its members. However, it was not until the influence of the activist Alphonse Desjardins that credit unions were really to take off in North America. Desjardins organised his first credit union in 1900. The passing of a crucial landmark Credit Union Law in Massachusetts in 1909 owed its existence to the work of Desjardins, along with Pierre Jay, Commissioner of Banks for Massachusetts, and Edward Filene, a wealthy Boston merchant who had been introduced to credit unions while in India. By 1921, three other states had passed similar laws authorising the organisation of credit unions.

In that same year, the Credit Union National Extension Bureau was established. It was financed by Filene, with the aim of securing the adoption by as many states as possible of credit union laws favourable to the further development of credit unions. Within only a few years, 32 states had passed appropriate legislation, and the efforts of the Credit Union National Extension Bureau were then directed at achieving growth in the number of credit unions and the establishment of a federal organisation to promote and supervise their activities. By 1934, the credit union movement in the United States had attained sufficient status to organise the Credit Union National Association (CUNA). A year after its establishment, CUNA created the industry's own Life Insurance Society—CUNA Mutual Insurance Society—as a means of meeting the need for adequate low-cost protection for borrowers.

Whilst, through the efforts of the early pioneers, credit unions were chartered under state laws, the introduction in the United States of a Federal Credit Union Act was achieved in 1934. State-chartered credit unions were regulated by an individual state's department of financial regulation, along with banks and savings and loans societies. Federally chartered credit unions were to be regulated by a separate regulatory body, the National Credit Union Administration (NCUA). Sustained growth and development has occurred in the US industry throughout this century.

The development of credit unions in Canada also originated at the turn of the century through the pioneering work of Alphonse Desjardins. The influential role that he played in the development of US credit unions has already been alluded to. Informed by a knowledge of European experience, plus a desire to prevent the evils of usury afflicting disadvantaged citizens, Desjardins established his first Canadian credit union, La Caisse Populaire de Levis in 1900. In doing so, he made two fundamental departures from European practice; first, he was determined that the dichotomy between urban and rural credit societies should not prevail, and, secondly, he rejected the principle of unlimited liability (Moody and Fite, 1971). The successful growth of credit unions in Canada can be judged by the fact that currently one in three Canadians is a member of a credit union or caisse populaire (Boreham and Bodkin, 1988).

The Canadian industry consists of three elements; local credit unions and caisses populaires, operating under individual provincial laws; central credit unions incorporated under provincial legislation; and two national central organisations, the Credit Union Central of Canada (formerly known as the Canadian Co-operative Society), operating under a charter granted by the Federal government in 1953, and La Caisse Central Desjardins du Quebec, which was set up in 1979 to look after the broad concerns of provincially incorporated caisses populaires.

Credit unions and caisses populaires are evolving into financial supermarkets and have a track record in Canada as innovators in product development. For example, they were the first Canadian financial institutions with extended hours of operation, daily interest accounts, flexible mortgage payment schemes, debit cards, internationally connected automatic teller machines, and other consumer features that have become the norm in financial services. The operation of the US and Canadian credit union industries will be revisited in the following chapter when a more detailed examination of these mature credit union industries is undertaken.

FUNDAMENTAL ORGANISATIONAL FEATURES OF CREDIT UNIONS

Before proceeding to consider a development typology for credit union industries, it is perhaps appropriate to first spell out the fundamental organisational features of credit unions. Credit unions follow distinctive rules of organisation and operation that give expression to those values originally enshrined in Rochdalian principles. The Rochdale rules have led directly to the formulation of current 'Co-operative Principles' adopted in 1966 by the International Co-operative Alliance as the benchmark against which to judge genuine co-operatives, including credit unions. Membership of a credit union is, accordingly, voluntary and open to all within the accepted common bond of association who can make use of its services and are willing to accept the corresponding responsibilities. Membership discrimination of any kind, whether social, racial, sexual, religious or political, is against fundamental 'Co-operative Principles'.

Genuine co-operatives are democratic organisations. Credit union members therefore enjoy equal rights to vote, i.e. 'one member, one vote', and have a right to participate in decision-making, regardless of the amount of their savings or the volume of business undertaken. In credit union support organisations or associations, voting is deemed to be proportional or representational, again in keeping with accepted democratic principles.

Rochdalian principles stressed limited interest payments for the use of capital and in credit unions this is the traditional constitutional case. Surplus monies arising out of its operation belong to the members. The distribution of any surplus may take a number of forms, including allocation among members in proportion to their transactions; the development of common services to benefit all members; or the development of the business of the credit union. A key element is that any surplus should be distributed in a way that avoids one member gaining at another's expense and the distribution mechanism employed should be under the democratic control of the membership.

To fulfil their dual economic and social role, credit unions place emphasis on the importance of education, which again echoes the principles of the Rochdale Pioneers. The economic, social, democratic and mutual self-help principles of credit unions are actively promoted through educational programmes for members, officers and the public in general. Awareness of the wise use of credit, and the rights and responsibilities that go with membership, are the main focus of educational programmes. Such educational investment is made to ensure that members understand the distinctive rationale that distinguishes the means—ends of credit union activities.

Perhaps the most unique characteristic of a co-operative, which strongly distinguishes it from ordinary business organisations, is its subsidiary nature. In other words, there is no profit motive involved in the operation of a credit union. Rather, it exists only to attain the economic and social goals of the people who comprise its membership (Croteau, 1963). How enduring this subsidiary nature can remain under current conditions of development in the United States and other mature credit union industries is a theme explored in later chapters.

THE IMPORTANCE OF THE COMMON BOND

Credit unions are unique financial institutions in that they are consumer co-operatives and are limited to serving the market for consumer credit and saving. A credit union can be thought of as a 'purchasing' co-operative from the standpoint of its borrowing members, and a 'marketing' co-operative from its saving members' point of view (Taylor, 1971). Since it deals exclusively with its members, a credit union can claim to be the purest form of all co-operatives (Croteau, 1963). It cannot do business with the general public because of charter limitations based on serving a membership that is characterised by a common bond. The definition of the common bond is the subject of legal regulation and confers on credit unions, alongside the Rochdalian principles of operation described above, a key defining characteristic. In addition, the common bond restriction on membership is assumed to reduce the cost of gathering credit information and, in consequence, minimises the exposure of individual credit unions to bad debt losses.

In theory, common bond relates to the existence of a common identity where the nature of social relationships stems from reciprocal interdependence typical of traditional community relationships. A common bond based on membership of a particular community is the purest expression of this concept of social relationships based on interdependence. Other forms of common bond are permissible and these are more associational types, perhaps reflecting the nature of industrialised society, which is not based on pure community relationships.

The scope of common bonds can be illustrated taking the example of current UK legislation. Under the Credit Unions Act 1979 the common bond is based upon either:

- following a particular occupation
- residing in a particular locality
- being employed in a particular locality
- being employed by a particular employer
- being a member of a *bona fide* organisation or being otherwise associated with other members of the society for a purpose other than that of forming a society to be registered as a credit union

and such other qualifications as are, for the time being, approved by the regulator—the Registrar of Friendly Societies.

The centrality of common bonds to credit unions has been neatly summarised by Burger and Dacin (1991):

> It is a multifaceted concept, interpreted tightly or loosely depending on the nature of the social, political, and economic environment. Common bond has been a strength of credit unions and also their Achilles' heel. It has aided the founding of thousands of credit unions, but over emphasis on common bond and disagreements over interpretation have also made it a weakness.

There is much debate within the credit union world about the relevance of definitions of common bond to the conditions of the late twentieth century. While the concept of the common bond is both appropriate and essential for the operation of credit unions, an important question for their future strategic development is whether traditional formulations of the common bond are too restrictive. A recent UK National Consumer Council Report (1994), for instance, stated that more than a third of UK credit unions felt that the definition of the common bond was a barrier to their future strategic development. In the US industry, the development of multiple common bonds based on fields of membership is a key initiative being pursued by CUNA.

Generally speaking, a common bond that is too restrictive may inhibit growth. The importance of growth for credit unions rests with the fact that it may enhance the achievement of cost efficiency and scale economies. The achievement of scale economies and cost efficiency may, in turn, enable credit unions to meet more easily their reserve requirements, generate a superior surplus performance and narrow the spread between borrowing and savings rates. It also reduces the incidence of bad debt by permitting credit unions to diversify more easily, particularly in terms of their customer base, as well as enabling them to become less dependent on donated labour, equipment and premises. With growth, and the attendant benefits of scale economies and cost efficiency, comes the real possibility that credit unions may, however, lose their subsidiary character. For example, developments in the United States show credit unions taking a business-like attitude to their operations with membership defined in less restrictive, and more pragmatic, terms in order to facilitate further membership growth. Examining in some detail the theme of credit union size and growth, and its potential effect on the traditional economic and social philosophy of the movement, is an important subject that we specifically return to as a recurring theme throughout this book.

THE POTENTIAL FOR MEMBERSHIP BIAS

The traditional concept of a credit union stresses the importance of co-operative values and the mutual economic interest of members. The assumption is that mutual self-help prevails over self-interest. Whilst all the members of a credit union bear the opportunity cost of foregoing market alternatives for their savings and credit, the fact that they can—theoretically at least—be divided into two distinct groups that can have different economic reasons for membership, i.e. savers and borrowers, implies that there is potential for a certain degree of conflict between these groups. In other words, credit unions may exhibit saver or borrower bias between savers and borrowers.

In an abstract economic model of credit unions (Taylor, 1971), at least the potential for conflict between savers and borrowers has been illustrated. In reality, members do not distinctly belong to either a savers' or borrowers' group; most members of a credit union usually engage in both economic activities—saving and borrowing. The logic of a credit union, in fact, encourages them to do so and not to adopt a restrictive stance as purely a saver or a borrower. In other words, the logic of a credit union is that it should exhibit a neutral stance between savers and borrowers. Whether neutral behaviour is, indeed, the norm is an important subject, given the philosophy of credit unions.

Where the membership of a credit union is defined in terms of a relatively narrow and restrictive common bond and, consequently, all other things being equal, insulates members from competition with each other, there is greater latitude for the emergence of preferential treatment in the form of either borrower-orientated or saver-orientated behaviour. This potential membership bias is likely to be exacerbated in a situation where, for instance, the regulatory regime subjects credit unions to a ceiling rate on both dividend payments and loan charges, such as in the United Kingdom where they are prohibited from paying a dividend that exceeds 8% per annum and are restricted from charging in excess of 1% per month (12.68 APR). Under these circumstances, it is not difficult to envisage how a borrower bias might emerge. In credit union industries that display more open membership policies, and where there is competition for members, the net effect is that loan and dividend rates may standardise across the industry. In such circumstances, and assuming that the credit union industry in question has a significant proportion of the savings and loans market, it is also likely that credit union interest rates will be dictated by market rates. This question of membership bias, and its impact on credit unions, is an issue that is the subject of in-depth consideration in Chapter 7.

DEVELOPMENT TYPOLOGY

At this point in the discussion it is necessary to elaborate more fully a development typology that can help to examine the various stages of development in credit union industries. On the basis of three distinct growth stages within country-specific industries, an assumption can be made about the existence of an evolutionary development path for credit union industries. In other words, they will potentially move from nascent through transition and on to a mature stage of development as a consequence of growth. Implicit in this typology is that there is a differential asset size associated with these three distinct development stages, with the mature stage representing the largest-asset-size position. Growth in asset size, as will be debated later, triggers a form of economic determinism that, in turn, helps to lead to changes in the ideology and operation of credit unions, based on a more business-orientated approach. Similarly, the economic environment within which any credit union industry operates is likely to have a profound effect, especially if this environment is deregulated and subjects it to competitive forces and market rate structures. Also, in an economic environment where electronic technology is a channel for the distribution of services and products, credit unions are pushed by a technological imperative towards a more business-orientated approach. Therefore, besides asset size, key features in the economic environment will create conditions for credit union industries to make the transformation to a mature industry.

Categorising development into a three-stage typology does not, of course, mean that a simple claim can be made about the homogeneity of any given credit union industry. For instance, in mature and transition industries there will be wide variation in the characteristics of particular credit unions, not only in terms of their asset size, but also, importantly, in terms of their characteristics and value position towards issues such as the need for greater business orientation. Caution therefore needs to be exercised in the application of such a broad industry typology since, in reality, credit union industries are, in fact, heterogeneous. Our typology, however, provides an ideal-type model of different industry growth stages. Although the actual descriptive reality will invariably prove to be more complex and involve greater variation than the neat abstract model about to be presented, the use of such an ideal model is still a useful heuristic device. In other words, our belief is that it is both easier to illustrate and to debate the dynamics of change occurring within credit union industries by abstracting the key features of different industry growth stages into such an ideal-type framework. The extent to which our typology is also a prescriptive one is an important point, but comment and debate on this should be postponed until the concluding chapter.

MATURE INDUSTRIES—KEY ATTRIBUTES

Table 2.1 highlights the key attributes to be found in a mature credit union industry.

To examine the attributes outlined for the mature credit union industries, the starting point is to look in some detail at the selective examples of the United States and Australia.

Table 2.1 Attributes of a mature credit union industry

Large asset size
Deregulation
Loose common bond
Competitive environment
Electronic technology environment
Well organised, progressive trade organisations
Professionalisation of management
Well-developed central services
Diversification of products and services
Products and services based on market rate structures
Emphasis upon economic viability and long-term sustainability of individual credit unions
Rigorous financial management of operations
Deposit insurance mechanism established

United States

The deregulation of US depository institutions in 1977 had a profound effect
on the nature of credit unions both in terms of the kinds of products and
services they can provide and in terms of their purpose and management as
financial institutions. The post-deregulation US experience provides a
demonstration effect of a credit union industry operating at a mature stage. It is
to the US credit union industry that we should, therefore, first turn for
discussion of the key attributes of maturity, given that the US industry matches
fully the attributes outlined in Table 2.1. To introduce a comparative dimension
to the discussion, reference is also made to the situation with the Australian
credit union industry, which similarly can be classified as mature. Consideration of these examples should be sufficient to test the validity of the framework
outlined for mature industries in our development typology.

Despite the growth experienced before deregulation, the US credit union
industry still remained small compared with other depository institutions. It
was characterised by a large proportion of small institutions and few large ones
(Pearce, 1984). Also, traditionally, the US industry has been dominated by
occupational credit unions, most of them being federal ones. The stability of
the sponsoring occupational organisation, and, in most cases, the financial aid
provided by it, contributed to the growth in the scale of this type of credit union
in the United States with their average size higher than for other types
(Brockschmidt, 1977).

The main effect of the deregulation of US credit unions was the introduction
of a less restrictive interpretation of the common bond requirement for
membership, thereby increasing potential membership and creating conditions
for mergers. Since deregulation in 1977, the US credit union industry has
undergone a period of consolidation. The net effect of this industry concentration has been a reduction in the number of individual credit unions. Those with
assets below $2 million have declined from over 65% in 1980 to 38% in 1992
(Kaushik and Lopez, 1994). Equally, for credit unions in the asset category
above $5 million, there has been consistent growth both in absolute size and in
relative terms. It is projected that this trend towards increased concentration is
likely to continue in the future.

Since deregulation, membership has grown consistently in the United States,
with some 25% of the population now belonging to a credit union. Widening
the scope of common bonds, making potential qualification for membership
broader, has played an important role in membership growth. Equally, the
attractiveness of US credit unions to consumers has been increased by
liberalisation of the products and services that they can offer. Deregulation has
enlarged the lending powers of US credit unions to include mortgages and
credit card operations. Similarly, improvements in their depository offerings,
including cheque book accounts, have also helped credit unions to operate

more effectively in meeting a fuller range of their members' financial needs in a deregulated, competitive, financial services environment.

Additionally, the management of credit unions in the United States has undergone 'professionalisation' as would be expected given the challenges of operating in a new deregulated environment. That the purely voluntary ethos has given way to a new breed of manager may not be entirely universal, but the US credit union industry is not based exclusively on the principles of a voluntary movement.

The defining characteristic of credit unions in a mature industry within our typology is the greater emphasis placed upon them as efficient providers of financial services. The US credit union industry displays a perfect fit with our mature classification. In other words, although still member-owned financial institutions, 'business principles' of growth and efficiency strongly prevail against more traditional co-operative principles to inform the strategy and operation of credit unions in the United States. The legal and regulatory framework in the United States obviously gives credit unions greater freedoms to operate in a more overtly business-orientated way. Deregulation and the loosening of traditional credit union common bonds has, therefore, provided a strong imperative towards membership growth and, in consequence, the further development of an already large industry asset base.

The existence of features such as credit union central services and the professionalisation of management also constitute defining characteristics of credit union maturity which, again, is well illustrated in the US example. Given the sophistication of a deregulated financial services environment, competing more effectively with mainstream financial institutions is obligatory if credit unions are to meet member expectations about the quality and range of products and services they offer. With moves towards greater diversification of products and services to members, credit unions in a mature industry increasingly take on more of the features of mainstream financial institutions, ultimately, perhaps, to converge at some future point with them.

Although still the subject of a fair degree of ideological debate in the United States, the discernible features of a greater business orientation by credit unions in a mature industry can, nevertheless, be seen to relate to changes in their institutional nature, to the provision of products and services based more on market rate structures, and to the more sophisticated financial management of credit union operations. This first point, the changed institutional nature of credit unions in a mature industry, can be described in fairly straightforward terms. Emphasis, for instance, is placed on 'visionary leadership' with greater use made of the skills of professional full-time salaried staff. Membership is deliberately sought from a more diverse base with an overriding aim to encourage growth. Business orientation, by definition, also includes greater emphasis on economic viability and encourages the goal of long-term financial sustainability for any given credit union. Equally, it discourages the automatic proliferation of credit unions that have no long-term economic sustainability.

Changes in the products and services offered by credit unions similarly provide a visible expression of maturity. Providing products and services based on market rate structures means that in a mature industry there is an intent to provide real positive rates of interest that are competitive with local financial markets. Equally, there is an aim that rates of interest should reflect accurately the risk of the activity that is being financed. By widening their product portfolios, credit unions are operating with an underlying belief that product diversification is what members themselves want and that greater business orientation is, therefore, to their ultimate benefit.

A rigorous approach to the financial management of credit unions is yet a third aspect of the greater business orientation associated with a mature industry. Better financial controls and disciplines are, therefore, emphasised in day-to-day operations. Improving their capital adequacy is an important aim that underwrites the emphasis placed on the economic viability of credit unions and their long-term sustainability. The creation of bad-debt provisions is similarly regarded as a further feature that helps to ensure the asset quality of credit unions, thereby contributing to continued long-term financial viability and sustainability.

Defining maturity, as seen from Table 2.1, involves consideration of multiple factors, so that placing any particular credit union industry in the mature category is, of course, a matter of judgement. This judgement is based upon the weight of industry features measured against the range of factors outlined in our ideal mature classification shown in Table 2.1. The weight of evidence supports the view that the credit union industries found in the United States and Australia should be classified as mature. The other credit union industries that can be classified as mature are to be found in Canada and Korea. As was indicated earlier, it is necessary to be selective in our treatment, so having considered the case of the United States, some brief attention should now be paid to Australia in order to comment upon a second example of a mature industry.

Australia

The first credit union was established in Australia in 1946. The establishment of credit unions in Australia owes much to the efforts of Kevin Yates, who propagated credit union ideals arising from his experience of Canadian credit unions when based in Canada while training in the Royal Australian Air Force. Currently, credit unions are amongst the strongest financial institutions in Australia. Three million Australians are now members of a credit union and this represents approximately 26% of the adult population. The combined assets of Australian credit unions stands in excess of $14 billion (CUSCAL, 1996).

By the 1950s, state associations or leagues had been established to promote the growth of credit unions in Australia. In 1966, the Australian Federation of Credit Union League (AFCUL) was formed by the leagues in New South Wales and Queensland, and by 1967 all state leagues had become federation members. The purpose of the federation was two-fold; first, to lobby for appropriate legislation conducive to the well-being of credit unions, and, secondly, through the pooling of resources, establish a strong trade body that could provide important services to all members. The first Australian Credit Union Act was passed in New South Wales in 1969 and since then further legislation has been enacted in all states to underpin the legal operation of credit unions nationally. In 1992, AFCUL and state credit union associations were centralised into a single national trade group—the Credit Unions Services Corporation (Australia) Ltd (CUSCAL) and the Credit Union Financial Services (Australia) Ltd (CUFSAL).

In 1992, the Australian Financial Institutions Scheme was introduced, which lays down stringent financial objectives that credit unions in Australia are required to meet. These objectives include the minimum prudential standards that must be maintained, and the provision of contingency funds and emergency liquidity support schemes, should they be required. As the Chief Executive of CUSCAL acknowledges (Harvey, 1995):

> The Financial Institutions Scheme has caused fundamental change in the way credit unions manage their business and has led to a maturing of our industry.

The changes brought about by the Financial Institutions Scheme has brought about structural and operational changes in the Australian credit union industry. For instance, there has been a decrease of 12% in the number of credit unions from 342 in 1992 to 299 in 1994, although the capital quality and strength of those remaining has improved. Over the period 1992 to 1994, Australian credit union assets increased by 21.5% to just over $13 billion. A growth in deposits has come from approximately 120,000 new customers attracted to credit unions since the enactment of the Financial Institutions Scheme.

Pickersgill (1995) argues that credit unions in Australia have shown themselves to be

> resilient and progressive, successful niche operators in the [deregulated] retail market.

As a group, Australian credit unions are the largest providers of personal loans; the largest issuers of internationally accepted debit cards (Visa); the second-largest providers of fixed-term deposit accounts; the second-largest providers of combined savings, investment and cheque accounts; and the second-largest providers of portfolio administration services. Credit unions provide transaction access via more automated teller machines (ATMs) and electronic fund transfer at point of sale (EFTPOS) devices than other institutions, and now process more than 20 million direct-entry transactions a year. The consideration of these mature industries would be incomplete without some evaluation of the impact of maturity on changing the philosophical and organisational characteristics of credit unions. Drawing from what has already been said about the US and Australian examples, it is possible to identify some of the key aspects involved in relation to the changed philosophical and organisational nature of credit unions.

Effects of Maturity

Credit unions, given their strong economic and social ideals, have traditionally targeted themselves at disadvantaged sections of society. In mature industries, such as in the United States and Australia, the membership base increasingly comprises affluent middle income groups. With the impetus towards further membership growth, the intention is to incorporate new members from diverse sectors of the population. The new realities facing US credit unions have been neatly summarised by Mason and Lollar (1986):

> ...the increasing sophistication of the credit union member base, attendant demands for more and varied services, and increased competition from other financial institutions all suggest the need for carefully developed competitive strategies as a key to survival and growth during the next decade. Such market driven strategies will require credit union executives to assume more of a role in strategy development and implementation than ever before.

Conventional wisdom on strategic development suggests that clarifying and ranking governing values is a prerequisite to the formulation and implementation of any strategy. Whether credit unions should, in fact, be market driven is a question that raises interesting value implications for them. It is possible to counterpoise their traditional values with more market-driven ones and consider the effect of these on the core activities of savings and loans. What is the effect, therefore, of market-driven interest rates, market-driven loan criteria and market-based definitions of share capital?

Ideally, credit union behaviour is supposed to be neutral between savers and borrowers, although, sometimes, loan interest rates tend to favour the borrower, being below market rates and negative in real terms. Making loan rates competitive with local financial markets would lead to the institution of real positive rates of interest. At the same time, market-driven rates would also more accurately reflect the risk of the activity that is being financed. Similarly, criteria for making loans are altered with a market-driven approach. Traditionally, credit union loans have been made to members on the basis of a multiple of savings; whereas, in a more market-driven approach, loans are usually made on the ability to repay, character and the borrower's own equity in a particular project. Changing the fundamental characteristics of a credit union can also be seen in the altering of its concept of share capital. Traditionally, there has been a blurred distinction between share capital (investment) and savings. A market-driven approach would strive to maintain share value and build member capital and stress more prominently the ownership dimension of share capital.

A more strategic market-driven approach has, therefore, a profound effect on the values surrounding core business activities. Further effects are equally evident once credit unions enter competitive financial mainstream markets. They have prided themselves on their democratic structures and the role of voluntarism in their affairs. The implication from the comments by Mason and Lollar (1986) that greater primacy should be given to the professionalism of credit union executives in determining future strategy poses interesting dilemmas for 'member democracy'. At the heart of this dilemma is the growth in the scale and complexity of credit union operations. Autonomous credit unions are not involved alone in the operation of their business activities. In reality, other agencies such as credit union central services and trade organisations create a web of interdependencies where the role of professional officials assumes increased importance. In other words, the growth of a credit union industry necessarily involves a degree of bureaucratisation, which can create tensions with the democratic ideal. Complexity requires increased levels of expertise that cannot be automatically assumed to exist amongst volunteers, so that, increasingly, the management of a credit union becomes the province of the professional.

In referring to competitive strategies as the key to survival and growth, Mason and Lollar (1986) indicate that competitive strategies for credit unions involve the management of risk in a market environment. Often, they have shown themselves to have inadequate capital positions. Adequate capital (reserves and undivided earnings) is a prerequisite for operating in the risky environment of mainstream financial services. Tightening levels of financial control, including the management of bad debt, is an additional feature that might be expected. Additionally, tightening of security requirements on loans would help to avoid risk and protect member capital. The changing nature of credit unions, and, in particular, their organisational basis, is a theme that will be revisited in the final chapter.

Having considered in some detail the attributes of the mature model, it is necessary now to consider the nature of transition credit union industries. The focus of our analysis in subsequent chapters concentrates specifically on the forces within a transition industry where we believe the 'economic determinism' of growth in assets, and the changing economic environment, play a significant role in the process of causing credit unions to seek a more business-orientated approach. In other words, the seeds of change within transition credit unions are sown much earlier than at the mature stage. The demonstration effect of what is happening in a mature credit union industry may lend support for protagonists of a market-driven approach. However, the dynamics of asset growth and the changing economic environment—particularly if it encourages deregulation—triggering the need for, and making possible, a business-orientated approach are played out in the earlier transition stage in the development of a credit union industry. It is for this reason that much of the focus of this book is on the transition model.

TRANSITION INDUSTRIES—KEY ATTRIBUTES

Table 2.2 summarises the key characteristics that can be applied to transition credit union industries. In keeping with the earlier discussion of mature industries, once again it is necessary to be selective in the choice of industries to be discussed as it is simply impossible to address all examples that fall into the transition category. Looking at the credit union industries in Ireland, Great Britain and New Zealand should provide sufficient examples for adequate discussion of the key attributes of transition industries. Taking each of these industries in turn, our attention can first be devoted to the case of Ireland.

Ireland

The legacy of the failure in Ireland of agricultural credit societies after the First World War was one of 'prejudices against co-operative credit' (Quinn, 1994). In the late nineteenth and early twentieth centuries, agricultural credit societies,

Table 2.2 Attributes of transition credit union industries

Large asset size
Shifts in regulatory framework
Adjustments to common bond
Shifts towards greater product diversification
Emphasis on growth and efficiency
Weakening of reliance on voluntarism
Recognition of need for greater effectiveness and professionalism of trade organisations
Development of central services

or, as they became known, 'land banks', were vigorously promoted by Sir Horace Plunkett in order to rescue rural communities from exploitation by shopkeepers, who lent money at exorbitant interest rates. Modelled on German Raiffeissen societies, there were, by the turn of the century, 76 such land banks in Ireland. However, there were a number of structural weaknesses that led to their eventual demise, and these weaknesses included insufficient deposits to match loans, inadequate control procedures and a dependency on state support. The land bank experience meant that it was not until the 1950s that Ireland again saw co-operative credit actively proposed as beneficial and worthy of large-scale support.

The successful formation of credit unions in Ireland owes much to the role of activists. At the risk of explaining the development of the credit union industry in Ireland purely in reductionist terms, the contribution of Nora Herily, Seamus MacEoin and Sean Forde resulted directly in the successful foundation of an Irish credit union industry. In the early 1950s, Ireland suffered economic depression, with all the attendant problems associated with such periods of economic downturn. High unemployment and emigration existed and this was also a period of extremely high interest rates. There was evidence of abuse in the form of exorbitant hire purchase charges and in the growth of illegal money-lenders, which contributed to debt problems for large numbers of people. In these conditions, the need for credit unions to alleviate such problems appeared, at least to the founding activists, as self-evident and worthy of support.

The process of diffusion, well tested in the transfer of the credit union ideal from Europe to North America, operated in a reverse order in the case of Ireland. In the early days of its formation, the credit union industry was encouraged by CUNA. Advice was offered on remedying the then lack of any specific legal recognition of credit unions in Ireland. The four credit unions existing in Ireland in 1960 had been registered under the Industrial and Provident Societies Act 1893. This was regarded by activists of the time as not being appropriate, since this Act's wide scope meant that commercial organisations and not just purely mutual organisations could be registered. Representation was made in 1960 by a CUNA official about the potential role and benefits of credit unions in Ireland to members of the Irish Government's Committee on Co-operation, which had been established in 1957 with a brief to examine the position of co-operatives. Practical assistance in providing training was also given by CUNA with, for instance, Nora Herily undertaking a three-month study tour of North American credit unions. In 1960, a Credit Union League of Ireland was established to foster the growth of credit unions and the League later became a member of CUNA. The League then evolved into the current Irish League of Credit Unions (ILCU). The ILCU, as the umbrella body of the Irish credit union industry, maintains an all-Ireland dimension. By 1964 the Irish League had formed Chapters based on groupings of credit unions in particular geographical areas to act as focuses for the interchange of ideas and experience in order to aid development.

The enactment in 1966 of a specific Credit Union Act—arising from the deliberations of the Government's Committee on Co-operation—marks the creation of regulatory conditions in Ireland that were more conducive to the establishment of a credit union industry. Following this legislation, a dramatic increase in the membership of Irish credit unions occurred. By 1994, 520 ILCU credit unions were in operation with a membership involving 1.5 million people and an aggregate asset base in excess of IR£1 billion. The vast majority of Irish credit unions (87%) are based upon a community common bond, often following the boundaries established by parishes within the Catholic church. The strong support of the Catholic church for credit unions has undoubtedly been a key element in the establishment of an industry in Ireland. In Northern Ireland, ILCU credit unions also took hold within the Catholic population with a significant role being played by John Hume, a prominent Catholic politician, in promoting their cause.

The history of the development of credit unions in Ireland can be viewed, therefore, as an original amalgam of diverse factors: the seeds of failure of earlier co-operative credit initiatives; the pressing economic and social needs generated by the depressed economy of the 1950s; the role of committed activists as catalysts for change; the establishment of a more supportive regulatory framework; the process of diffusion of North American experiences; the support of the Catholic church. All these various factors have, in combination, contributed to the successful growth of an Irish credit union industry.

In our development typology, Ireland is classified as being in the transition stage of development. Compared with North America, Irish credit unions lag behind in terms of many of the features of a mature industry, although in terms of asset size there is scope, certainly, in Ireland to adopt a more business-orientated approach. Already, reforms are being discussed and, for instance, changes are likely to be mainly in the form of the diversification of the products and services provided by credit unions. Current debate about issues such as professionalisation of the industry, deposit insurance schemes and so on, indicate that, to a large extent, the US mature credit union industry is providing a demonstration model for Irish credit unions regarding the possible direction of their future development path.

Great Britain

Although, as was discussed earlier, Great Britain can point to a long history of co-operative initiatives, credit unions have been slow to take hold. The first credit union was established in Great Britain in 1964. It was only with the passing of a Credit Unions Act in 1979 that any headway was made in terms of growth, with around 70 credit unions formed in the period up to 1982. However, a tightening of reporting requirements by the regulator—the Registrar of Friendly Societies—plus the effects of the economic recession, which undermined some employer-based credit unions, led to a period of stagnation in terms of further growth in the period thereafter. Dating from the late 1980s, credit unions have, however, achieved a revival of growth, with a four-fold increase in formation. The industry in Great Britain can be categorised, therefore, as a young, vibrant and high growth one.

The industry in Great Britain differs from its counterpart in Ireland in that, generally, credit unions are of a much smaller asset size. Also, there is a proliferation of trade organisations in Great Britain rather than, as is the case in Ireland, a single trade body. Besides fragmentation into a number of rival trade organisations, credit unions in Great Britain show a greater variety of credit union types than in Ireland with, for instance, more employer-based credit unions in evidence, particularly within the public sector. As in Ireland, there is current debate about the barriers to future growth with, again, consideration being given to the US credit union industry as a model that might be emulated. Debate about the future of the industry in Great Britain has led to pressure to allow credit unions:

- greater product freedom
- enhanced flexibility in the determination of their common bond
- the opportunity to avail of potential scale efficiencies through the raising of loan volumes and membership ceilings

In terms of much of the subsequent analysis undertaken throughout this book, our focus lies in addressing the dynamics operating within the UK transition credit union industry. By definition, this includes those based in Great Britain and in Northern Ireland. The reason for this strong UK focus stems from our access to a computer database of all credit unions in this country and also from the fact that the United Kingdom constitutes a recognised industry framework. Taking a UK perspective provides a useful test-bed for the rigorous interpretation of the economic and financial dynamics involved in a transition industry moving along the development continuum. The UK industry provides an interesting and relevant forum to evaluate a transition credit union industry against its mature counterparts. By drawing out the appropriate lessons for the wider movement, the analysis of the UK credit union industry has generalised applicability to many other transition industries throughout the world.

New Zealand

New Zealand provides another example of a transition industry. With 115 credit unions representing 126,000 members nationally, New Zealand credit unions collectively have assets of over \$229 million. However, there has been a period of consolidation and the number of credit unions has fallen from a highpoint of 312 in 1985. Besides this reduction in numbers, there has also been a realignment towards community credit unions, with membership rising over the last 10 years from 50% to 75% of total membership. This particular change is a reflection on the harsh economic climate affecting workplace credit unions as a consequence of firm closures and unemployment.

At the same time as the membership base is changing from predominantly work-based to community, the New Zealand credit union industry faces unprecedented competition from other financial institutions as a consequence of deregulation. New credit union legislation is awaited 'to remove the unfair burden placed upon us in a deregulated environment' (New Zealand Association of Credit Unions, 1995). At present, credit unions in New Zealand are governed by the Friendly Societies and Credit Unions Act 1982. If credit unions view this legislation as restrictive, the government, in turn, has reservations both about the tax exemption and the adequacy of the prudential standards contained in the provisions of this existing Act. Therefore, in the consultative process regarding legislative reform, three major proposals for change have been put forward for discussion by the government to the New Zealand industry. These are:

- that many of the present regulatory restrictions on credit unions' operations be lifted. This includes relaxing the common-bond requirement, reducing the limits on the size of deposits and shares and removing restrictions on borrowing, lending and investing in land.

- that the larger credit unions be put under the same taxation regime as other financial-sector companies.

- that the new legislation enhances the prudential safeguards governing credit unions.

Interestingly, the legislative change proposals put forward by the New Zealand government indicate that credit unions might not need separate legislation, but that credit unions could undergo a change of status to bodies corporate with limited liability for members and fall, therefore, under the coverage of companies legislation. Additionally, if credit unions were to reregister under the Companies Act, their tax exemption on income earned from dealing with members would no longer apply. This suggested loss of tax exemption is, however, being suggested only for large credit unions, which, for this purpose, are defined as those with gross assets in excess of \$5 million.

Whilst the New Zealand industry obviously welcomes the proposed liberalisation of the rules governing the operation of credit unions, the attitude towards the loss of tax-exempt status and registration under the Companies Act is problematic. It is likely that the legislative proposals will be modified by the industry to the extent that retention of separate credit union legislation, based upon credit union status, will be sought. Whether it is possible for the New Zealand industry to retain its tax-exempt status is a matter of some interest, although all the signs are that there will be changes in this direction.

The New Zealand Association of Credit Unions (NZACU) provides trade association services to 96 of New Zealand's 115 credit unions. Much effort is being exerted in strengthening the role and function of this trade association. The NZACU is possibly the first credit union trade association in the world to take the significant step of separating the governance of business from the governance of membership activities. The role of the trade association is increasingly seen as that of innovator, particularly in the area of technology-based products and services. More generally, efforts are being placed on new product development, with both mortgage lending and retirement savings products being planned.

In terms of our classificatory typology, the New Zealand example matches many of the features of a transition industry. There is an emphasis on future growth and efficiency, a shift towards greater product diversification, greater emphasis on professionalism, and a deliberate policy to enhance the provision of central services.

The final category to be addressed in our development typology is nascent industries and, as before, the same rider applies regarding selectivity in the examples examined.

NASCENT INDUSTRIES—KEY ATTRIBUTES

Table 2.3 contains a summary of the key attributes of nascent credit union industries.

Table 2.3   Attributes of nascent credit union industries

Small asset size
Regulated
Tight common bond
Emphasis on voluntarism
Serve weak/poor sections of society
Single savings and loans product
Require sponsorship from wider credit union movement to take root
High commitment to traditional self-help ideals

The development of nascent industries should be understood in the context of what can be termed a global associational revolution. In other words, there is a striking upsurge under way around the globe in organised voluntary activity and the creation of private, non-profit or non-governmental organisations. The scope and scale of this phenomenon are immense and, as argued in the introductory chapter, we are in the midst of a global associational revolution that may prove to be as significant to the late twentieth century as the rise of the nation-state was to the nineteenth century.

In the developing countries of Africa, Latin America and the former Soviet bloc, the need for self-help organisations is well recognised and their potential importance is, as indicated above, highly significant. Recent historical events have added to this potential. For instance, the worldwide potential for credit unions has dramatically increased with the removal of the Iron and Bamboo curtains. Countries such as Russia, Central and Eastern Europe, China and Vietnam offer the potential for an explosion in global development. The commitment of the movement to creating such global development is a testament to the distinctiveness of credit unions. They are not merely financial institutions but also, in respect of development issues, agencies with a strong social purpose. In other words, economic development is seen as inseparable from the empowerment of individuals and the emergence of democratic institutions. The credit union movement is a mechanism that facilitates the involvement of individuals and communities in decisions that affect their own economic well-being.

The credit union movement, through the auspices of the World Council of Credit Unions (WOCCU) is, therefore, active in promoting growth in developing economies. WOCCU is implementing long-term development in Africa, Asia, Central and South America and Central/Eastern Europe. In developing countries, it is estimated that there are more than 36,000 credit unions with over $3.4 billion in total assets serving 11.5 million member owners. Credit union development strategy primarily focuses on the mobilisation of local savings as opposed to reliance on outside funding. By generating local resources, credit unions have become one of the most important sources of financing for small-scale entrepreneurs in developing countries.

In 1994, WOCCU launched a People-to-People Programme aimed at bringing people from different credit union industries face-to-face through internships, study tours, partnerships, a speakers' programme and a volunteer technical assistance programme. The US Agency for International Development provides funding to help strengthen fledgling credit unions in developing countries. This funding amounts to some $5 million in grants for credit union programmes in developing countries. As a matter of deliberate policy, and aided by US government funds, WOCCU is anxious to nurture the emerging credit union industry in developing countries. The United States is not the only country with a programme like People-to-People. For example, Canada has its Partnership Programme; Australia has Volunteers to the South Pacific; Ireland has an exchange programme; and Taiwan and Korea have been sending volunteers to the People's Republic of China.

Central and Eastern Bloc Countries

The infant credit union industries in Central and Eastern bloc countries provide a good example of nascent industries. Referring to these countries simply as Central and Eastern bloc countries should not obscure the cultural and linguistic diversity and the multifarious traditions of the individual countries involved. The broad description of this vast geographical area as a bloc can be refined if it is further disaggregated into Central Europe, comprising the Czech Republic, Slovakia, Poland and Hungary; Russia and the Commonwealth of Independent States, which formed out of the former non-Russian Soviet states; and the South Central Region of Europe (the Balkans), Rumania, Bulgaria, Albania and the former Yugoslavia.

The countries of Central Europe have rich democratic traditions and a history of close relationships with the West, whereas, in the former Soviet Union, communism was more deep-rooted and suspicion of the West more pro-nounced. The legacy of a communist economic system has had a profound influence in all of these countries. A command economy, dominated by the military–industrial complex and quota-based production targets, the former communist economic system did much to restrict the ability of individuals to control their own economic destinies. This is not to say that, in the face of harsh economic conditions and an autocratic government, there did not flourish strong traditions of mutual support and collectivism, particularly in rural peasant communities.

The start-up of credit unions in developing countries critically requires sponsorship from the wider movement and this is applicable in the case of Eastern and Central Europe. The focus on self-help, voluntary principles and development in this new context is echoing the history of the early credit unions in Europe. An immediate concern is to seek the legal recognition of credit unions and establish an appropriate regulatory framework. Credit unions are here typified by the traditional single savings and loans product, and their assets in Eastern and Central Europe are modest. In terms of economic regeneration, the potential contribution of credit unions is important, not least because of a long absence of democratic institutions and the lack of a free market economy, but also because they can mobilise whole populations to invoke the principle of self-help in addressing the severe economic problems facing many Eastern and Central European countries.

Africa

African credit unions can similarly be classed as a nascent industry. They have been operating much longer than in Eastern and Central Europe and are to be found in over 30 African countries. They provide financial services to segments of the population, both consumers and producers, who do not have access to formal financial markets. The level of structural organisation of credit unions in Africa is more advanced than in Eastern and Central Europe. The African Confederation of Co-operative Savings and Credit Associations (ACCOSCA) was established in 1968 to assist credit unions to organise, expand, improve their economic performance, and integrate their financial role within the social, economic and monetary development of African countries (ACCOSCA, 1993). Asia, Latin America and the Carribean have developed similar national and regional structures. Manrell (1995) argues that these nascent industries share common challenges:

> They are all faced with divergent and ongoing problems of getting and maintaining a foothold in their respective financial communities. In many ways, the credit unions of these areas are fighting the same battles the [mature industries] fought decades ago; the governmental and banking hegemonies, local apathy, lack of national leadership, public image and so forth.

The African industry has a long way to go before it realises its full potential. By 1990, ACCOSCA-affiliated credit unions were successful in mobilising $503 million in savings. However, this needs to be put in the context that African credit union savings and loans activity averages approximately 1% of commercial bank savings and loans. With large segments of the African population outside the credit union system, there is still a major task in expanding their membership and growth.

Consideration of nascent industries is a powerful reminder of the social ideology of credit unions in operation, and the perspective offered by the role of the movement in the developing world confirms the difficulty in holding a unitary perspective on them. Obviously, there are vast differences between credit unions in terms of the development continuum mapped out in our typology. The strategic development of credit unions will, undoubtedly, be driven by ideological values surrounding their purpose and function and this is an issue that will be returned to in the concluding chapter.

CONCLUDING COMMENTS

This chapter selected key aspects of the historical, ideological and developmental features of credit unions. This selectivity, of course, involves an amount of bias on our part. The juxtaposition of the traditional with a more market-driven, business-orientated model of credit unions suggests that there is a forced choice to be made. Although the value sets involved in traditional and market driven credit unions are often divergent, they may be less so if their mission is accepted as better serving the needs of a larger number of consumers than in the traditional membership base. If credit unions are a good idea then they are a good idea for everyone. This places the growth and further development of credit unions centre-stage as a new century approaches. In the United States for example, an ambitious programme 'Moonshot 2000' aims to increase membership from the 1994 level of 66 million members to 100 million members by the end of the decade. The further growth and strengthening of the credit union movement, whether it be in mature, transition or nascent industries, can only be of economic and social benefit to the vast untapped membership that exists.

By examining the historical dimensions of development, the distinctive means–ends rationale of credit unions was emphasised. There are core organisational and operational principles that are deemed to matter and that distinguish credit unions from other providers of financial services. As member owned, democratic institutions, credit unions stand out from other organis- ational forms not only through an emphasis on self-help and voluntarism, but also in respect of their wider social objectives concerning educational and developmental concerns, particularly for weaker, disadvantaged segments of society. Retaining this distinctive ethos of credit unions is paramount in the eyes of many activists, officials and members. Reconciling more business- orientated credit unions with their historical and distinctive ethos is, therefore, an important dimension in the future strategic development of the movement.

Notwithstanding the concerns about their distinctiveness, their growth, and the mechanisms by which these are achieved, are still the major issues that will impact on the future strategic development of credit unions. In this chapter, the development typology put forward offers a workable framework within which to examine credit union growth and change issues. Examining the challenges involved in the start-up and formation of credit unions in, for example, developing countries in Africa, and in the newly liberalised Central/Eastern bloc countries, is critical to their future strategic development. The role that credit unions can play as democratic institutions in improving the economic well-being of the large populations of these countries is a significant concern when evaluating the role and purpose of the movement.

Similarly, the position of more established credit union industries embarking on regulatory reforms that will take them into a more market-driven environ- ment is certainly worthy of close scrutiny. Providing an in-depth case study of the UK credit union industry, we believe, can illuminate the specific growth issues for established industries yet to enter a mature phase of development. Finally, the position of the North American industries provides an important backdrop to our considerations of credit union growth and development.

Drawing out the lessons demonstrated by changes within these credit union industries can give pointers to the future direction of the transition model. With this in mind, we should now turn to a more in-depth case study analysis of North American experience in order to gain a deeper appreciation of the changing purpose and function of credit unions operating in a deregulated, competitive financial services market.

3

Mature Credit Union Industries—the United States and Canada

INTRODUCTION

The US and Canadian credit union industries are examined in this chapter against the attributes identified as the distinguishing features of a mature credit union industry within our development typology. Initially, the focus is on the US industry: the Canadian industry is examined in the latter part of the chapter. With over $347 billion in assets, the US industry now holds a 7.8% market share of the assets in all depository institutions compared with a 3% market share in 1974. Well over 550 credit unions are of an asset size in excess of $100 million and there are now 12 billion-dollar-asset-sized US credit unions. This growth in asset size in the United States has been a function of deregulation and competition in financial services markets where many of the smaller credit unions have voluntarily merged with larger ones in order to compete more effectively as multi-product providers of financial services. As will be examined in this chapter, the economic trauma experienced by the industry in the late 1970s and early 1980s created pressure for change and innovation, which, in turn, led to an irresistible momentum for deregulation.

Deregulation of the US industry profoundly affected common bond and fields of membership concepts, transforming both of these into more permissive terms that helped to underwrite the successful growth in new membership and a rationalisation of the industry structure through increased merger activity. Equally, it also created conditions whereby credit unions were able to diversify their products and services, so that no longer were the traditional core activities of savings and consumer loans seen as the sole features of credit union identity. Importantly, deregulation also freed the US industry from the strictures of imposed interest rate ceilings and replaced them with a market-based interest rate structure. The establishment in the 1970s of a Federal Deposit Insurance Fund further established the credentials of the US industry within the wider financial services market and added additional weight to its classification as a 'mature industry'.

The last few decades have also witnessed great strides being made in the provision of sophisticated central services. The development of the Corporate Credit Union Network, which provides liquidity and investment expertise for the industry, is an important innovation introduced in the 1970s. Equally, the position of CUNA as the premier trade organisation within the credit union movement has been consolidated through the continuing development of an extensive range of services offered to credit unions by its various constituent organisations. The federal credit union trade organisation, the National Association of Federal Credit Unions (NAFCU), is also vibrant in contributing to the continuing development of federal credit unions and the wider credit union system in the United States. Similarly, the National Federation of Community Development Credit Unions (NFCDCU) provides back-up services for those community development credit unions that serve predominantly low-income communities. It is not only the professionalisation of formal support structures within the credit union system that deserves comment; the increased professionalisation of management within US credit unions in general must also be acknowledged.

Since the mid-1980s the number of full-time employees in the industry has increased by 56% to 125,400 and another 29,000 staff are employed part-time. The nationwide payroll for the industry is now over $4 billion. This increased professionalisation within the industry can perhaps be gauged from the fact that the remuneration paid to chief executives in mid-sized, $100+ million-asset-based credit unions jumped from an average of $69,000 in the early 1980s to an average of $109,000 in the early 1990s. Besides the evident professionalisation of staff and support structures, perhaps of even more significance is the operational environment within which credit union managers work in a mature industry.

The complexion of this new environment might be gauged from changes in the language surrounding the operation of credit unions, where concepts such as strategic competitive advantage, marketing, full service, and so on, are nowadays part of everyday management language. This has led some commentators (see, for example, Crecelius and Comrie, 1994) to claim that there has been a fundamental ideological shift in the US industry away from the traditional paradigm of credit union activities:

> The playing field has changed, the rules of the game have changed, the fences around the industry's ballpark (barriers to entry) have been torn down, many new teams have joined the league, and the new competition is threatening to put yesterday's dynasties in the bottom of the standings. To play and win in this more dynamic league requires new fundamentals, new team skills and competencies, great aspirations, and a strategic—not tactical—approach to achieving those aspirations. It requires competitive advantage.

Obviously, the competitive environment has changed the rules of the game and placed greater emphasis upon the economic viability and long-term sustainability of individual credit unions. In this respect, greater attention is paid to the 'bottom line' and the last few decades have seen the introduction of more rigorous financial management of the operations of credit unions. In the unpredictable, innovative financial services market of the 1990s, credit unions have faced unprecedented challenges and opportunities, which have led to greater emphasis on strategic management. The extent to which this represents a fundamental ideological shift in the US industry away from genuine credit union values and principles is a question best left for the moment in order to consider one further feature that is highly significant to the US mature industry.

In a study undertaken by Ernst & Young and the American Bankers Association of US and Canadian banking practices, it was found that home banking, telebanking, automated teller machines and other non-traditional banking channels accounted for 45% of all banking transactions. The expectation was that, by 1998, this proportion would increase to some 60% of transactions. Similarly, the continuing development of the internet offers vast potential to revolutionise the business practices of financial service providers and credit unions will undoubtedly be greatly affected by this when designing new delivery channels to better serve the needs of their members. Technological and production innovations, therefore, seem to constitute imperatives in the operating environment of mature US credit unions.

The broad aim of this chapter is to provide a comprehensive overview of the historical and structural development of the mature US industry alongside a less detailed comparative examination of the main features of the Canadian credit union industry. The major dynamics of the US industry's development will be examined, particularly with respect to the part played by economic forces in driving the process of change towards a more business-orientated approach. Also, the key adjustments that have been made progressively to the regulatory regime will be traced and the impact of these assessed in changing the complexion of the credit union industry's operating environment. Besides offering a chronology of major historical events, an appraisal is contained in the conclusion to this chapter of the central role of credit union values in the US industry, and some of the debates surrounding particular issues will be highlighted. The analysis of the Canadian industry receives less weight in this chapter and is undertaken only to the degree that it can serve as a broad comparator to the US industry.

The choice of the US industry and, to a much lesser extent, the Canadian industry, to illustrate the dynamics of a mature industry is necessarily a selective one. Other industries, for instance, Australia, could just as easily have been the subject matter for this chapter. Taking an in-depth look at the US industry, and considering the broad features of the Canadian industry, does, however, provide sufficient opportunity to rigorously examine important issues. Obviously, undertaking selective case studies entails a trade-off between wider comparative dimensions and the in-depth characteristics afforded by a detailed case study approach. However, it should be noted that most, if not all, of the issues discussed in respect of the US industry are exportable and relevant to other mature industry contexts and, therefore, have a significant, generalised importance.

THE EARLY US CREDIT UNION INDUSTRY

From their early inception in Europe, emphasis was placed by credit unions on a member's character as the most effective security for a loan. The hallmark of the early US industry lay in the fact that it was established on the basis of tight common bonds, thereby guaranteeing close knowledge of the character and antecedents of any given member. Burger and Dacin (1991) have argued that the use of a restrictive common bond and a narrow field of membership was, in fact, advantageous in the early formation of the US industry:

> The use of common bond, although encouraged as a basis for founding a credit union, was largely voluntary during the early stages of the credit union movement. However, by focusing on founding credit unions on the basis of common bond, the credit union industry began to flourish. Common bond became the basis for bringing groups of individuals together to form new credit unions. It proved to be a viable mechanism with which to found new credit unions and easily spread credit union principles across the United States. Additionally, the relational aspects of the common bond requirement enabled credit unions to achieve economic benefits such as loan safety as well as moral responsibility and loyalty towards the organisation.

Defining credit unions in terms of restrictive common bonds gave the early US industry a competitive advantage over other financial institutions in the small consumer loans segment of the financial services market. Small consumer loans, by definition, involve high fixed costs. Economically, the early US industry was well positioned to serve this niche market, where the cost of collecting information on loan applicants was lowered because of the explicit knowledge of a member's character in organisations founded on a common bond. The voluntary nature of credit unions also conferred economic advantage in that they did not incur labour costs. The fact that credit unions often also enjoyed subsidies from employers and other sponsoring organisations similarly helped to reduce their operating costs. Occupation-based credit unions, in particular, offered low-cost information on the income and job security of prospective borrowers and also offered the capability to process loan repayments inexpensively through payroll deductions. The feasibility of making small loans to people who otherwise would not have access to main-stream financial institutions was, consequently, underwritten by the benefits that flowed from restrictive common bonds as the organisational basis of the early US credit unions.

During these early years, credit unions formed on the basis of occupational and community common bonds flourished. With the establishment of the Credit Union Extension Bureau in 1921, pressure was exerted by the industry—as mentioned in Chapter 2—to see the enactment of state laws supporting the formation and operation of credit unions. By 1933, 38 states had passed legislation that legally recognised the role and function of credit unions. However, the lack of uniformity in state legislation created a somewhat fragmented legal framework governing the credit union industry as a whole. Criticism of this, plus the fact that states could conceivably repeal their legislation relating to credit unions (and also bearing in mind that many states were not covered by such legislation) led the Credit Union Extension Bureau to agitate for the passing of a Federal Credit Union Act that would establish national standards for the organisation of the industry.

The question of the regulation of the US financial system was, in the early 1930s, sharply in focus given the events of the Great Depression, which led not only to large-scale unemployment and the decline of industrial production, but also to the failure of many financial institutions. Interestingly, the US industry actually strengthened its position during the Depression years with overall growth in credit union numbers. From a figure of 900 in 1929, they rose to 1500 in 1932. By 1939, the US industry comprised 7859 credit unions, with an aggregate membership of some 2.3 million members. The shambolic state of the US financial system in the early 1930s created an urgent need for the US government to restructure the financial system along more tightly regulated lines, with little, if any, permissible competition between the segments making up the financial system. Different financial institutions were, instead, to be regulated in ways that allocated them to distinctive and well-defined separate segments of the financial services market.

With the passing of the Federal Credit Union Act in 1934, the role and function of credit unions was, not surprisingly, tightly prescribed, with an explicit common bond requirement specified in the Act. The 1934 Act allowed for three types of common bond, namely:

- occupational
- associational
- residential

A more expansive role for credit unions had, in fact, been considered by industry representatives and suggested to Congress prior to the passing of the Federal Credit Union Act. Such representation was unsuccessful, however, in shaping the legislation finally enacted, primarily because of the government's resolve not to allow a repetition of the severe problems in the financial system of the early 1930s that led to the failure of so many financial institutions. The suggestions put forward at the time for a more expansive role for the US credit union industry are, however, worth noting.

Roy Bergengren, co-founder of the Credit Union National Extension Bureau, had been attracted to the proposition of credit unions becoming more like 'people's banks'. His colleague Edward A. Filene thought specifically in macroeconomic terms about the possible future role of credit unions, believing that if the industry were to concentrate more on consumer instalment credit, then it might help shift the US economy out of recession through the stimulation of growth in consumer spending. The Federal Credit Union Act, in the end, permitted no room for any sort of permissiveness concerning the role and function assigned to the industry, and it would not be until the late 1970s, with the advent of deregulation, that the industry would broaden its service and membership basis. The US industry remained, by the provisions of the Federal Credit Union Act, tied to a market niche of small, short-term consumer loans—a market niche that other major financial institutions regarded as inherently unprofitable.

GROWTH, CHANGE AND DEREGULATION

This narrow regulatory policy established by the Federal Credit Union Act also impacted upon state-chartered credit unions, where the standards set in the Federal Act became a bench-mark for their regulation. Changing social and economic patterns, which resulted in the enlargement of potential membership groups, could not be entirely capitalised upon, given both the narrow definition of common bond and the strict interpretation of fields of membership contained in the Federal Act. It has been argued that the common bond requirement, where membership groups 'be extensively acquainted with each other', stood at variance with changing social and demographic patterns within US society (Burger and Dacin, 1991). Equally, the same authors argued that the strict interpretation of field of membership limits, where geographical fields of membership were tightly restricted, family membership was narrowly defined, and community credit unions were subjected to arbitrary limits on the numerical size of their field of membership, meant that field of membership became a restrictive, rigidly defined concept.

With the exception of a decline during the Second World War, the US industry continued to thrive despite the narrowness of this legally defined role for credit unions. By 1960, there had been a doubling in their number to over 20,000 with a four-fold increase in membership to over 12 million. Also, at this time, the US industry's aggregate shares and deposits stood at $5 billion. The US industry continued to grow substantially in the 1960s and early 1970s.

During the period from 1961 to 1976, the aggregate assets of credit unions grew at an annual rate of 12.8% and credit union deposits grew an average of 13.7% a year. Over the same period, the credit union share of total consumer instalment credit rose from 9.3% to 16.1%. Membership increased nearly three-fold, reaching some 34 million members by 1976 despite the fact that the number of credit unions remained relatively constant (Pearce, 1984).

In 1967, the National Association of Federal Credit Unions (NAFCU) was founded with the aim of shaping the laws and regulations under which federal credit unions operate. In the ensuing period of growth, change and deregulation, NAFCU was active in promoting the various reforms discussed later in this chapter, including the Federal Share Insurance Fund, the establishment of NCUA, the establishment of a Central Liquidity Facility, expansion of fields of membership and the powers of credit unions, and also reform of the regulatory regime governing federal credit unions. The central position of common bond definitions as the limiting factor on credit union powers and operations—and as the key determinant of membership growth potential—made it an important matter not only for NAFCU, but all parties in the credit union industry. This being the case, the following overview of changes made to the common bond can help explain the growth patterns referred to above and also why subsequent growth occurring within the industry can invariably be traced to liberalisation of the common bond and fields of membership regulations.

The growth of credit unions described earlier lies in an easing of the regulatory definition of the common bond in 1972. The previous requirement that members 'know each other' was removed and replaced with a definition that was more in keeping with the social and demographic realities of US society. Thus, the revised definition of the common bond now reads

> Common bond is a characteristic prerequisite to the fulfilment of group objectives and when present among persons of related interests and purposes, these persons could be expected to effectively operate a credit union (Burger and Dacin, 1991).

At the same time as this changed definition was introduced, it was also deemed acceptable under the rules that employees of one nationwide company could be considered a legitimate field of membership. These revisions to the common bond and field of membership requirements obviously facilitated growth. Other measures, such as an increase in the membership limit of community credit unions and more responsive fields of membership in respect of employment; for instance, in office complexes, industrial parks, and shopping centres, also helped to foster credit union membership growth. Liberalisation of the credit union mergers policy further assisted in growth and the establishment of a more concentrated industry structure.

After being the responsibility of a succession of government agencies, federal credit unions came under the control of their own independent agency, the National Credit Union Administration (NCUA) in 1970. This organisation undertook the management of the National Credit Union Share Insurance Fund (NCUSIF). Establishing such a deposit insurance mechanism finally placed the industry on an equal footing with other depository financial institutions. All federally chartered credit unions were required to be members of the deposit insurance fund and state-chartered credit unions could apply for membership.

Further key changes occurred in the industry in the late 1970s as a consequence of deregulation. Not only did this deregulation eradicate regulatory constraints, but it also propelled the industry into a significantly more competitive environment. At the same time, new sources of liquidity were opened up to credit unions, since their trade associations could now provide access to money markets. These factors, in turn, enabled the industry to widen the scope of its financial services and, increasingly, the US industry began to acquire those attributes of a mature industry that we described in Chapter 2. A major driver for change at this time is to be found in the volatile dynamics of the broader US financial services market where pressure had built up for deregulation. Briefly tracing the contours of the changing US economic environment during the 1960s and 1970s will help to put into context the nature of the pressures that had built up for deregulation.

The hallmark of the US financial services industry up until the mid-1960s was its stability and limited rate of innovation. From the early 1950s, the US economy had experienced low inflation and relatively stable interest rates. The US economy enjoyed an expansionary phase in the early 1960s. However, a sharp increase in government spending associated with the Vietnam war, and the emergence of inflation, were predictors that price and interest rate stability was under threat. Spending demand by government and industry fuelled a demand for credit that resulted in market interest rates rising to record levels. Similarly, the consumer price index rose rapidly. Consequently, 1966 saw the introduction of a policy of monetary restraint, which has been labelled 'The Credit Crunch of 1966'.

An important element of this restraint policy was the use by the Federal Reserve, for the first time, of Regulation Q ceiling rates on time deposits as a means of restricting commercial banks' ability to extend credit. Although the banks had not aggressively sought time deposits until the late 1950s, these had become increasingly significant to them by the early 1960s. The response by the banks to Regulation Q was, however, to seek to avoid it by devising new liabilities that were free of interest rate ceilings and reserve requirements. For instance, the banks began to compete directly for household savings by issuing small-denomination, non-negotiable certificates of deposit, avoiding the Regulation Q maximum rate of 4% on passbook savings. Credit unions felt the effect of this increased competition from the banks; growth in shares fell to 9.8% in 1966 compared with the average 13.1% growth throughout the 1960s. This increasing force of competition caused the US industry to make calls for the liberalisation of restrictions on interest rates and on restrictive common bonds and mergers policy.

Innovation was also a force impacting upon the transition away from a highly regulated, stable and segmented financial services market in the United States. As financial services began to enter a more competitive era, there was an incentive for institutions to introduce financial innovations in an effort to gain competitive advantage. From this period onwards, a high rate of product innovation became the norm within the US financial services industry.

Further major changes took place in the 1970s in the profile of the US credit union industry. The most obvious feature concerned the declining number of credit unions. From a peak of 24,876 credit unions in 1969, the mid-1970s witnessed a gradual decline in credit union numbers that was to accelerate over the next two decades. In effect, the US industry was becoming more concentrated, with the number of credit union members and total assets continuing to grow throughout most of the 1970s. The industry successfully expanded its share of the consumer instalment credit market, although this market share began to decline in 1979. Additionally, the introduction of a deposit insurance fund in 1970 affected the composition of credit union share accounts, whereby large accounts were displacing smaller accounts to the extent that the proportion of large accounts doubled from 29% in 1970 to over 56% by 1977, with the monetary value of large accounts amounting to some $14.5 billion.

During the 1970s, a number of important changes were also made that allowed greater scope in the provision of financial services by credit unions. Following a pilot programme in 1974, the limited implementation of share drafts (cheque book facility) occurred in the credit union industry. By 1976, some 940 credit unions offered their members share drafts. Permanent authority to offer share drafts occurred in 1980 with the passing of the Depository Institutions Deregulation and Monetary Control Act, although this contained a stipulation that credit unions should meet the same reserve requirements as other depository institutions. Later, the Garn–St Germain Depository Institutions Act excluded from the reserve requirement credit unions with less than $2 million in checkable deposits, which, in effect, excluded the vast majority of credit unions.

Legislation enacted in 1977 also granted credit unions additional powers to engage in variable savings accounts, mortgage loans and consumer loans. Credit unions were now permitted to offer variable rates and maturities for savings accounts and could offer share certificates. This legislation, the credit union 'mini-bill', also enabled credit unions to establish self-replenishing lines of credit for their members and thus removed entry barriers to the credit card market. CUNA sponsored a pilot credit card programme with Visa in 1976, which involved 22 credit unions. The lending powers of credit unions were also enhanced by increasing the maturity on non-residential loans to 12 years and eliminating the $2500 limit on unsecured loans.

Soaring interest rate levels in the late 1970s dramatically intensified competition in the financial services market in the United States, and 1978 proved to be a difficult year for the credit union industry. The trigger for the intensification of competition was clearly identified by Black and Dugger (1981):

> The money market certificates authorised for banks and savings and loans in the summer of 1979, radically altered the competitive posture of credit unions with respect to the return that could be earned on large savings accounts. The same attributes that enabled market forces to be resisted by credit unions in previous years now made them vulnerable to credit tightening. Though also authorised to issue money market certificates in November 1978, credit unions found themselves in a freely competitive market consisting of strong new competitive elements in the form of money market mutual funds.

Credit unions suffered disintermediation with much of the loss of savings in the form of interest-sensitive large share accounts. In 1979, faced with a slow growth of savings, plus the high cost of funds and the outflow of funds, consumer lending was halted by many credit unions. A large proportion of the US industry experienced severe earnings and liquidity problems in 1979. The regulator took cognisance of this by waiving the required annual statutory reserve transfer due from federal credit unions in that year.

In 1978, under the Financial Institutions Regulatory and Interest Rate Control Act, a Central Liquidity Facility (CLF) was established under the administration of NCUA. Previously, credit unions had no access to a lender of last resort such as the Federal Reserve. Both federal- and state-chartered credit unions were eligible to join the CLF provided they were prepared to subscribe 0.5% of their unimpaired capital. Members experiencing short-term liquidity problems could turn to the CLF in order to secure a short-term loan. Access to the Federal Reserve System was also opened up to the credit union industry. Consequently, credit unions could now buy services directly from the Federal Reserve and they also had legal access to the discount window.

To summarise, therefore, the 1960s and 1970s were important decades for the development of the US credit union industry. The legislative changes introduced, particularly in the 1970s, established the foundations for a major process of change in the financial services sector in general, but also specifically for credit unions. From this period, the traditional segmented markets in the financial services sector were at an end and the new powers granted to the credit union industry allowed it to operate more effectively in an environment where competition and innovation were increasing everyday realities.

THE GROWTH IN CREDIT UNION CENTRAL SERVICES

The deregulation measures so far described provided US credit unions with the opportunity to offer their members a wider range of services. However, to do this successfully, especially in a competitive marketplace, required a strengthening of the central services provided by CUNA. The help of this trade association was required to overcome those inherent weaknesses within the industry that placed credit unions at a competitive disadvantage. For instance, the relatively small size of many credit unions prevented them from reaping economies of scale in areas such as data processing or investment. Similarly, the lack of finance expertise of voluntary officers put credit unions at a disadvantage vis à vis mainstream competitors such as the banks. In the 1970s, the new deregulated environment encouraged the development of a range of central services by CUNA that potentially integrated US credit unions and their respective leagues into a single, unified credit union financial network.

An important innovation that started under the umbrella of CUNA in the mid-1970s was the Corporate Credit Union Network (CCUN), which provides liquidity and investment expertise for the industry. It operates on a pyramid structure with individual credit unions at the bottom, corporate central credit unions in the middle and the US Central Credit Union at the top. These corporate central bodies, which are owned by their member credit unions through capital subscriptions, are intended to act as a 'credit union for credit unions'. In effect, the CCUN allows credit unions to channel investment funds through the corporate centrals to one portfolio run by US Central, thus obviating the need for financial expertise within individual credit unions to achieve competitive returns on investments. The role of the CCUN, and the ongoing development and growth of central services will be returned to later in this chapter. As the early 1980s proved to be a particularly traumatic time for the US credit union industry, where the difficulties experienced were of such a severity that some commentators predicted its death, it is necessary, perhaps, to consider this historical episode in detail in order to continue our chronology of the events that helped shape the US industry.

THE EARLY 1980s—TRAUMA AND RECOVERY

The early years of the 1980s were very difficult times for the credit union industry. With the US economy falling into recession, unemployment rose to over 10% with much of the economic downturn in the industrial sector, and this adversely affected credit unions through the closure of sponsoring firms that had supported employee-based organisations. The early 1980s also witnessed interest levels reaching record heights, which, combined with interest ceilings on loans and deposits, led to a rising tide of disintermediation of savings at credit unions. This was particularly the case in respect of interest-sensitive large accounts. At the same time, the yield on money market investments was rising, which resulted in a substantial shift in the structure of credit union balance sheets and a dramatic reduction in consumer lending with funds, instead, channelled into investments. In net terms there was a relative decline in consumer loans from about 80% of assets in 1976 to below 60% in 1983 (Pearce, 1984).

The depressed economic environment of the early 1980s resulted in a rapid rise in credit union failure and, by the end of 1982, the total number of credit unions had declined by some 4000 from a peak of 23,876 in 1969. However, the membership still continued to grow during this troubled period, but at a much reduced rate. By the end of 1982, about a quarter of federal credit unions were in a loss-making situation. Pressure on the Deposit Insurance Fund intensified in the early years of the 1980s with payouts jumping from $19 million in 1979 to $78.6 in 1981. The problems occurring in the industry at this time urgently required further changes to be made in the way it operated.

The Depository Institutions Deregulation and Monetary Control Act had permitted credit unions new freedoms to compete more effectively with other financial institutions. Within this Act there had been a provision for the orderly phase-out of interest rate ceilings on deposits, which, in effect, was overtaken by the turbulent environment of the early 1980s. The Garn–St Germain Act, mentioned earlier, accelerated the deregulation of the financial services industry and introduced the most significant regulatory changes for credit unions since the 1934 Federal Credit Union Act. The NCUA's Annual Report for 1982 summarised the importance of the consequences of the changes introduced:

> 1982 was the year federal credit unions began looking to themselves for answers rather than to the government. NCUA deliberately stepped out of the way, stripped away the red tape, and allowed credit unions to decide what savings plans they should offer, what dividends they should pay, and whether or not they should form credit union service organisations.

In keeping with this more liberalised regulatory stance, NCUA's policy towards the interpretation of the common bond and fields-of-membership issues became more permissive. For instance, the 25,000 membership limit placed on community credit unions was eliminated and, instead, cases for expansion were to be dealt with by the regulator simply on the merits of any particular submission. Relaxation also occurred in respect of membership policies relating to family membership when, in 1983, NCUA allowed credit unions to establish their own approach about the eligibility of members' relatives for membership. Similarly, changes were made to the fields-of-membership policies governing occupational and associational credit unions. In 1982, these types of credit union could now add groups with a similar common bond to their membership. Again, in 1983, this policy was further liberalised to allow such credit unions to add select or small employee groups with common bonds dissimilar to their own. In such instances, NCUA had to be assured that the group had asked to be incorporated, that the receiving credit union had the ability to provide the required service and that potential overlap conflict with other credit unions was negligible.

This treatment of select groups permitted small groups to gain access to much fuller credit union services. For receiving credit unions there were also obvious advantages; for instance, in terms of economies of scale that expansion through select groups offered, and, similarly, diversification away from total reliance on a single common bond, where the consequences of difficulties—such as evidenced in the case of occupational unions with plant closures—could be lessened. The impact of these fields of membership changes were fairly immediate in transforming the complexion of the US industry. This view was held by Burger and Dacin (1991):

> Although many credit unions remained tied to a single employer, many others used the new policies to expand their fields of membership. During fiscal year 1983, 1,416 federal credit unions received one or more amendments to expand their fields of membership and 8,553 groups were added as a result of amendments. The percentage of credit unions serving more than one employee group rose to over 30 percent by the end of 1983. In 1984 there were 3,805 fields of membership amendments for federal credit unions, through which 2.7 million persons became eligible for membership.

Easing merger restrictions, in that NCUA could now merge a failing federal credit union without regard to geographical area and field of membership, also made it easier to manage those with problems without having recourse to liquidation. The latter consequently fell from 251 in 1981 to 50 in 1983. Mergers increased from 333 in 1981 to 706 in 1983. This transformation removed the threat to the NCUSIF posed by continuing liquidations of large numbers of credit unions. Predicting the death of the credit union industry proved, therefore, to have been premature, although it had indeed been through extremely difficult times. The regulatory changes to the common bond and fields of membership had a beneficial effect on the operation of credit unions and the industry in general. At the same time, economic conditions began to improve dramatically in 1983 as a result of a period of economic expansion that has continued up to the present time.

It should be noted that, in 1985, federally insured credit unions recapitalised the NCUSIF by depositing 1% of their shares into the Share Insurance Fund. Backed by the 'full faith and credit of the United States Government', the Share Fund has three fail-safe features. These are that:

●   federal credit unions must maintain a 1% deposit in the Fund

●   premiums can be levied by NCUA if necessary

●   when the equity ratio exceeds 1.3%, NCUA pays a dividend to credit unions.

Since 1985, NCUA has charged credit unions a premium only once, in 1991. Given the healthy financial growth of credit unions in the 1990s, the Share Fund has prospered. In 1995, the NCUSIF reached 1.33% equity ratio and the NCUA board issued dividend payments to 11,836 federally insured credit unions totalling $103.5 million.

THE US INDUSTRY—COMPETITIVE ADAPTATION

Returning to the effects of the relaxation of fields of membership regulation and mergers policy, the impact of this policy can be traced out in figures concerning a continuing trend toward industry concentration. In the period 1983 to 1993, membership grew by 34% from 47.5 million to 63.5 million and total assets grew by 370% from $93 billion to $437 billion, despite a 32% reduction in the number of credit unions (Crecelius and Comrie, 1994). The number of unions with assets of less than $5 million decreased by 3620 between 1987 and 1992. Correspondingly, the number of those with assets greater than $5 million increased by 817 and it was within the $20 million to $50 million asset range that the most pronounced growth was seen during this period (Tripp and Cole, 1994).

The overwhelming driver for industry concentration was the increased use of mergers. Between 1986 and 1992 some 3336 mergers occurred within the industry, the bulk of which were voluntary. During this same period, the establishment of new credit unions was occurring at a reduced rate compared with earlier periods of industry growth. In the increasingly competitive business environment of the late 1980s and early 1990s, the motives for smaller credit unions seeking mergers are not difficult to determine. One reason concerned the benefits that are perceived to accrue from greater size *per se*. In other words, it was anticipated that by merging into larger credit unions there would be a beneficial effect in terms of economies of scale and scope, and that the average operating costs within the merged organisations would be reduced, thereby providing a better competitive basis in the financial services market. Another important reason why smaller credit unions sought mergers related to the difficulties experienced in coping with regulatory compliance burdens, and in mounting viable product diversification strategies. Finally, the dominance in the industry of employer-based credit unions also provided an impetus towards mergers, given the difficulties experienced by these types of credit union in periods of economic downturn, where merger helped guard against the effects of the closure of a host employer organisation.

Although described as deregulation, the measures introduced in the 1980s have by no means removed the onus placed on the industry to comply with a wide array of regulatory requirements, to the extent that some commentators nowadays talk about reregulation. There is, therefore, an ongoing debate about the appropriateness of the level and form of regulation imposed on the industry.

The motives, for instance, of smaller credit unions in seeking to escape from the burdens of regulatory compliance requirements can be easily understood when the volume of regulation of their activities is considered. As Dunn (1995) puts it, federal regulation is only the beginning:

> A menagerie of rules from about a dozen other federal regulatory agencies directly affect credit unions, either because credit unions are financial institutions or because they are employers. These rules range from Truth-In-Lending (T-I-L) from the Federal Reserve Board, to backup withholding and dividend reporting from the Internal Revenue Service, to the recently released regulations under the Family and Medical Leave Act from the Department of Labor. These are just the federal rules; state and local requirements can be pretty hefty, also.

There is the prospect of financial institution regulatory relief legislation being enacted in the future. Regulatory relief legislation aimed at scaling back the provisions of Truth-in-Savings and Truth-in-Lending and other consumer laws would help alleviate the concerns voiced about the burden of regulation placed upon credit unions. Further consideration of the role of regulation and supervision of the industry will occur later in this chapter, since this is currently an important issue. Returning to the competitive adaptation of the US industry, perhaps the most tangible sign of this can be seen in the transformation that has occurred in the product portfolios of US credit unions.

Diversification of products and services has been the hallmark of the US industry in a deregulated competitive environment, whereby extensive diversification from the traditional core business base of offering share accounts and consumer loans has occurred. The transformation to multi-product financial institutions has, in the late 1980s and early 1990s, been quite dramatic. In a study conducted by CUNA in 1992, it was found that 37% of credit unions offer first mortgages, 33% offer credit cards and 46% offer interest-bearing share drafts. Additionally, it was found that 27% offer ATM cards and 6% member business loans.

Product diversification is regarded as a means to avoid the risks associated with being reliant on a limited product range, although such diversification incurs its own risks. For this reason, diversification usually entails tighter regulatory control with regard to safety and soundness, which smaller credit unions can find difficult. Product diversification also calls for a level of expertise that is more likely to be found in the larger, professionally staffed organisations. The continuing trend of product diversification should, therefore, support continuing merger activity within the US industry. Indeed, predictions have been made, on the basis of a poll of credit union executives and board members, that of the credit unions that currently exist each has a one-in-two chance of being around in ten years' time when the overall number surviving in the US industry is likely to be in the 6000 to 7000 range (see, Crecelius and Comrie, 1994).

If the position of smaller credit unions in the competitive environment of the 1980s and 1990s has driven many of them to seek mergers with larger bodies, the position of those in the middle range also seems to have its own difficulties. In a recent research study it was postulated that after an asset size of $50 million is reached, further increases in size increase the rate of failure and merger until the $250 million mark is passed (Amburgey and Dacin, 1993). This study also suggests that adverse selection occurs in credit unions of this asset-range size and that they face the greatest risk of failure. The conclusions drawn from this research are that mid-sized credit unions are, in terms of their business strategy, often caught in the middle in that they are neither highly focused on a narrow product/service line, nor large enough to have the resources to offer a full range of services and compete effectively with other full-service financial institutions.

The pursuit of membership growth appears to be the touchstone of the US industry. 'Access for all Americans' to credit union services is an ambition underlying CUNA's drive in the 1990s to push for fields of membership expansion that ensures continued membership growth yet, at the same time, maintains credit union co-operation. Credit unions were created to accomplish a social purpose, as is clearly indicated in the 1934 Federal Credit Union Act:

> An Act to establish a Federal Credit Union System, to establish a further market for securities of the United States and to make more available to people of small means credit for provident purposes through a national system of co-operative credit, thereby helping to stabilise the credit structure of the United States.

Because of this social purpose, credit unions have historically enjoyed a special status and legal privileges. In other words, they are exempt from taxation and Community Reinvestment Act requirements and, in addition, enjoy a separate, dedicated regulatory agency to oversee the industry. With the continuing push for membership growth and the increasing business orientation of US credit unions, the industry faces acrimonious legal challenges from the banking sector claiming that this special status is unwarranted and gives an unfair competitive advantage to credit unions. Before considering the conflict with the banking sector, it is important to consider that serving 'people of small means' is an important philosophical precept of credit unions, notwithstanding the new commercial ideology found in a mature industry. In a CUNA Task Force Report (1994), which examined the implications of yet further expansion of fields-of-membership operating principles, emphasis was placed on the continuing need by the US industry to serve low-income families and communities.

Because serving low-income individuals and communities is consistent with traditional credit union philosophy, this does not mean that it automatically runs counter to the business-orientated approach found in the US industry. A study examining the strategic opportunities in serving people with low to moderate incomes concluded that this population is under-served by mainstream financial institutions and, therefore, serving individuals and communities with low to middle incomes affords credit unions good market opportunities. The authors of the study also concluded that serving this market would help to diversify the membership base which, it is argued, helps spread risk and better ensures the stability of a credit union (Burger and Zellmer, 1995).

Serving the needs of members and communities with low to middle incomes is regarded by many as being necessary to remain true to credit union philosophy. It also appears that there are sound business reasons for serving this market. Also, if the special status for credit unions can be shown to be illusory and that the financial services market is not a level playing field, then it can be anticipated that the banking sector will continue its legal attacks on the tax-exempt status of credit unions.

With the expansion of fields of membership has come increasingly bitter criticism from the banking sector, which claims that credit unions have overstepped their legal boundaries and have moved away from their unique social purpose. Since 1990, banking organisations have taken this argument to courts in eight states. The banks believe that the lower fee structure of credit unions is a direct result of the fact that they are not paying taxes. (It should be noted that while federal credit unions are exempt from all income tax, state-chartered credit unions pay state income tax.) The banking industry believes that since credit unions increasingly desire to compete with them, they should do so without the competitive advantage of tax-exempt status. With only 8% of the $4.1 trillion assets held by US banks, the US credit union industry is mounting a vigorous campaign to retain its tax-exempt status. As mutually owned co-operatives, credit unions return any surpluses to their members in the forms of lower loan rates, higher savings rates, and new and improved products and services. Since they earn no profit, should credit unions be forced to pay taxes this would have to come from their reserves, making them more susceptible to the vagaries of the marketplace and the economy. Additionally, credit union managers could be pressurised to eliminate free and unprofitable services, such as small loans, financial counselling and small share cheque accounts.

In the context of attacks from the banking sector, the role of credit unions in serving the needs of disadvantaged groups and individuals in order to lay claim legitimately to a unique social purpose is an important issue. Some commentators speculate that there is a possibility that Congress, in order to enforce lender bias laws and ensure expanded financial services for the poor, might pass legislation requiring financial institutions to offer lifeline banking services and cheque book accounts to people of modest means. This further highlights the importance of the issue of serving disadvantaged sections of society and this issue will be considered again in the concluding section of this chapter.

DEBATE AND RENEWAL

Recent development of the industry has continued positively, although it is obvious to industry-watchers that the US industry has entered a period of re-evaluation of key elements of its philosophy and operation. Perhaps the trigger for this has been the events surrounding the activities and management of corporate credit unions. Concern began to be expressed in the early 1990s about perceived deficiencies in the corporate credit union system and NCUA's supervision of these institutions. The issues surrounding corporate credit unions put into focus the question of how far, in a mature industry, credit unions can proceed from their fundamental purpose and methods of operation. The events surrounding the Banco Espanol de Credito (Banesto) affair, involving US Central and the failure of the CapCorp Corporate Credit Union, have brought into sharp focus a number of issues, including the role of NCUA as regulator, the role of CUNA and questions around the professionalisation of credit unions and the position of membership accountability through the role of credit union directors.

When originally established, corporate credit unions were intended to be a safe and sound liquidity facility for their members. However, by the 1990s there was evidence that some were drifting away from their 'matched-book' approach of the past to a riskier 'managed-book' approach, which involves a higher yield but a more risk-laden approach to investment. In the early 1990s it was also recognised that for institutions of their asset size, corporate credit unions were undercapitalised. Minimum-risk-based capital requirements were therefore introduced in 1992. The weaknesses of the corporate credit union system were further exposed when US Central Credit Union was criticised for placing its solvency in jeopardy through a single investment of $255 million in the troubled Banesto. Although US Central fortunately did not lose its investment, NCUA immediately imposed a moratorium on corporate centrals engaging in such foreign investments. Additionally, NCUA established a Corporate Credit Union Study Committee to conduct a review of the corporate credit union system.

The major recommendations of this study committee concerned four major issues.

1. The committee believed that both primary and risk-based capital levels ought to be increased as it considered that capital levels were still insufficient despite the earlier increase made in 1992.

2. The committee thought that NCUA itself needed to improve the expertise of its corporate examiners through better training.

3. The committee called for the promotion of competition and increased efficiency through an expansion of corporate credit unions' fields of membership.

4. The committee took the view that corporate credit unions should be stand-alone institutions where the interlock relations with CUNA and other trade organisations should be deliberately lessened.

Underlying these recommendations, and implicit in the analysis offered by the study committee, lies a particular perspective on the philosophy of corporate credit unions with a reminder of the importance of member accountability even where, as in this case, members are other credit unions. In his testimony before the Subcommittee on Financial Institutions and Consumer Credit of the Committee on Banking and Financial Services of the US House of Representatives, Norman D'Amours, the Director of NCUA, articulated the importance of this key issue of membership accountability in corporate credit union affairs:

> There have been significant changes in the credit union system since the 1960s and 1970s when most of the existing corporate credit unions were first established. CUNA and the credit union leagues were instrumental in establishing a much needed corporate credit union system to provide liquidity sources to credit unions. However, it is time for corporate credit unions to declare their independence from politically controlled trade associations and stand on their own. The boards of directors of corporate credit unions should be comprised of individuals who rcprcscnt, and are accountable to, the natural person credit unions that they were established to serve. For there to be integrity and confidence in the corporate credit union system, there must be no conflicts of interest, or even the appearance of conflicts of interest, between corporate credit unions and trade associations (D'Amours, 1994).

CUNA and the other trade organisations, as might be expected, hold a somewhat different perspective on the new 'interlock rule' introduced by NCUA in early 1996, which debars the majority of directors of a corporate credit union being officers, directors, agents, or employees of the same credit union trade association. Criticism from CUNA has followed the introduction of this regulation, and legal action has ensued from CUNA challenging the validity of this regulation.

Mention was made earlier of the debate surrounding the position and role of directors in corporate credit unions. As lay volunteers, directors are the personification of the membership democracy highlighted in Chapter 2 as an important tenet of credit union philosophy. A link has been made, in the thinking of the regulator, that in meeting the desire of credit unions for even greater deregulation, a concomitant need still exists for NCUA to be able to fulfil its statutory supervisory role. In this respect, increased emphasis is being placed by NCUA upon the role of directors as having a primary supervisory role, with the NCUA's role being seen as secondary back-up. Notwithstanding the comments made earlier about the volume of regulation surrounding the activities of credit unions, attempts continue to be made to lessen regulatory burdens. For instance, loan participation rules have recently been relaxed, as have guidelines for some fields of membership expansion, where streamlined procedures have also been introduced. The interesting point about current debates concerning regulation is the emphasis being placed on credit unions, through directors, taking primary responsibility for the supervision of their activities.

From the analysis undertaken of the US industry in particular, the attributes considered in our typology to be the hallmark of a mature industry can now be judged. Within the context of changes in the economic and social environment, the deregulation of financial services introduced a new competitive era where products and services became based on market rate structures. Equally, greater emphasis was placed on the economic viability and sustainability of individual credit unions. Professionalisation has become a touchstone of credit union operations and is reflected in more rigorous approaches to the financial management of operations, the development of central services and the operation of vibrant, well-organised trade organisations. The introduction of a deposit insurance mechanism marked an essential component if credit unions were to be serious players in the more competitive, deregulated environment. The technological imperative that currently exists in the financial services market has also been grasped by credit unions and they have shown themselves to be innovative in the use of electronic technology. Finally, underlying the trend towards industry concentration is a continued growth in assets and membership. As they stand, these are significant and mark out the industry as an important component of the broader US financial services scene. Taken in combination then, these attributes do seem to confirm that the US industry is, indeed, mature. As will be shown shortly, the Canadian industry similarly fits this mature classification. Underlying these largely descriptive attributes is, however, an ongoing dynamic relating to the ideology of credit unions. So far, the dominant ideology is still that of co-operative ideals; if this were to shift towards a more pronounced mainstream commercial stance, then, of course the industry might not be seen to have matured, but rather converged or trans-formed. This is an issue that will be considered in more detail in the final chapter where a discussion is offered on the importance of values to credit union identity.

THE CANADIAN CREDIT UNION INDUSTRY

In our examination of mature credit union industries, the evolution of the Canadian credit union industry deserves attention, since it, too, provides a good comparator against which to measure the attributes of maturity as defined in our typology. The analysis offered of the Canadian industry is less detailed than that provided for its southern neighbour, and only those key features that help to confirm the industry's maturity are discussed. In 1991, nearly 10 million

Canadians belonged to either a credit union or caisse populaire and the combined asset base of Canada's credit unions and caisses populaires was $80 billion. The Canadian credit union industry has built up a reputation for developing flexible, convenient and innovative financial products and services, and it is clearly at a mature stage of development.

The origins of the Canadian credit union industry at the turn of the century have already been alluded to and, in keeping with its US counterpart, it has enjoyed steady growth, particularly in the 1950s and 1960s. In Canada, the caisses populaires founded by Desjardins historically precede credit unions. As the only financial co-operatives in the first quarter of the century, caisses populaires were initially linked to the Catholic church and were heavily concentrated in Quebec. Credit unions, in contrast, typically originated as industrial and community-based organisations and drew their inspiration from a co-operative education programme launched at St Francis Xavier University in Antigonish, Nova Scotia in 1928, known as 'The Antigonish Movement'. The key historical distinction between caisses populaires and credit unions in Canada is highlighted by Zinger (1994):

> While caisses populaires promoted the virtues of thrift, credit unions placed a greater emphasis on providing a convenient and inexpensive source of credit for personal borrowing needs. As a result, the percentage of members who were also borrowers would tend to be much lower at a typical caisse populaire. Historically, caisse populaires encouraged members to accumulate their savings via deposit accounts, whereas credit unions tended to favour the purchase of credit union shares.

As was indicated in Chapter 2, the Canadian industry consists of three elements:

1. Local credit unions and caisses populaires operating under individual provincial laws.

2. Central credit unions incorporated under provincial legislation.

3. Two national central organisations, the Credit Union Central of Canada (CUCC) (formerly known as the Canadian Co-operative Society), operating under a charter granted by the federal government in 1953, and La Caisse Central Desjardins du Quebec, which was set up in 1979 to look after the broad concerns of provincially incorporated caisses populaires.

At the local level, most credit unions are full-service financial institutions with a wide range of products to match member needs. Although linked provincially and nationally to other credit unions, each credit union operates independently. Provincially, local credit unions hold membership in a 'central' which provides them with important corporate financial services and development support. Centrals also constitute important links to government and to the national co-operatives.

Thus, as in the United States, the Canadian industry has developed a sophisticated framework. Provincial legislation, which governs 'locals' stipulates matters such as reserve requirements, types of investments, permissible sources of funds and individual loan limits. 'Centrals' operate as umbrella organisations and their main purpose is to supervise the financial well-being of their locals. The services provided by centrals include a liquidity source at provincial level, access to deposit insurance, marketing, electronic data processing, and educational, public relations and legal services. Centrals are regulated provincially, with most of them also subject to federal legislation in the form of the Co-operative Credit Associations Act. This credit union financial system has at its apex the CUCC, which is the industry's main trade organisation and is federally regulated. The CUCC provides a further tier of liquidity support to the credit union system and also provides a vast array of support services. It represents the interests of the credit union system to the government and liaises with the Desjardins caisses populaires and the wider international credit union movement. It should be noted that three other national organisations, the CUMIS Group, the Co-operators Group Limited, and the Co-operative Trust Company of Canada also offer insurance and trust services to Canadian credit unions.

The organisation of the caisse populaire system differs from Canada's anglophone credit union system. With Quebec as its stronghold, the 1327 caisses populaires located in that province constitute nearly one half of the locals in Canada and generate approximately 50% of the credit union system's annual revenues (Zinger, 1994). La Confederation des caisses populaires et d'economie Desjardins du Quebec has direct supervisory powers over its caisse populaire locals in Quebec and other provinces. La Confederation is regarded as one of the most progressive financial groups in Canada and has subsidiaries engaged in business financing, life insurance, stock brokerage, leasing, general insurance, trust services, electronic funds transfer systems, and—through an investment division—has interests in transportation, chemicals and steel. In Quebec, it is a significant player in the financial services market and in 1990 controlled 30% of the province's residential mortgage market, 31% of consumer loans and 22% of industrial and commercial loans. Total assets grew from $2 billion in 1972 to over $40 billion by 1990, and with over 34,000 employees it is amongst the province's largest employers (Zinger, 1994).

A DYNAMIC MARKET PLACE: CHANGING CONTOURS OF THE CANADIAN INDUSTRY

There are many trends that have affected the Canadian industry that mirror those of the US experience. For instance, during the 1970s and 1980s the Canadian industry faced the trials of periods of high inflation, volatile interest rates and recessionary pressures. Equally, the financial services market has proved dynamic in the pace of change with emphasis on intensified competition, new product development and increasing use of electronic service delivery. The Canadian financial services industry has engaged in a process of deregulation in the context of this dynamic environment. The Canadian industry, like its neighbour, has seen a concentration in the number of credit unions. From a peak of 5000 in 1965, the number of credit unions declined to 4117 in 1975 with a further reduction to 2664 in 1991. This increasing industry concentration, again in keeping with the US experience, has been brought about by mergers. This merger process was due to the adverse economic environment within which Canadian credit unions operated, particularly during the 1980s.

The 1980s and 1990s have been decades of innovation, and the caisses populaires, in particular, gained a reputation as innovators, having pioneered financial products such as daily interest savings accounts, variable rate mortgages, debit cards, and weekly payment mortgages. The Canadian industry also evolved a sophisticated ATM network, which, by 1988, encompassed 17 different financial institutions and was being used for upwards of 60% of deposits, withdrawals and transfers. At the same time, these decades have witnessed ever-intensifying competition from rival financial institutions, particularly in the areas of consumer lending and residential mortgages (Zinger, 1994). In the light of this increased competition, some credit unions have been attracted to business financing as an alternative to consumer lending and residential mortgages. However, whether the industry has a strong enough capital base has been questioned by La Confederation des caisses populaires et d'economie Desjardins. As Zinger (1994) points out:

> Another serious problem that has continued to plague financial co-operatives stems from their difficulty in maintaining a stable capital base, due in large part to the absence of outside investors.

There are restrictions, which vary from province to province, that limit the extent to which credit unions can engage in activities such as commercial lending in support of the small business sector. For instance, in Ontario, total commercial loans held by a credit union cannot exceed 7% of capital and surplus. Consideration of ways to improve the capital base of the credit union industry in Canada is the subject of debate and has led to a number of suggestions on devices that might be introduced to improve capital adequacy in the industry. For example, one suggestion is to increase compulsory member equity and create non-voting share and debt instruments carrying competitive rates of return. Additionally, it has been suggested that the practice of placing restrictions on members' shares could be scrutinised as another mechanism for stabilising the capital base of the industry (Canadian Co-operative Association, 1991).

The Canadian credit union industry, in terms of its designation as a mature industry, comes out as a sophisticated variant. Indeed, its characteristics could support the view that it displays a potential to go beyond maturity and move towards convergence with the banking sector. This, of course, is not certain, but there is a danger that this might be the strategic direction of the industry should the distinctiveness and uniqueness of credit unions be forgotten. In his study, Zinger (1994) identifies the force of this trend:

> There is little doubt that the competitive environment will continue to pose some serious threats, insofar as chartered banks can be expected to continue their dominance of the financial services market. Also, smaller trust companies, as part of large conglomerates, or insurance companies will attempt to position themselves in 'credit union-dominated communities'. In response, many of the larger credit unions and caisses populaires have become more like banks in terms of their policies, procedures, and product offerings. In light of the new financial services legislation, many industry insiders considered it imperative that the movement continue to proceed in this direction.

In keeping with the current renewal debate in the United States, the Canadian industry likewise faces a need to evaluate a mature industry against the principles and values of member-owned co-operatives. Ensuring the continuing primacy of co-operative ideals in a mature competitive industry appears to be an issue of debate in both of the industries considered. The importance of this debate will again be considered more fully in the final chapter.

CONCLUDING COMMENTS

Both the credit union industries in the United States and Canada are mature, sophisticated providers of financial services to their members. No longer operating as limited product institutions in segregated financial services markets, credit unions in the United States and Canada have undergone a transformation as a result of deregulation and the growth of a more competitive marketplace. Structurally, both industries have undergone a process of increased concentration with a reduction in the overall number of credit unions. The asset size of both industries, and the asset size of their constituent credit unions, continues to grow. Growth in membership and the ambitious plans for further growth reveal a confidence in these industries about their future.

The trigger for the transformation of the US industry has been reforms of the common bond and fields of membership requirements. Credit unions are distinctive organisations, and they owe much to their historical origins, where strong values associated with democratic, self-help organisations have played a prominent role in defining as important their function in serving the needs of disadvantaged individuals and communities. With the liberalisation of the common bond and fields of membership, the opportunity to extend membership more universally has been seized, although not without complaint from competitors. As the US industry has developed it has established a trade support infrastructure that befits a major industry and the industry has a good track record for safety and soundness in handling the financial affairs of its millions of members.

The US industry, as our primary case study of a mature industry, displays all those characteristics that we held to be important in defining maturity. One question raised in our discussion was, 'how far does the credit union industry proceed before it escapes the bounds of maturity to transform itself into some other form of financial institution?' From our analysis it is still the case that the benefits of mutuality are well-recognised in the US industry. This extends beyond the purely pragmatic question of tax-exempt status, and recent developments within the industry—such as the issue of the governance of corporate centrals, serving the needs of the poor, the supervisory role of directors, and even whether to charge fees to non-profitable members—trigger debates about the true role and function of credit unions. Despite the shift to a more business-orientated and professional approach by credit unions, the central value system of co-operative-member-owned institutions is still alive and well. The core value set of credit unions, of course, has to be reinterpreted in the light of constantly changing conditions and adapted to suit evolving conditions, and the evidence is that this entails a constant process of realigning credit union principles and practice. In the final chapter there will be a more extended discussion of credit union values once the opportunity has been taken to consider examples of transition and nascent industries, as this will provide a better-balanced appreciation of the significance of credit unions.

In the chapters that follow, a detailed case study is offered of the UK credit union industry. Because it is much smaller than the US industry, it is possible to offer really detailed analysis on issues such as scale efficiency and membership bias, and also to offer comprehensive coverage in terms of the performance appraisal of this industry. Prior consideration of mature industries will help in locating much of the material on the UK industry, given the assumption that, as a transition industry, it will wish to replicate the experience of the successful US and Canadian industries.

4

A Structural Analysis of UK Credit Union

INTRODUCTION

Croteau (1963) stated that:

> Credit unions seek to protect the weak, to save them from the exactions of usurers. They emphasise voluntary action, the democratic dream, the development of latent abilities found in the common man. These explicit values are not amenable to economic analysis, but they cannot be ignored by anyone who would understand the credit union.

This is a statement that is true about the credit union movement in its formative stages of development, but one that is less obviously true as credit unions progress along the developmental spectrum. In the context of the United Kingdom, Croteau's statement, while still relevant for a sizeable section of the movement, has, over time, become much less relevant for an increasing number of institutions. This latter group now appear to be at a start point in a new phase of their development and, to progress through this phase, a necessary prerequisite is that they are freed from the constraints and strictures that currently govern the UK credit union industry. Indeed, at present, and in line with the economic determinism debate detailed in Chapter 2, pressure has mounted to allow UK credit unions:

- greater product freedom
- enhanced flexibility in the determination of their common bond
- the opportunity to avail of potential scale efficiencies through the raising of loan volume and membership ceilings

The UK credit union movement, in this its transition period, can, therefore, be employed as a test-bed for our hypothesis that, given the appropriate industrialised setting there is an inbuilt logic that encourages and supports the development of credit unions into full-scale and main-line financial institutions.

In addition to the industrial and developed setting in which the UK credit union industry is based, and the fact that the industry is now in a period of transition, there are, of course other advantages in focusing on the UK credit union industry. Perhaps the foremost of these relates to the fact that transition by, and the transformation of, financial institutions has become a regular and accepted feature of the UK financial services industry—the most recent case in point being that of the UK building society industry (see McKillop and Ferguson, 1993). Prior to the 1986 Building Societies Act, building societies were highly specialised firms with a key position in the UK market in solely mortgage and savings products. Today, as a consequence of the new legislative freedoms gained post-1986, many of the top building societies can be viewed as multi-product institutions heavily involved with other high street rivals in competition for market share.

Another advantage in choosing the UK credit union industry is that it occupies a halfway position along the developmental spectrum and, in consequence, more developed movements such as those in the United States, Canada and Australia may be employed as a demonstration model for those in the UK, while the latter can, in turn be held up as an intermediary role model for those institutions still very much in the formative (nascent) stages of their development. Reference on this latter count is primarily to credit unions in Africa and to those in countries of the Eastern bloc. The movements in these countries are explored in Chapter 11.

The somewhat dichotomised nature of UK credit unions, between, on the one hand, those that wish to continue to focus on community development, self-help and small units, and, on the other hand, those that are more in favour of modernisation, diversification and expansion, is also likely to be advantageous to the study. More specifically, this dichotomy will enable a compare-and-contrast methodology to be adopted during this and the forthcoming chapters, which will, in turn, provide a clearer perspective on the factors driving change and the consequences of change. The final advantage in the choice of the UK credit union industry rests with the fact that the industry is easily identifiable and of a size that lends itself to quantitative and statistical analysis. As of 1994, there were 611 credit unions registered for business in the United Kingdom. (Fourteen, all recently formed, have not as yet completed annual returns for the Registry of Friendly Societies. Consequently, the majority of the data analysis in this and later chapters is conducted with reference to 597 credit unions.) Such a number is sufficiently large to allow confidence to be placed in any statistical or data-based findings that might emerge during the course of the analysis, but not so large (as in the case of the US position) that generalities about the industry are, to all intents and purposes, meaningless.

In this chapter, an attempt is made to document the legislative and structural framework within which UK credit unions operate. An effort is also made to highlight salient trends within the sector, with emphasis, in this instance, placed on trends that have emerged, particularly, over the period 1991 to 1994. The chapter also endeavours to analyse the relative importance of the three main trade organisations—the Association of British Credit Unions (ABCUL), the Irish League of Credit Unions (ILCU) and the National Federation of Credit Unions (NFCU) (brief comments will also be made about the Scottish League of Credit Unions, which was formed in 1993 and now has 16 credit unions affiliated to it, most of which have been poached from either the NFCU or ABCUL). In addition, an overview of the literature recently published on UK credit unions is provided.

The main purpose of this chapter is, therefore, in terms of its provision of background information. This information is then drawn on and built upon in the next six chapters. The areas under investigation in Chapters 5 to 9 are dictated by the development typology documented in Chapter 2, which, as indicated, lead to the categorisation of credit unions in the United Kingdom as typically within the transition stage of development. These areas include: the operational efficiency of the UK movement; economic viability and service provided within a risk–return context; consequences of a shift from the current narrow and focused definition of the credit union common bond to the much broader concept of fields of membership; the rationale for, and the appropriate form of, a deposit insurance mechanism; differences in the roles of community-based and employer-based credit unions; and the identification of membership biases within the industry. Chapter 10, which concludes this UK section of the book, endeavours to embrace all that has gone before and, within the framework of the development typology, provide markers as to whether the UK movement is capable of repositioning itself within the mature categorisation of our typology.

LITERATURE REVIEW

A useful starting point in this analysis of UK credit unions is with an overview of pertinent literature. In this chapter we focus solely upon material specific to the United Kingdom. Research based on material from other countries, which, in many ways, has been important in shaping the operational features of UK credit unions and the regulatory environment within which they operate, is introduced at appropriate points in future chapters.

Even a cursory examination of the literature reveals that there is a significant shortfall of research undertaken into UK credit unions. A number of reasons may be advanced to explain this shortfall. First, the importance of credit unions in the UK, as demonstrated by a sustained growth in their numbers, is only a relatively recent phenomenon. Secondly, while the absolute size of individual credit unions has increased, they are still extremely small in terms of the general size range of other UK financial intermediaries. Thirdly, a relatively accessible and comprehensive database on UK credit unions, upon which to base research, has not been available. This current research, for example, was only made possible through the laborious process of transferring paper-based annual account information on Northern Ireland credit unions (provided by the Registry of Friendly Societies at its offices in Belfast) into a form compatible with that available on disk on credit unions located in England, Scotland and Wales (provided by the Registry of Friendly Societies from its offices in London).

Research on UK credit unions has tended to have a strong policy emphasis, concentrating on legislative changes to enable credit unions both to develop and to provide a more appropriate service to their constituent customer base. The earliest and by far the most comprehensive work of this kind is by Berthoud and Hinton (1989). The authors begin by describing the scale of credit union activity in the United Kingdom. They focus initially on what they call the well-developed movement in Northern Ireland, before detailing the structure of the relatively weak, but expanding, group in Great Britain. The report then proceeds to concentrate upon the role of the leadership and membership within credit unions. In the case of the former, emphasis is placed on development and administration from a leadership perspective while, in the latter case, the authors examine what sort of people ordinary members are; what they want from their union; how much they participate in its activities; how members go about using savings and loans services and how this varies according to their income and other circumstances as well as with their use of other financial institutions. The authors conclude by attempting to assess the successes and failures of the credit union movement and the policy measures that should be adopted to further promote the movement in the United Kingdom. The analysis provided by Berthoud and Hinton (1989) could only be described as well-balanced and comprehensive. It does, however, suffer from the fact that it is somewhat insular in its coverage. The study, for example, does not attempt to place the UK industry in a more general framework and, consequently, does not consider issues pertinent to credit unions outside the United Kingdom that may also have relevance for the movement in this country. On this count, issues such as membership bias, efficiency, risk exposure and the role of deposit insurance are all issues omitted from coverage. It should also be noted that the study by Berthoud and Hinton is based on returns for the years 1986 and 1987 and is, therefore, somewhat dated.

McArthur, McGregor and Stewart (1993) employed a case study method-ology, based on interviews with 556 members from 14 credit unions, to examine their contribution to disadvantaged residents in low-income communi-ties. The authors find that, although community-based unions are located in

economically disadvantaged communities, they are not exclusively used |
poor. They also find that while better-off groups save and borrow m__, _
greater proportion of low-income users would not have purchased goods and
services in the absence of a credit union. The position taken by the authors is
that credit unions are making useful, although marginal, contributions to the
credit and debt problems of low-income families. McArthur, McGregor and
Stewart suggest that much more could be achieved if additional resources were
made available, although they stress that inappropriate external funding runs
the risk of damaging the strong mutual aid foundations upon which credit
unions are based.

Crow, Howells and Pick (1993) also focused on community-based credit
unions (the authors indicated that this study has its origins in previous work;
see, for example, Griffiths and Howells, 1991, 1993). The objectives of their
study were to investigate the support available to community-based unions, the
extent to which development agencies and development workers were reaching
people who needed them, and to make recommendations regarding the most
effective use of resources to promote the growth of community-based credit
unions. The research methodology was based on a case study and question-
naire. The report made a total of 12 recommendations aimed at enabling the
more effective development of community-based credit unions. A number of
these recommendations centred upon the promotion of educational policies for
credit unions and development workers, whereas others addressed the issues of
a reformulation of the common bond and the adoption of a much more cohesive
approach by the two main trade organisations in Great Britain—ABCUL and
the NFCU.

The National Consumer Council (1994) published a report that endeavoured
to map out a strategy for the growth of the credit union movement in Great
Britain over the next three to five years. The report was put together by a
working party drawn from officers and members of credit unions, development
workers, academics and representatives from local authorities and the Registry
of Friendly Societies. The working party examined the role of the various
bodies within the movement, considered the viability of individual institutions
and the movement as a whole, looked at what credit unions themselves view to
be the problems and barriers hindering growth and development and concluded
with 26 recommendations for change. A number of the recommendations were
targeted at improving the functioning and operation of credit unions, others
focused on the need for specified legislative change, while yet others were
geared towards the achievement of a more cohesive and co-ordinated structure
within the movement. In totality, the recommendations were all about Great
Britain achieving in the twenty-first century a sound and flourishing network
of credit unions.

Thomas and Balloch (1994) reviewed the involvement of metropolitan
authorities in promoting credit unions. The authors surveyed metropolitan

districts and London boroughs in March 1993. They achieved a total of 52 usable responses. This then enabled the authors to assess the problems in establishing credit unions, to measure the assistance provided to them by metropolitan authorities and to identify measures that need to be adopted to make credit unions more effective instruments of community regeneration. One of the key points raised by Thomas and Balloch (1994) was the unstable nature of the funding upon which much of the development work is based and they evidence this by the fact that, increasingly, local authorities and development workers spend significant amounts of time in seeking sources of finance.

McKillop, Ferguson and Nesbitt (1995a) employed a paired difference approach to investigate for the existence of scale economies in the United Kingdom. The analysis was conducted for both credit unions in aggregate as well as a number of subgroups, with the latter defined in terms of their umbrella organisation. Furthermore, unlike the aforementioned studies, this study did not confine itself to credit unions located in Great Britain. Rather, it adopted a UK perspective and included in the analysis credit unions based in Northern Ireland. The discussion revealed that significant efficiency gains were available through credit unions adopting a policy of asset growth. This finding held good irrespective of the umbrella organisation to which the credit unions belonged, although the analysis also revealed that the opportunity for efficiency gains was not so pronounced for the members of one of the trade organisations—the NFCU. The authors argued that this finding was owing to the latter's much more overt emphasis on self-help and community development, particularly in areas of economic disadvantage.

In a more policy-orientated paper, McKillop, Ferguson and Nesbitt (1995b), employing 1992 annual reports and accounts information, examined the structure and performance of UK credit unions. The authors revealed that a significant dichotomy has emerged in the cost structure, capital adequacy and profit performance between small and large organisations. Larger credit unions had much superior levels of capital adequacy than smaller ones and also managed to achieve a much stronger profit performance. The key to the healthier position of the larger unions centred upon the fact that there were significant scale economies to be achieved within the industry. Policy measures advocated by the authors related to an easing of the restrictions on both membership limits and loan volume, but only when financial safeguards were introduced to underwrite the industry. The financial safeguards in question referred to mechanisms to ensure the protection of depositors' funds.

On an annual basis, on a previous year basis, the Registry of Friendly Societies (from its offices in London) provides an overview of general developments within the industry for England, Scotland and Wales. This overview takes the form of providing details of new registrations; the geographical spread; a breakdown in terms of asset size; and a time-series analysis of membership, loans, other assets and liabilities. Any legislative changes occurring in the previous year are also detailed in the report. Similar information is provided on Northern Ireland credit unions by the Registry of Friendly Societies from its offices in Belfast.

Finally, the respective trade organisations each provide practitioner-orientated material for members and organisers. This material includes information on starting a credit union, the services provided for its members, an association rulebook and perhaps also a copy of the 1979 Credit Unions Act.

From this discussion it should be clear that, as stated at the outset, much of the material published on UK credit unions has a strong policy emphasis. In this and future chapters we also propose to highlight policies to promote growth and development. The intention is, however, to first provide additional research information vis à vis those issues that have come under scrutiny in other countries, where credit unions are at a more advanced stage of development. A start is made in this chapter by now examining the current structure and framework within which those in the UK operate.

ORIGINS AND DEVELOPMENT OF UK CREDIT UNIONS

Credit unions in Northern Ireland

In a British Isles context, credit unions were first established in Dublin at the end of the 1950s. The movement spread to Northern Ireland in 1960 with the first Northern Ireland credit union established in Derry in 1960. Under the auspices of the trade organisation, the Irish League of Credit Unions (ILCU), the movement in Ireland has flourished. The ILCU was itself established in 1960 and it is a non-statutory, all-Ireland body organised voluntarily from within the credit union movement. The principal objectives of the ILCU are to promote, service and develop credit unions in Ireland. This is achieved by offering a central financial service providing loans and stand-by facilities to credit unions for such purposes as capital equipment purchase and to ensure liquidity during peak business times. Through its Star Plan, insurance cover for affiliates, such as public indemnity, fire and burglary, is also provided. The ILCU also operates a common fund that invests on behalf of, and in the interest of, all participating members. This service does not extend to affiliated unions in Northern Ireland. The ILCU also provides formal training for credit union officers and supplies an extensive range of educational and promotional material. Affiliates pay 10% of their income into an insurance scheme, the aim of which is to provide savings and loan protection. Profits from this scheme are employed in funding the services that the trade organisation provides to affiliates.

The perception is that the credit union movement, not only in Ireland as a whole but also in Northern Ireland, is concentrated almost exclusively within

Catholic communities. That such a perception is held is perhaps not unexpected in that, especially in its formative years, the movement was strongly supported across Ireland by the Catholic church. In addition, as argued by Quinn (1994), Catholic communities based on the parish system provide fertile roots for the development of the movement. The success of the movement in Ireland did not, however, go unnoticed by the Protestant community, and following strong interest among the Protestant community the now Newcastle upon Tyne (formerly Bradford) based NFCU set up a regional office in Northern Ireland in 1985. It should be noted that, in 1995, as a consequence of an internal dispute, the Northern Ireland credit union affiliates of the NFCU broke away to re-establish under the banner of the Ulster Federation of Credit Unions, UFCU. In that a 1994 database is employed in our analysis of the UK industry, we will continue to classify UFCU members in terms of their pre-1995 NFCU affiliation.

At the end of 1994 there was a total of 152 credit unions in Northern Ireland. Of that number, 104 were affiliated to the ILCU and 41 to the NFCU. Of the remaining seven, three were classified as independent and four followed the Antigonish model of Nova Scotia.

Credit unions in Northern Ireland are supervised by the Registry of Friendly Societies in Belfast, which has substantial powers in the registration, inspection, control and prudential supervision of credit unions. The initial legislation to regulate the operation of unions in Northern Ireland was passed in 1969 as a subsection of the Industrial and Provident Act. This legislation was, in turn, brought into line with the 1979 Credit Unions Act, which governs credit unions in Great Britain, by the Credit Unions (Northern Ireland) Order, 1985. In recent years the main changes to the latter would have been implemented as a result of Credit Unions (Loans and Deposits) Order (Northern Ireland) 1993 which increased the maximum shareholding of a credit union member and the maximum borrowing limit of a member from £5000 to £10,000 in both cases.

In the Republic of Ireland, legislation is currently being drafted at the Department of Enterprise and Employment that will allow credit unions to introduce ATM facilities and cheque books for their members. By improving the range of services that they offer, credit unions in the Republic of Ireland are deliberately targeting members from middle incomes to extend their clientele beyond the confines of the less-well-off sections of society. It is unlikely that Northern Ireland will remain untouched by the impact of reforms set to take place in the Republic of Ireland. The Registrar of Friendly Societies in Belfast is faced with a particularly complex situation in revising the legislation, as many of the dimensions are historically specific to Northern Ireland. The industry displays dual characteristics, with a large segment of strong, well developed ILCU credit unions and a much weaker NFCU (as highlighted, since 1995, this group has gone under the banner of the UFCU) segment. As the former is a major force representing the interests of its members in an all-Ireland context, it can be anticipated that it will desire a large degree of compatibility and consistency in the powers granted to credit unions in both parts of Ireland.

Credit unions in Great Britain

The first credit union was established in 1964 and although the Crowther Committee (1971) report on consumer credit made an early and impassioned call for credit union development, it was not until the passage of the 1979 Credit Unions Act that the movement gained significant positive impetus. Somewhat perversely in that the Credit Unions (Northern Ireland) Order, 1985 was introduced to bring legislation in Northern Ireland into line with the 1979 Act, which applied to credit unions in Great Britain, the 1979 Act itself was introduced to bring legislation in Great Britain into line with that provided for by the Industrial and Provident Act in Northern Ireland.

The central requirement of the 1979 Act is that all credit unions should be registered with the Registry of Friendly Societies. Before permitting a credit union to register, the registrar must be assured that it has a satisfactory common bond, meets the objectives of the movement and is functioning under an appropriate set of rules. Once a credit union is operational, the function of the registrar then becomes one of monitoring its quarterly and annual returns and management capabilities. The registrar also has powers to suspend a credit union's operations, cancel its registration or, indeed, prosecute. Other key aspects of the 1979 Act include:

—there should be a minimum of 21 members and a maximum of 10,000 members, although the Registrar has the right to permit higher numbers.

—the objectives of the credit union must be the promotion of thrift among its members by the accumulation of their savings; the creation of sources of credit for members' benefit at fair and reasonable rates of interest; the use and control of members' savings for their mutual benefit; and the training and education of members in the wise use of money and in the management of their financial affairs.

—admission to membership is restricted to persons each of whom has, in relation to all other members, not less than one common bond.

—no member shall have, or claim an interest in, shares of the credit union exceeding £5,000 or such sum as may be determined by law.

—a dividend on members' shares at a rate not exceeding eight percent per annum (or such maximum rate as may be prescribed by law) may be recommended by the board of directors for declaration by the members at the annual general meeting.

—the credit union may make to a member who is of full age a loan for a provident or productive purpose, upon such security (or without security) and terms as these rules provide.

—the credit union shall have a lien on the shares of a member for any debt due to it by the member or for any debt which the member has guaranteed, and may set off any sum standing to the member's credit, including any shares, interest rebate and dividends, in or towards payment of such debt.

—the credit union may at the end of any year of account transfer to general reserve from the profits of that year, or transfer from general reserve to the revenue account such sum as the credit union may determine, provided that the general reserve is not thereby reduced to less than 10 percent, or increased to more than 20 percent.

Most credit unions prior to registration with the Registry of Friendly Societies simply adopt a set of prespecified model rules. These model rules are prespecified by the appropriate trade organisation. As earlier indicated, the two main trade organisations for credit unions in Great Britain are the NFCU and ABCUL. The latter, in some ways, can be viewed as a sister organisation to the ILCU in Ireland in that both are affiliated to the WOCCU and have similar philosophies. Of more minor importance, at least in terms of credit unions under their auspices, is the Scottish League of Credit Unions and the Forum of Credit Unions in Salford, both of which had their model rules recognised by the registrar in 1993 (an examination of the structure and ethos of the two main trade organisations and differences in their affiliates is undertaken later in this chapter).

In the three years after the introduction of the 1979 Act there was a sharp increase in credit union formation in Great Britain so that, by 1982, some 73 had registered. During the mid-1980s, a downturn in new formations took place. This downturn was due to the introduction by the registry of additional reporting requirements on existing credit unions, as well as additional competency requirements for its officers prior to registration, the net effect of which was to raise the opportunity cost of registration. A further factor important in the decline in new formation was the economic recession of that time, which undermined, in particular, some employer-based credit unions. Between 1983 and 1985 only seven were started and a total of six were closed.

The period since the mid-1980s has witnessed unprecedented growth in the number of credit unions formed in Great Britain. Over the period 1987 to 1994 there has been a four-fold increase in registrations. There were 108 registered for business in 1987, with the number by 1994 rising to 459. These new institutions have, by definition, a relatively small membership and asset level. However, over the period it has also been the case that credit unions already in existence have become significantly larger, and, consequently, growth in both asset volume and membership levels for the movement as a whole have outpaced the growth in new credit unions. Membership increased from 27,162 in 1987 to 138,251 in 1994, with asset volume over the same period increasing from £7.03 million to £60.74 million. This is approximately a five-fold increase in membership and an eight-fold increase, in nominal terms, for total assets.

As in Ireland, a dissatisfaction has arisen in Great Britain with regard to the legislative framework within which credit unions operate. In recognition of this the Treasury issued a consultation document (Treasury, 1995) on proposed amendments to the 1979 Credit Unions Act. The close date for responses to this consultation document was May 1995. In July 1995 the government laid before parliament proposals that were enacted in January 1996 and gave credit unions more freedom in the way they operate. In summary, the proposals are as follows:

- Credit union membership is to be extended to employees or residents in a particular locality

- There will be a relaxation of the limit on a member's shareholdings and loans

- The maximum loan permitted is to be £5000 above a member's shareholding or 1.5% of total credit union shareholding at the last balance date

- Registration is to be allowed on the basis of a statutory declaration that a common bond exists

- Credit unions are to be permitted to grant loans on the security of a member's shares, provided that those shares exceed the loan

- Credit unions may make loans to non-qualifying members in excess of their shareholding

- The maximum repayment period for unsecured loans is to be increased from two to four years and the maximum repayment period for secured loans increased from five to ten years

This took the form of an Order under the new deregulation procedure created by the 1994 Deregulation and Contracting Out Act (see Department of Trade and Industry, 1994). In general, the above has been welcomed by the movement and is seen by many as a means of further increasing the growth potential of credit unions. Aspects of these changes, particularly those that impinge on the common bond and those that relate to revisions in the membership and asset-level ceilings, are considered in more depth in later chapters.

CREDIT UNIONS: THE REGIONAL DIMENSION

This rapid growth in credit union numbers in Great Britain has tended to concentrate in selected areas. The geographical spread of the UK industry is detailed in Table 4.1. Information is presented on credit union numbers, membership and the size of total assets.

Table 4.1   Geographical spread of credit unions, 1994

Region	Number of credit unions	Members	Total assets
London	30	12,162	7,985,941
South East	22	4091	2,278,677
South West	7	1359	706,728
East Anglia	7	473	102,241
West Midlands	51	12,573	5,754,984
East Midlands	12	2956	1,300,480
Yorkshire and Humberside	45	7847	2,990,864
North West	93	25,395	10,717,829
North	74	8394	2,228,741
Wales	21	2711	643,758
Scotland	97	60,290	26,032,564
Northern Ireland	152	209,885	183,933,671
Total	611[a]	348,136	244,676,478

[a] As indicated, 14 credit unions, most of which are recently formed, have not as yet completed annual returns. Consequently, membership and total assets figures relate only to 597, which have supplied the relevant information.

Unlike most other financial intermediaries, there is clearly no extreme tendency amongst credit unions to cluster around London and the South East. It is also clear from Table 4.1 that the industry in Great Britain is not geographically spread in terms of some uniform distribution, but, rather, occupies pockets of significant strength in specific areas. There are, for example, very few credit unions in the highly rural regions such as the South East and East Anglia. Sizeable concentrations can, however, be found in the urban areas of West Yorkshire, Tyne and Wear, Merseyside, Greater Manchester, Greater London and the West Midlands. In Scotland, the majority are located in Glasgow and in its satellite towns, while in Wales, West Glamorgan is the favoured area for establishment. It is also interesting to note the relative strength of ABCUL and the NFCU in Great Britain. ABCUL is particularly strong in London, the West Midlands, the North West, Wales and Scotland. The actual numbers affiliated to ABCUL in these regions are 25, 47, 60, 21 and 77, respectively. In contrast, the NFCU has a strong presence in Yorkshire and Humberside, the North West, the North and Northern Ireland. The number of NFCU affiliates in these regions are, respectively, 33, 31, 42 and 41 (again note that the UFCU is now the trade body for this latter group of 41 credit unions).

The urban concentration of credit unions in Great Britain contrasts markedly with that for Northern Ireland, where in excess of 75% are located outside the two main urban areas—Belfast and Londonderry. The high incidence of rural credit unions in Northern Ireland reflects the fact that in excess of 80% are community-based. The initial impetus, and, indeed, continued support once formed, for these community-based credit unions emanates, in the main, from the parish system upon which the Catholic church is based. The common bond is simply that of church parish boundaries.

From Table 4.1, an analysis of the data reveals that, in 1994, credit unions in Northern Ireland had, on average, 1380 members per credit union and £876 in assets per member. No other region in the United Kingdom comes close to the penetration level reached by the Northern Ireland movement. Scotland is next in line in terms of average credit union membership. For 1994, average credit union membership in Scotland was 622 (assets per member in Scotland were calculated at £432). London, after Northern Ireland, had the next highest ratio of assets per member, computed at £657. The number of members per London-based credit union stood, however, at a mere 405. The average figures for Great Britain as a whole turn out to be a membership of 311 per credit union and an asset size of £439 per credit union member. The differential between Northern Ireland and Great Britain should not be that surprising in that the credit unions in the former are at a much more mature stage in their development. This rests with the fact that they started earlier, were strongly supported by the Catholic church and, at least until 1979, operated under a much more favourable legislative framework.

Over recent years, however, the growth rate of credit unions in Great Britain has significantly outpaced that of their Northern Ireland counterparts. Earlier, it was noted that, over the period 1987 to 1994, credit unions in Great Britain had achieved a four-fold increase in numbers, a five-fold increase in membership and an eight-fold increase in asset size. This has not been matched by Northern Ireland. In 1986 there were 93 credit unions in operation with this figure rising by 1994 to 152. Over the same period, asset volume increased from £49.55 million to £183.93 million, while membership rose from 122,860 to 209,885. At one level, this differential performance is not unexpected in that, as argued, credit unions in Northern Ireland, in general, are at a much more mature stage in their development. Northern Ireland is now covered by a web of credit unions with, at present, a density of 12% of the adult population. This compares with a penetration level of 0.2% of the adult population in Great Britain. It is, therefore, clear that there is much more scope for growth in Great Britain and, in consequence, the superior growth rate should be of little surprise.

It may also be of interest to note that those new credit unions that have formed in Northern Ireland are, in the majority case, affiliated to the NFCU (as earlier indicated, all NFCU affiliates in Northern Ireland subsequently established their own trade body—the Ulster Federation of Credit Unions) rather than the ILCU. This would tend to signify that these new credit unions are being formed to service sections of the Protestant community, which, given the history and development of the movement in Ireland, have only recently begun to embrace the credit union ideal. Of course, there has also been growth over the period by ILCU affiliates. This growth has concentrated on existing credit unions increasing their membership levels and asset volume. This, as will be highlighted in Chapter 6, has had important consequences for the achievement of scale economies and, hence, the opportunity for these credit unions to generate cost-efficiency savings in their operations.

COMMUNITY-BASED CREDIT UNIONS IN GREAT BRITAIN

The more urban focus of credit unions in Great Britain stems primarily from the origin of the support sources for the movement. Local authorities are one of the principal sources of support for the establishment of credit unions. Thomas and Balloch (1994) believe that they support the credit union ideal primarily because they help provide a source of reasonably priced credit to disadvantaged groups not usually eligible for other forms of credit. In particular, the authors refer to many of the community groups in inner cities and in peripheral housing estates. Additional, although somewhat subsidiary, reasons for local authorities supporting development include the fact that setting up and running a credit union can provide training for the unemployed and low waged, as well as the fact that credit unions encourage the introduction of a savings philosophy amongst groups that might not otherwise be exposed to such a philosophy.

Thomas and Balloch indicate that the power of local authorities to support credit unions is derived from Section 69 of the Weights and Measures Act 1985, which allows local authorities to provide advice to, or for, the benefit of consumers of goods and services, including financial services. The authors classify the support provided by local authorities into four distinct categories:

- financial assistance
- support in kind
- support for development workers
- the establishment of credit union development agencies

Financial assistance relates to the provision of start-up grants, usually between £500 and £2000, and grants to cover the costs of training credit union members and committees by outside agencies. Support in kind refers to local authorities providing premises for the credit union to conduct its business, directly assisting in the training of staff and the sponsoring of events. In their article, Thomas and Balloch argue that perhaps the most effective method local authorities have of supporting credit unions is through the employment of development workers—the responsibility of the development worker being to promote credit unions not only amongst community groups but also in the workplace. Finally, a number of local authorities have also established specialist bodies, such as development agencies, to meet the diverse requirements of the credit unions in their areas. These agencies are companies limited by guarantee that employ their own development workers to advise and support new, and, indeed, existing, credit unions.

Credit unions in Great Britain are not, of course, solely community-based as a sizeable number are now established in particular employment sectors to provide low-interest loans and savings opportunities. Local councils appear to be the employee grouping that has most embraced the credit union ideal. There are, at present, 20 credit unions scattered across Great Britain, linked to different local councils. The police service is also well represented within the credit union movement, with a total of 12 credit unions linked to constabularies. The movement has also a presence within the transport sector, with post office workers, within the fire service and the health service as well as within a growing number of high-profile workplaces, including British Airways, British Aerospace, News International, Pitney Bowes and Lloyds Bank Employees. In Chapter 8 we will refocus attention on employer-based credit unions in order to determine whether there is the same potential for expansion within this segment of the movement as has occurred in the United States.

SIZE CHARACTERISTICS OF UK CREDIT UNIONS

On the basis of asset size, information is presented in Table 4.2 on relative asset share, credit union numbers and membership levels. This information has been obtained from annual returns for the year up to the end of September 1994.

It is apparent from Table 4.2 that the distribution of credit unions in numerical terms is very much skewed towards the lower end of the distribution.

Table 4.2 Assets and members of UK credit unions, 1994

Asset range (£)	Assets of groups as a percentage of the total	Number of credit unions	Number of members
Over £1,000,000	71.51	59	190,638
£500,000 to £999,999	14.72	49	55,900
£250,000 to £499,999	6.06	42	27,644
£100,000 to £249,999	3.90	59	23,852
£50,000 to £99,999	1.44	49	13,000
£613 to £49,999	2.37	339	37,102
Total	100.00	597[a]	348,136

[a] The total does not include those credit unions, 14 in total, that while registered, have not as yet completed an annual return for the Registry of Friendly Societies.

Approximately 57% have an asset base between £613 and £49,999. When credit unions are, however, viewed in terms of their membership, the picture obtained is somewhat reversed in that the top group (assets greater than £1 million) account for 55% of total membership. Although there is an obvious concentration in membership, which has itself been increasing over time (in 1991 the top group of credit unions accounted for only 43% of the membership), it may be the case that such concentration would be even more pronounced were it not for the 1979 Credit Unions Act, which initially placed an upper ceiling of 5000 (now increased to 10,000) on membership. It should be noted, however, that the registrars of friendly societies can grant exemption from this maximum limit if they are satisfied that exemption would be in the public interest. Nevertheless, this restriction does raise the question of whether, for example, legislation has, in the past, adversely impacted upon the ability of credit unions to avail of scale economies in their operation.

A decomposition of the asset structure is documented in Table 4.3. The breakdown is again provided on the basis of asset size.

An analysis of Table 4.3 reveals that for all credit union groups the majority of assets are tied up in the form of loans to members. For the most part, net loans contribute in excess of 75% of total asset volume, the exception is with respect to the end, low-asset-volume group—£613 to £49,999—where the share of net loans is 60.5%. The explanation for the disparity appears to be that for smaller credit unions liquidity constraints have necessitated that a larger proportion of their assets are held in the form of cash (38% for the asset range £613 to £49,999), which, in turn, reduces the proportion of funds available for on-lending to members.

Drawing together information from Tables 4.2 and 4.3 and computing the ratio, assets by number of members, it transpires that the larger unions are considerably wealthier than the smaller unions. Indeed, there is a marked downward trend in the ratio, in that for the top credit union group, assets per member stand at £902 and fall to a mere £157 for the smallest group (the comparative figures for 1991 were £701 and £125, respectively). Therefore, it is

Table 4.3 UK credit unions asset decomposition, 1994

Asset range £	Net loans to members, £	Investments, £	Cash in hand cash at bank, £	Other assets, £
Over £1,000,000	136,378,127	10,018,557	21,803,364	3,699,300
£500,000 to £999,999	26,151,531	2,359,540	6,163,036	129,129
£250,000 to £499,999	10,916,627	580,837	2,832,417	150,212
£100,000 to £249,999	7,368,721	298,283	1,715,837	85,510
£50,000 to £99,999	2,659,239	77,018	794,481	15,478
£613 to £49,999	3,521,050	40,742	2,190,479	67,383
Total	186,995,295	13,374,977	35,499,614	4,147,012

clear that there is a significant relationship between size and wealth within the sector, with this relationship having become much more pronounced over time. This apparent dichotomy between small and large credit unions may, again, suggest the existence of scale economies in the operation of the UK industry.

Details of the liability structure of the UK movement are presented in Table 4.4.

Table 4.4   UK credit unions liability structure, 1994

Asset range (£)	Share capital (£)	Other liabilities (£)	General reserves (£)
Over £1,000,000	150,804,274	8,835,176	15,369,354
£500,000 to £999,999	31,240,977	1,065,543	3,216,132
£250,000 to £499,999	12,796,836	710,450	1,316,681
£100,000 to £249,999	8,558,106	339,633	635,559
£50,000 to £99,999	3,046,014	216,607	252,693
£613 to £49,999	5,176,152	260,911	368,118
Total	211,622,359	11,428,320	21,158,537

In that credit unions are not permitted to accept deposits from any persons except by way of subscriptions for their shares, it is clear that share capital is essentially their deposit base. In aggregate, share capital accounts for, on average, 86% of liabilities. There is a marginal difference between large and small credit unions, with the latter group tending to have a share capital base 2% to 3% larger than the former. One of the remaining components of the liability base of credit unions encompasses deposits by persons too young to be members. Under the 1979 Act, a credit union may take deposits up to a total of £750, or such higher maximum as may be prescribed by law, from a minor under the age of 16 who would otherwise not be qualified to become a member of that credit union. Other liabilities are: borrowings from authorised banks or from other credit unions; plus general reserves. With respect to the latter component of the liability structure, credit unions in the United Kingdom are required to hold at least 10% of total assets in the form of reserves. As will be highlighted in later chapters, a sizeable number of credit unions fall far short of the 10% reserve ratio with the problem being more acute for the smaller-asset-range organisations. Indeed, it is this shortfall in reserves that has artificially presented smaller-scale credit unions as having, at least in relative percentage terms, a greater proportion of their liabilities as share capital.

TRADE ORGANISATIONS

Earlier in this chapter it was noted that UK credit unions belong primarily to one of three umbrella organisations—the Association of British Credit Unions

(ABCUL), the National Federation of Credit Unions (NFCU), and the Irish League of Credit Unions (ILCU).

ABCUL, which is affiliated to the World Council of Credit Unions (WOCCU), represented, in 1994, 308 solely British-based credit unions (10 of that number are newly formed and did not make a return to the registrar for 1994 and, hence, are not included in the tabular analysis presented in Table 4.5). ABCUL, while representing a significant number of community-based credit unions, represents almost all those that are based on a workplace or occupational group: for example, in 1994 there were 63 employer-based credit unions and ABCUL represented 51. It provides advice, information and assistance to both those groups planning to establish and those already established. In addition, ABCUL provides a set of model rules that fulfil the registrar's registration criteria. To finance activities, ABCUL receives support from the US-based CUNA Mutual, the insurance company owned by credit unions that serves the international credit union movement. Finance is also generated through an annual levy placed on affiliates, with the amount determined by membership size, and also through commission earnings from acting as a broker for the fidelity bond insurance that all credit unions in Great Britain must have as a requirement of the 1979 Act.

The ILCU is also affiliated to the WOCCU and, in 1994, represented a total of 560 credit unions in Ireland, of which 104 were based in Northern Ireland. In that this part of the book focuses on the UK industry, we are only interested, from an analytical viewpoint, in the 104 ILCU members based in Northern Ireland. The ILCU plays a vital role in the development, training, administration and supervision of the Irish credit union movement. It provides a set of model rules to aid credit union establishment. Through the ILCU and its associated ECCU Assurance Company Ltd., credit unions provide life assurance protection for both savings and loans. Members' savings are also protected by a savings protection scheme operated by the ILCU to cover credit unions in financial difficulty. The ILCU, as a mature trade organisation within the WOCCU is also involved in European Union-led initiatives to encourage development in countries within the Eastern Bloc.

The NFCU, as of end 1994, represented 165 credit unions in the UK (four of that number are newly formed and did not make a return to the registrar for 1994 and, hence, are not included in the tabular analysis presented in Table 4.5). Until the haemorrhage in 1995 of NFCU, affiliates to the UFCU, the NFCU had a strong presence in Northern Ireland, with 41 of its 165 affiliated credit unions located there. Given that the database on which the discussion is based pertains to 1994, we will, as earlier stressed, classify these 41 unions as NFCU affiliates. As with the other trade organisations, the NFCU provides advice, information and assistance to credit unions both prior to establishment and after their formation. It also has its own set of model rules that credit unions may adopt, which, in many ways, are less complicated than those of the other trade organisations. The structure of the NFCU is itself much simpler than that of the other bodies, with a single committee responsible for all its functions. In terms of funding, the NFCU earns commission income from acting as a broker for the fidelity bond insurance. In addition, it places a levy on each credit union, the size of which is determined by the membership size, and has also, at different times, obtained bursaries from charities and grant-awarding bodies.

In a UK context, an important point of note is the difference in emphasis between the NFCU and ABCUL. The primary focus of the former is on community development, self-help and small units. Its members consider the role of credit unions not only in terms of the provision of financial services, but also in the promotion of self-help and community development, particularly in areas of economic disadvantage. While encouraging its members to become economically viable by developing to a size appropriate to the needs of the members and the local community, it nevertheless prefers credit unions not to exceed a few hundred members. Expansion, where it occurs, should be in the development of new unions.

ABCUL, which would have the same ethos and philosophy as its sister organisation, the ILCU, in Ireland, in contrast to the NFCU, is very much in favour of a growth-orientated strategy. While it also has experience of community-based and community-orientated institutions, attention is more sharply concentrated upon individual credit unions achieving significant critical mass. This is then expected to result in the generation of business efficiency and scale economies, with the credit unions eventually occupying a significant position in the savings and loans market.

ABCUL, in recent years, has been very much to the fore in pushing for changes in the rules under which credit unions conduct business. Indeed, many within the credit union movement would argue that ABCUL has been the main force behind the proposed changes to the 1979 Act that were passed in 1995 and came into effect from January 1996. It is also likely that, in the future, ABCUL will be agitating for further changes, particularly with respect to the range of products credit unions can provide. While the NFCU argue that such proposals could be seen as beneficial, their concern is that credit unions occupy a particular niche and philosophy of co-operation and self-help and, under such proposals, this would be negated and they would become just another financial institution.

Information on the respective trade organisations is detailed in Table 4.5.

It is evident from this information on credit union numbers, membership and asset size that ILCU affiliates occupy in strength the upper size brackets for both membership and asset share and, while there is significant overlap in size range between NFCU and ABCUL, it is clear that, overall, a larger proportion of both NFCU unions and members occupy the smallest size bracket, £613 to £49,999.

Table 4.5   Trade organisations, 1994

Asset range (£)	Number of credit unions	Number of members	Total assets (£)
ABCUL			
Over £1,000,000	14	45,964	32,161,920
£500,000 to £999,999	9	11,589	5,914,938
£250,000 to £499,999	14	10,934	5,070,007
£100,000 to £249,999	30	11,929	4,528,338
£50,000 to £99,999	29	8604	2,090,703
£613 to £49,999	202	24,687	3,635,078
Total	298[a]	113,707	53,400,984
NFCU			
Over £1,000,000	0	0	0
£500,000 to £999,999	3	3914	1,694,693
£250,000 to £499,999	8	5176	2,743,860
£100,000 to £249,999	13	5461	2,148,410
£50,000 to £99,999	14	2877	1,021,131
£613 to £49,999	123	10,858	1,890,907
Total	161[b]	28,286	9,499,001
ILCU			
Over £1,000,000	43	141,647	140,759,796
£500,000 to £999,999	35	37,873	26,932,917
£250,000 to £499,999	16	9109	5,713,345
£100,000 to £249,999	9	3087	1,570,989
£50,000 to £99,999	0	0	0
£613 to £49,999	1	143	35,851
Total	104	191,859	175,012,898

[a] There are a further 10 credit unions registered with ABCUL that did not make a return for 1994.
[b] There are a further four credit unions registered with the NFCU that did not make a return for 1994.

Given the ethos of the respective trade organisations, coupled with differences in the time period over which each has been in operation, the results documented in Table 4.5 are as expected. The pattern of a heavy skew in union numbers and members in the two bottom-rank classifications for the NFCU fits in with its emphasis on community development, self-help and small units. In a similar respect, the greater incidence in the larger scales for the other associations accords with their more overt growth-orientated strategies. In that these two trade organisations, as already indicated, are considered sister organisations, with both affiliated to the WOCCU, the larger scale of the ILCU relative to ABCUL rests with the fact that the former has been in existence for a significantly longer time period.

In terms of progress during the 1990s, the impression is that ABCUL has led the way. Between 1991 and 1994 a further 100 credit unions registered under its banner. The net effect was that total membership doubled and total assets increased from £21.6 million to £53.4 million with the most pronounced increase being for the top asset category. (Between 1991 and 1994, for the asset-range category over £1m, membership increased from 9446 to 45,964, while total assets increased from £7.2 million to £32.16 million.) The NFCU also made considerable progress between 1991 and 1994 with the registration of an additional 44 credit unions, membership increasing from 13,512 to 28,286 and total assets rising from £2.7 million to £9.5 million. In contrast to the NFCU and ABCUL, the ILCU had very few new formations in Northern Ireland with only two new credit unions established between 1991 and 1994. As argued earlier, this is to be expected in that Northern Ireland is already well covered by credit unions, particularly the Catholic community, to which the ILCU is orientated. Much more impressive was the membership and asset growth of existing ILCU credit unions. The membership level in Northern Ireland increased by 60,000 between 1991 and 1994, while total assets rose by £78 million. Particularly important from the perspective of the viability of the movement is that most of this increase took place within the asset range 'over £1 million'. For this category, membership, over the period 1991 to 1994, rose from 89,361 to 141,647, while total assets increased from £63.2 million to £140.76 million.

When the number of credit unions affiliated to these three trade organisations are added together it still leaves 34 unaccounted for. In the main, these are small in terms of their membership and assets under their control. Only two, for example, would have an asset level in the range 'over £1 million'. A total of nine of these credit unions are unaffiliated, three follow the Antigonish model of Novia Scotia, four are classified as independent, two have adopted the Forum of Credit Unions in Salford (FOCUS) model rules (the indication is that no other credit unions are likely to follow the FOCUS model) and the remaining 16 are affiliated to the Scottish League of Credit Unions (SLCU).

The latter was established in 1993 and has experienced good growth in the intervening period. It was established to exploit and, indeed, foster the Scottish identity and, consequently, its membership is solely based in Scotland. In addition to the introduction of three new credit unions, the SLCU has enticed seven ABCUL affiliates, four NFCU members and two unaffiliated unions to transfer to their model rules. As with the other trade organisations, the majority of credit unions affiliated to the SLCU are small in asset size (seven are in the asset range '£613 to £49,999', while their largest member has assets in the category '£500,000 to £999,999'. What is, nevertheless, impressive about the SLCU is the manner in which they harnessed and built upon the Scottish identity.

CONCLUDING COMMENTS

The discussion has identified the UK credit union industry as regionally diverse, young, vibrant and high growth, particularly over the course of this last decade. Evidence of the strong growth performance of the UK movement can be seen in the growth of credit union numbers, members and the total asset volume under their control. This rapid movement by UK credit unions along the developmental growth spectrum is not unexpected in that the UK economy has numerous demonstration models as to how financial institutions, once established, can be expected to develop. In addition, it is clear that the regulator for credit unions, the Registry of Friendly Societies, has demonstrated considerable flexibility in the creation of a framework within which credit unions can best develop. In the formative years the registry focused heavily on the economic soundness and financial credibility of credit unions. The registry now appears to believe that credit unions have progressed considerably in the establishment of their economic worth and, consequently, it has been proactive in the introduction of legislative amendments aimed at permitting credit unions to enter a new stage in their development. A further factor of importance in the rapid movement by UK credit unions along the developmental spectrum relates to the fact that in the United Kingdom they are essentially part of an advanced industrial economy. The implication, in this instance, is that although credit unions service the more disadvantaged of the population their clientele, nevertheless, are well aware of the potential range, quality and cost of financial services available elsewhere and, consequently, are likely to be continually pressing for enhanced services.

While progress in the UK has to date been good and the framework is now being established to further encourage growth, it would be unwise at this juncture in time to overstate the contribution of credit unions to the overall financial community. What, however, we will argue is that if the pattern of development in Great Britain follows in any way that in Northern Ireland, where the movement was established some five years earlier and now has a membership that covers 12% of the adult population, credit unions by the end of this century are likely to occupy a significant position within the UK financial services industry.

The analysis also revealed that a considerable dichotomy has emerged in the relative wealth of large and small credit unions. The larger credit unions have an asset level per member some six times that of their smaller counterparts. The key to the healthier position of the larger credit unions relates to the fact that they have been established for a much longer period. It was also intimated that the differential in relative wealth may point towards the existence of significant scale economies within the industry, an issue that will be explored in Chapter 6.

While the discussion in this chapter has provided insight into both the structure of UK credit unions and the legislative amendments aimed at encouraging the growth of the movement, it should also be clear that the industry in the United Kingdom remains very much under-researched. As yet, nothing is known about the member group orientation of credit unions and its impact upon total member benefits; the optimal scale and efficiency level in the operation of credit unions; the risks inherent in credit union activity; and the potential benefits and costs with respect to risk reduction from the introduction of deposit insurance. It is these issues and others that we turn to in the forthcoming chapters.

5

Economic Viability of, and Service on Offer from, UK Credit Unions

INTRODUCTION

A twin-track approach is adopted to the analysis in this chapter, with the tracks themselves necessarily intertwining at times. In the first instance, the chapter focuses on the viability of credit unions. The *modus operandi* in this instance is to examine the income and expenditure account of three credit unions at very different stages in their development—the point to highlight being that viability, and, in particular, financial viability, is subject to a myriad of both definitions and interpretations. To some it means survival, in terms of paying essential bills and meeting the requirements of the Registry of Friendly Societies. To others, the concept of viability is synonymous with self-sufficiency and the achievement of a critical scale in its operation. Yet others may consider consistent asset growth as evidence of financial viability, while a further group may hold the view that viability is not achieved until a credit union has adequate reserve levels, pays a dividend on members' shares and has an adequately diversified loan book. No doubt, the definition chosen is very much influenced by the stage a credit union has reached along its developmental spectrum. Self-sufficiency, for example, is likely to be the objective of a credit union in the initial years after its formation, while achieving adequate reserves, paying a dividend and operating a diversified loan book is likely to be a target that is only achievable by those at a more mature stage of development.

The second part of the analysis is an examination of the quality of service, in terms of price, that UK credit unions provide for their members. This aspect of the discussion concentrates upon the dividend rate paid by credit unions to their members and the loan rate levied on their members. This gives some insight into the relative position that individual credit unions adopt to their savers and borrowers. Such a discussion would, however, be deficient if it were not placed within a risk framework. Consequently, the relative riskiness of credit unions is assessed through the computation of a number of financial ratios, including: a capital ratio that measures a credit union's ability to absorb loan loss; a bad-debt write-off ratio to measure the quality of the loan portfolio and a bad-debt provision ratio to examine the potential future losses to which credit unions may be subject.

The intertwining aspect of the analysis relates to the hope that the discussion will discover that as credit unions become more economically viable they become able to offer a better quality service in a lower-risk environment. To test this hypothesis, the analysis of the quality of service provided by credit unions, and their relative riskiness, is assessed on the basis of credit union size. The expectation is that it is large credit unions that will prove to be more economically viable and more able to balance the treatment of borrowers and savers in a lower-risk environment. As the discussion unfolds, as a tangential theme, effort is also made to determine whether the trade organisation to which the credit union belongs has an influence on the quality of service and the risk environment within which that service is provided.

The discussion begins with the examination of the income and expenditure accounts of the three credit unions—one recently formed, another 10 years in operation and the third over 30 years in existence, with the latter credit union one of the unambiguous successes of the movement in the United Kingdom. This part of the analysis then feeds into a model of the four stages of growth necessary prior to a credit union being classified as self-sufficient. The analysis then breaks from this tack to examine the service on offer by credit unions and the risks faced by their members. The chapter is completed with some concluding comments, the emphasis of which is on the drawing together of the two tracks pursued in the body of the discussion.

CREDIT UNION VIABILITY

As a starting point in the examination of viability, consider the information documented in Table 5.1 on the three credit unions. This material pertains to the income and expenditure during the 1994 year of account. Also detailed are a number of related financial ratios.

Credit union A

Credit union A was formed in 1992 with its common bond defined on the basis of a small localised community. Consequently, even at this early stage, it can

Table 5.1   Income and expenditure profile for three credit unions, 1994

	A	B	C
Expenditure			
Salaries	0	700	86,079
Accommodation	0	1564	11,391
Printing and stationery	23	834	7535
Loan and share insurance	42	1509	41,817
General insurance	35	498	4049
Audit and accountancy fees	0	705	3525
Training	0	0	2880
Bank interest and charges	0	664	6652
Bad debt write-offs	0	1790	34,147
Bad debt provisions	0	300	15,000
Other expenditures	105	2240	34,999
Total expenditure	205	10,804	248,074
Income			
Interest from members' loans	197	16,814	392,391
Other interest	18	1972	15,544
Other income	21	598	8374
Total income	236	19,384	416,309
Surplus (Income − Expenditure)	31	8580	168,235
Asset size	5024	269,359	4,163,112
Membership	34	736	6327
Dividend (%)	0	3.23	3.07
Loan/asset ratio (%)	41.88	57.37	89.65
Reserve ratio (%)	4.26	6.44	9.37

be said that if credit union A's common bond remains as currently defined there is little potential for it achieving significant critical mass. At present, credit union A has a membership of 34 and an asset base of £5024. Credit union A has achieved a reserve-to-asset ratio of 4.26% and on-lends 41.88% of its total assets to members, which for 1994 amounted to a total 20 loans, but has not as yet paid a dividend to members on their savings.

The income generated through making loans to members may be viewed as a credit union's lifeblood and it is through such self-generated income that a credit union eventually achieves self-sufficiency. As will later be demonstrated, most credit unions lend in excess of 70% of their asset base, with Copson (1992) stating that many credit unions operate on the principle that a minimum of 75% to 80% of savings must be out on loan over the course of a year to ensure financial efficiency. It is clear that credit union A is not operating within this financial efficiency band and there may be one of two reasons for this. First, it may simply be the case that credit union A faces an insufficient demand for loans. Copson indicates that just such a problem is faced by a number of credit unions. He further argues that they need to strike a balance between overstretching financial resources and underutilising them. This is achieved by ensuring a sufficient flow of funds into the credit union, through the repayment of loans, plus the interest on them, and new savings, and by a regular outflow of borrowing. Credit union A has not, at this point, achieved the required balance. A second reason why credit union A is not within the target efficiency band may relate to its new formation and the fact that in this formative period there are significant start-up costs, which reduces the ability to on-lend to members. The National Consumer Council (1994) documents some of the core start-up costs. In the main, the most significant costs centre on those levied by the trade organisation to which the credit union is affiliated. Common costs across the respective trade organisations include a registration fee—£200 (payable to the Registry of Friendly Societies); stationery starter pack—£90; fidelity bond insurance—£90 and manuals £35. ABCUL, in addition, levies an initial affiliation fee of £250 and may charge up to £500 for initial training of the credit union's officers. The NFCU does not charge an initial affiliation fee and provides training free of charge. Of course, credit unions will also require resources to equip their offices and will be subject to a range of running costs, some one-off, others recurring. A flavour of some of these expenditures may be obtained through examination of credit union A's expenditures detailed in Table 5.1.

It must be clear from the analysis that survival, let alone self-sufficiency, is only possible for credit union A if it obtains, in these its formative years, grant aid from bodies outside the movement and the services of unpaid volunteers to carry out the administration and operation of the union. Details of the range and types of grants available to credit unions were mapped out in Chapter 4. The main grant aid support that individual credit unions receive relates to one-off grants, invariably of the order £1000 to £2000, to help them pay their start-up costs. Without such outside support it is clear that credit union A, and others like it, would find it extremely difficult to establish. It may also be the case that many small localised community-based credit unions, with limited growth potential, will continue to require such outside funding for their survival, although, in this context, it should be noted that such outside help mitigates against the whole concept of self-help and is frowned upon by certain sections of the credit union movement (see Berthoud and Hinton, 1989).

What, however, is certainly the case is that the formation and continued survival of credit union A would not be possible without unpaid volunteer labour. Credit union A relies totally on volunteer staff to service its various functions. Its members would have elected a board of directors with officers such as chairperson, secretary and honourary treasurer. This board of directors then appoints credit committees to consider loan applications, while members, as an extra precaution, elect supervisory committees to carry out functions such as examining the books and records of the credit union. In addition, members are required to perform the tasks of taking deposits, issuing loans and book-keeping, as well as to aid in general office management. In the case of credit union A, the various functions and services were provided by the membership for the membership on an unpaid basis. Indeed, irrespective of their asset size, all credit unions, to a lesser or greater extent, depend on unpaid volunteers to service at least some of their functions.

Credit union B

Credit union B was established over 10 years ago, and, as with credit union A, its common bond is community-based, although its population catchment is considerably larger, which consequently provides it with enough potential scope for the achievement of financial viability. At present, credit union B has a membership of 736 and an asset base of £269,359. It has accumulated a sizeable capital base with its reserve to asset ratio currently standing at 6.44%. It made some 235 loans in 1994, on-lending 57.37% of its total assets and also managed to pay a dividend to members that averaged 3.23% over the course of the year.

Our second case study, in line with most other soundly established credit unions in the United Kingdom, has experienced strong asset growth in recent years. (Its asset level has grown by an average of 26% in each of the years from 1991 to 1994.) This asset growth has brought with it additional problems. In the first instance credit union B no longer operates from premises free of charge. Significant accommodation expenses are now incurred (see Table 5.1). These expenses include rent, rates, heating, lighting, cleaning, repairs and renewals of fixtures and fittings. Credit union B, unlike credit union A, is subject to expenditure on salaries. It would be extremely unlikely that a credit union of this size could be run solely by unpaid volunteer members. One person is employed on a part-time basis to manage the office. In 1994, salary and national insurance costs amounted to 7.61% of total management expenses. In that this 7.61% equates to £700, it is evident that a high level of unpaid volunteer work is still needed.

Credit union B also pays auditor's fees as well as bank charges. For 1994, audit fees amounted to £705, while bank charges were £664. For many credit unions, audit fees are a serious financial burden. Only those credit unions whose receipts and payments do not, in aggregate, exceed £5000, and whose membership does not exceed 500, are permitted to carry out lay audits (for more details see National Consumer Council, 1994).

Although subject to these additional costs, credit union B is in a position to pay a dividend on member shares. This dividend in 1994 amounted to 3.23%. The payment of a dividend is a necessary step for financial viability. It is only through the generation of a steady stream of new savings that credit unions can continue to on-lend to members and, through this process, generate the critical mass required for financial viability. While credit union B appears to be financially viable (in 1994 it had a reserve ratio of 6.44%, generated a surplus of £8580 and had a negligible bad-debt problem) it has not achieved an adequate level of financial efficiency. Over the course of 1994, 57.37% of savings were out on loan to members, which is considerably short of the optimal target range, 75% to 80%. The shortfall may be owing to the fact that credit union B is still adjusting towards the financial efficiency target, or it may be the case that, at this point in its development, considerable additional costs are faced, notably on premises and salaries, which are disproportionately high given its current asset size.

Credit union C

Credit union C was formed in the mid-1960s and, as with the other two case studies, the common bond between members is that of community. In this instance, the community is located in a somewhat disadvantaged area of an inner city. Credit union C has a significant catchment area for members and has been relatively successful over the years in attracting members, which currently number 6327. The asset size is £4.16 million. The reserve-to-asset ratio is 9.37%, which almost meets the 10% reserve ratio stipulated by the Registry of Friendly Societies. Loans granted during 1994 were 5639, equivalent to a loan/asset ratio of 89.65%. A dividend of 3.07% was paid for the year.

During the 1990s, credit union C has grown rapidly. For example, over the period 1991 to 1994, total assets increased by more than 25% per year, while membership rose annually by approximately 10%. In terms of expenditure, the dominant cost was that of salaries, which, in 1994, amounted to 47% of management expenses. This percentage figure is the norm for credit unions of this asset size and reflects the fact that to provide an efficient service to the membership, salaried staff must be employed, although, as stressed earlier, credit union C, as with all credit unions, still relies heavily on volunteer staff.

Loans written off as bad debts at £34,147 (2.76% of total assets) is also a significant cost. Growth in size necessarily implies that the informal information that the loan committee may have on individual borrowers may not be as good as in the case of a small credit union. Consequently, the expectation is that asset growth and bad-debt write-offs are positively correlated. A problem for credit unions once they reach a critical mass to allow financial viability and self-sufficiency is that this should not be put in jeopardy by an increase in loan default.

Most credit unions, once they reach the size of credit union C, have in place procedures to minimise bad-debt write-offs. All credit unions, as a matter of course, monitor accounts on an on-going basis, with any found to be in arrears dealt with by the arrears control committee. The arrears control committee contact the defaulting member and request that the loan repayment shortfall is made good. If this fails, the committee may contact a solicitor with a view to taking legal action to recover the money due. This step is taken only as a last resort. Credit unions do not like taking legal action, although it must be stressed that they do have a legal obligation to protect members' savings. Finally, credit unions of a size comparable to credit union C may also retain the services of a debt collector to deal with specific cases. Bad debt as a problem for all credit unions is explored in more detail later in this chapter.

With 89.65% of savings out on loans to members generating interest of £392,391, credit union C is operating above the upper end of the financial efficiency target range. It is also informative to examine briefly the other sources of interest income available to it. If savings are not being loaned to members, the balance either remains unused or attracts interest on deposit, although the interest gained is somewhat lower than that available through on-lending to members. Credit union C received £15,306 in the form of bank deposit interest (this is classified within the subcomponent 'other interest' in Table 5.1, the rest of which consists of £28 in interest from investments and £210 in interest from loans to other credit unions).

Although the relative size of the return from lending to other credit unions (£210) is small, an interloan market in the industry is to be encouraged. The arrangement results in a better rate of return for the lending credit union than that available on deposit and can be extremely helpful to a credit union requiring additional short-term funds for on-lending to its members. This internal loan market permits credit union C, and others that have achieved financial viability and self-sufficiency, to aid smaller unions in their achievement of these objectives.

To conclude this part of the chapter it is perhaps informative to reproduce material published by the Birmingham Credit Union Development Agency, which identifies four broad levels of growth that lead to self-sufficiency.

Level 1
This is the basic level and occurs when the credit union has approximately £20,000 in assets including at least £12,000 on loan to members. Taking account of some limited slow payment of loan interest, yearly income should, with deposit account interest, exceed £1,300. This should be sufficient to pay all the credit union's costs, provided accommodation is rent free. There will, however, be very little surplus.

Level 2
This level occurs when a credit union has assets of £40,000, including over £24,000 on loan. Deposit account and loan interest should generate an income

of approximately £2,600 a year. This will enable the credit union to cover its expenditure, build up the financial reserves of the credit union or pay a small dividend.

Level 3
When a credit union has reached £160,000 in assets with over £96,000 on loan to members, income should exceed £10,400 a year. At this point, as well as covering the expenditures of Levels 1 and 2, the credit union should be in a position to pay a part-time worker. Further progress will also have been achieved in the build-up of reserves and in the payment of a dividend to shareholders.

Level 4
With £400,000 worth of assets and over £240,000 on loan to members, income should be approximately £26,000 per year. In addition to covering the expenditures detailed in Levels 1 and 2 the credit union should be able to employ either a full-time staff member or a number of part-time employees. At this juncture the credit union should have a reserve asset ratio in place which meets the requirements of the 1979 Credit Union Act as well as providing an adequate dividend rate on members' shareholdings.

For each level, the Birmingham Credit Union Development Agency model also assumes that at least 60% of assets are on loan to members over the course of the year and that slow payers and bad debts are kept to a minimum.

Returning to the three credit unions initially examined, it is clear that credit union A, with only £5024 in assets in 1994, has not even achieved a Level 1 stage of development. Credit union A cannot, however, be viewed as an outlier. Out of the 611 registered credit unions in 1994, a staggering 237 would not have achieved Level 1, as defined by the Birmingham guidelines. A total of 92 credit unions are currently at the Level 1 stage of development. It is, however, our opinion that the criteria utilised is somewhat harsh. Many credit unions of an asset size between £10,000 and £20,000 are generating the required surplus, on-lending in excess of 60% of members' savings and building up reserves, with some even paying a dividend. (Of the 93 credit unions with an asset size between £10,000 and £20,000, a total of 31 pay a dividend to their members.) Consequently, we would consider an asset size of £10,000 as a more appropriate threshold for the achievement of Level 1 development.

Taking Level 2, as classified by the Birmingham Development Agency, there are 105 at this stage of development. A further 55 are at the Level 3 development stage, while 122 are at Level 4. It is this latter group of 122 credit unions that are defined as self-sufficient and economically viable under the criteria utilised by the Birmingham Development Agency.

For the remainder of this chapter attention is focused on various return and risk measures for UK credit unions. The rationale for this is to provide further reinforcement for the argument that, as credit unions increase in asset size, they provide a better return for their members and are less risky as an institutional form. As a concurrent theme, we will also investigate whether the trade organisation to which the credit union belongs has any influence on its risk and return performance. The starting point for this part of the discussion is an examination of the surplus generated by credit unions.

SURPLUS PERFORMANCE

In determining the surplus or deficit resulting from the operations of a credit union during any year of account, all operating expenses in that year must be taken into account (including payments of interest) with provision made for depreciation of assets, for tax liabilities and for bad and doubtful debts. No provision is made in respect of amounts to be paid by way of dividend. On the basis of asset size, the 1994 surplus performance of credit unions in aggregate, and under the auspices of the respective umbrella organisations, is presented in Table 5.2.

An analysis of Table 5.2 reveals a number of points of note. If we initially concentrate upon the column headed 'all credit unions' it is clear that a pronounced inverse relationship emerges between size and the surplus ratio. For example, the largest group (over £1,000,000) generates, on average, over 5p for every £1 held in assets, while the smallest size category (£613 to £49,999) generates less than 3p per £1 in assets held.

In terms of the manner in which the surplus ratio is computed, there may be a number of competing explanations for this inverse relationship. One explanation is that large credit unions may be able to avail of scale economies

Table 5.2   UK credit unions' surplus performance, 1994

Asset range (£)	All credit unions: Surplus after tax/total assets	ABCUL: Surplus after tax/total assets	NFCU: Surplus after tax/total assets	ILCU: Surplus after tax/total assets
£1,000,000	0.0518	0.0500	—	0.0522
£500,000 to £999,999	0.0432	0.0459	0.0343	0.0424
£250,000 to £499,999	0.0440	0.0354	0.0495	0.0453
£100,000 to £249,999	0.0316	0.0301	0.0312	0.0479
£50,000 to £99,999	0.0278	0.0237	0.0310	—
£613 to £49,999	0.0271	0.0292	0.0244	0.0114
All credit unions	0.0484	0.0440	0.0357	0.0505

in their operations and, in consequence, are more efficient than their smaller counterparts. While such an explanation is likely to hold good for most types of financial institutions, it is not immediately obvious for credit unions. This rests with the fact that smaller credit unions rely almost exclusively upon donated inputs (premises and labour) as well as a range of subsidies and grants, while large credit unions are more likely to be subject to the marketplace and the going price in obtaining their inputs. Consequently, on an *a priori* basis the expectation might be that per-unit costs actually increase as the credit union increases in asset size. This issue of whether there are scale economies in credit union operations is investigated further in Chapter 6. Suffice to say, at this stage there may be some evidence, although it is subject to question, that the industry is characterised by increasing returns to scale.

Another explanation for the superior surplus performance of larger credit unions may relate to the fact that they are subject to a lower level of certain non-management expenses, in particular: loans written off as bad debts, provisions for doubtful debts and provision for taxation. With respect to the provision for taxation, this appears in the revenue account as a zero expenditure for most credit unions and therefore has little or no explanatory power. More sizeable items in the revenue account of many credit unions are bad-debt write-offs and bad-debt provision. As will be evidenced later in this chapter, there is little difference in the bad-debt exposure of large and small credit unions.

Turning now to the credit unions affiliated to the respective trade organis-ations, it appears from Table 5.2 that across most size classifications, and certainly in terms of the average performance, ILCU affiliates outperform those credit unions affiliated to the other trade organisations. This would, therefore, tend to suggest that a further important factor in the generation of an adequate level of surplus rests with the length of time a credit union has been established. That is, it may take a number of years before those involved in the running of the credit union have progressed up the learning curve and are in a position to generate the maximum potential surplus.

In addition, while the inverse relationship between size and surplus performance broadly holds for ABCUL and NFCU credit unions, the pattern is less evident for ILCU affiliates. This may, therefore, suggest that time in existence is more important than scale economies in explaining the inverse relationship, because, across each of the size classifications, ABCUL and NFCU unions are of a more recent origin than ILCU affiliates. The expectation is that, at best, the documented inverse relationship for ABCUL and NFCU credit unions and the industry in aggregate is transitory.

In terms of the application of the generated surplus, the credit union has a number of options. First, it may transfer a proportion to general reserve. Indeed, if at the end of any year of account the amount standing to general reserve is less than 10% of total assets, the credit union is obliged to transfer to general reserve not less then 20% of its surplus for that year. Secondly, the generated surplus may be employed to pay a dividend on members' shares. A dividend, at a rate not exceeding 8% per annum, may be recommended by the board of directors for declaration by the members at the annual general meeting. Such a dividend is declared on all full shares held during the preceding financial year. Shares held for less than a full year are entitled to a proportional part of the dividend. Thirdly, provided that a dividend on shares at a rate of not less than 3% per annum has been recommended by the board of directors, a proportion of the surplus may be used as a rebate of interest paid by, or due from, members who have received loans. Such rebates are calculated as an amount proportional to the interest paid by, or due from, the members of the credit union during that year of account. Finally, a percentage of the surplus may be used by the credit union for social, cultural or charitable purposes. Again, limitations are placed on expenditure under this category. No more than 10% of the surplus may be used for these purposes, with a total block placed on such spending unless the credit union has that year paid a dividend of at least 3% on all paid-up shares.

In terms of the relative percentages, credit unions, on average, spend less than 2% of their surplus on social, cultural or charitable purposes. Not surprisingly, given the above noted constraints, smaller credit unions spend a lower percentage than their larger counterparts. Rebate of loan interest accounts for, on average, 3% of the surplus. Transfers to reserves in 1994 accounted for, on average, 30% of the generated surplus, while the remaining 65% was distributed to shareholders in the form of dividend payments. It should be noted that, with respect to these latter percentages, a significant dichotomy emerges between small and large credit unions. Indeed, it is almost as if a structural break exists between credit unions with an asset base greater than £250,000 and those with assets less than £250,000. Those with assets in excess of £250,000 transfer, on average, 27% of their surplus to reserves and 67% goes towards a dividend payment. Credit unions with less than £250,000 in assets divert approximately 47% to reserves and pay out 52% in dividends. The dichotomy is because smaller unions are more recently formed and have not, as yet, built up their reserves to a level that they, or, for that matter, the Registry of Friendly Societies, would view to be adequate. Consequently, prudent management dictates that they transfer a relatively large share to reserves. With the exception of cultural, social and charitable expenditure, we now consider in more detail each of the other competing demands on the surplus of a credit union.

DIVIDEND RATES

As indicated, a dividend on members' shares, at a rate not exceeding 8%, is payable by credit unions. The dividend rate paid in 1994 is detailed in Table 5.3 for the industry as a whole and for the respective umbrella organisations.

Table 5.3   UK credit unions' dividend rate, 1994

Asset range (£)	All credit unions: dividend (%)	ABCUL: dividend (%)	NFCU: dividend (%)	ILCU: dividend (%)
Over £1,000,000	0.0409	0.0344	—	0.0424
£500,000 to £999,999	0.0331	0.0282	0.0297	0.0329
£250,000 to £499,999	0.0343	0.0294	0.0305	0.0394
£100,000 to £249,999	0.0161	0.0133	0.0162	0.0216
£50,000 to £99,999	0.0171	0.0138	0.0201	—
£613 to £49,999	0.0070	0.0071	0.0068	0.0071
All credit unions	0.0161	0.0287	0.0212	0.0406

An examination of the average dividend paid across the respective asset classes again reveals the relationship to be inverse in form. This is not surprising in that the dividend is payable from the surplus generated by credit unions, which, as we saw, was itself inversely related to asset size. There is, however, one break in this inverse relationship and it occurs for each of the credit union categories. On average, credit unions in the asset range £250,000 to £499,999 offer a higher dividend rate than those in the asset range £500,000 to £999,999. (Note that a similar break in the relationship between the surplus ratio and size, Table 5.2, also emerges.) One explanation that will be explored further in the next chapter is that credit unions in the larger-asset-size group face a much broader range of input costs, particularly on labour, than the smaller-asset-size category, these costs not being offset by achieving increased operational efficiency through scale economies. It is only when credit unions enter the asset category over £1 million that the scale effect outweighs the broader portfolio of input costs and causes a further upward movement in the operational efficiency, thus permitting them to offer relatively higher dividend rates.

Of course, there are some larger-scale credit unions that have continued to rely heavily on donated inputs. A case in point is that of the fifth largest in the United Kingdom, the Clonard credit union. It has an asset base of £5.1 million, an expenditure-to-income ratio of 27%, no salary outlays and provides a dividend rate to its members of 6.3%. Indeed, of all the 611 UK credit unions, the Clonard's 1994 dividend rate was the highest. Most of the large credit unions pay a dividend to their members. In the top three asset categories, only eight credit unions failed to pay a dividend to their members in 1994. This compares with 251 out of 335 credit unions in the asset class £613 to £49,999 not offering a dividend.

A final point of note with respect to Table 5.3 is that the dividend rate offered by most credit unions with assets in excess of £250,000 is highly competitive vis à vis the deposit rates on offer from both the banks and building societies during 1994. A customer of any of the high street financial institutions with a small-scale sum for investment, the norm for most credit unions, would have been hard-pressed to find an account offering in excess of 4%. That is not to say that credit unions are actively competing against retail financial institutions in their respective localities, although the deposit rates on offer elsewhere must have some influence on the dividend rate recommended by their board of directors. Support for this hypothesis may be obtained by examination of the average dividend rate over time. For example, in 1991, the average dividend rate in each asset class, for the credit union industry as a whole as well as for each of the groups based on trade association affiliation, was approximately 1% higher than the percentage rate detailed in Table 5.3 for 1994. Market rates were, of course, much higher during 1991 with the base rate averaging 12% compared with 5% in 1994. Therefore, while credit unions' dividend rates are in no way dictated by market forces, it is clear that credit unions keep an eye to the market in setting dividend rates.

LOAN RATES

Credit unions must endeavour to balance the interests of savers and borrowers. They, however, have difficulty in the achievement of this objective. Member savers want the highest possible dividend return on savings, but this can only occur if borrowers are subject to high loan charges. In contrast, borrowers want to minimise the interest rates levied on loans, which, in this instance, can occur only if the dividend rate paid to saving members is minimised. In Chapter 7 we will investigate in detail whether credit unions are borrower orientated or saver orientated or, indeed, neutral in their treatment of members. For the present, consider some preliminary data on the interest rate policy of UK credit unions. The majority of them, at least in terms of their 1994 returns, adopted the policy of charging the maximum allowable under the 1979 Act, that of 1% per month (annual percentage rate of 12.68%). For example, only one credit union in Northern Ireland levied a rate less than the maximum allowable percentage, and while a greater number of credit unions in Great Britain opted for a rate lower than the maximum, 19 in total, they were still obviously very much the exception rather than the rule. The rate recommended by an individual credit union's board of directors may not, however, give a true reflection of the cost of the loan in that the board of directors may also recommend a rebate of interest provided that a dividend of 3% or more is paid. In 1994, a total of 28 credit unions recommended a rebate of interest. This rebate was calculated as a percentage of the total interest payment made by a credit union's membership over the course of the year. The rebate varied between 1% and 15%, with the average rebate, for those making such a recommendation, averaging at 8%.

Even without loan rebates or rates levied beneath the maximum allowable, credit unions provide an extremely low-cost loan service for their members,

with interest rates well below the average percentage rates charged by the high
street financial institutions. Credit unions are able to charge such low rates of
interest not only because they have low overheads but also because of the
security, in the form of a member's savings, that is held to offset the risk of
default on a loan.

> The credit union shall have a lien on the shares of a member for any debt due to it by
> the member or for any debt which the member has guaranteed, and may set off any
> sum standing to the member's credit, including any shares, interest rebate and
> dividends, in or towards payment of such debt (Credit Union Act, 1979).

Furthermore, in order to qualify for a loan, the borrower must be a member of
the credit union and must have saved for a certain period of time, with, at
present, the maximum amount that can be borrowed being £5000 in excess of
the member's shareholding or 1.5% of total shareholding (at last balance date if
this is higher). Taken together, these features create a low-risk framework for
credit unions to conduct their business. The next task in this chapter is to
investigate whether this low-risk framework manifests itself in low-risk credit
unions.

RISK PROFILE

As outlined in the introduction to this chapter, the relative riskiness of credit
unions is assessed through the computation of a number of financial ratios,
including: a capital ratio that measures the ability to absorb loan loss; a bad-
debt write-off ratio to measure the quality of the loan portfolio and a bad-debt
provision ratio to examine the potential future losses. The opportunity is taken
to produce, in Table 5.4, the respective ratios for both 1991 and 1994.

Table 5.4   Risk profile of UK credit unions, 1991 and 1994

Asset range (£)	Reserves/total assets		Bad-debt write-offs/ total assets		Bad-debt provision/ total assets	
	1994	1991	1994	1991	1994	1991
Over £1,000,000	0.0878	0.1017	0.0028	0.0045	0.0162	0.0252
£500,000 to £999,999	0.0893	0.1044	0.0037	0.0037	0.0161	0.0226
£250,000 to £499,999	0.0888	0.1045	0.0028	0.0048	0.0137	0.0219
£100,000 to £249,999	0.06667	0.0905	0.0023	0.0029	0.0194	0.0195
£50,000 to £99,999	0.0719	0.0565	0.0036	0.0012	0.0173	0.0171
£613 to £49,999	0.0634	0.0737	0.0024	0.0015	0.0129	0.0093
All credit unions	0.0865	0.1004	0.0029	0.0041	0.0161	0.0234

The first financial ratio examined is the capital ratio, that of reserves/total assets. The ratio gives an indication of the proportion of total assets that could be called into question as a consequence of loan default and be absorbed by the capital surplus. A decrease in this ratio would indicate a riskier credit union, all other things being equal. If attention is initially focused on the 1994 reserve ratio, the picture to emerge is that, generally speaking, large credit unions are subject to less capital risk than their smaller counterparts, although the differential between them is by no means marked. Nevertheless, the industry as a whole operates a lower reserve ratio, 8.65%, than the 10% prescribed under the 1979 Act. In the opinion of the authors, this should not be interpreted as indicative of a high-risk industry, but rather as supporting evidence of an industry gravitating towards the optimal capital ratio as prescribed by the regulator. Indeed, many commentators would view institutions with a reserve ratio of approximately 8% as relatively low risk, all other things being equal, and, consequently, the regulator's stipulated ratio of 10% as overly cautious. Of course, it would be wrong to portray the industry in too glowing a light as the category averages do mask the fact that a number of credit unions have worryingly low reserve ratios. For the most part, these credit unions are small scale in terms of asset size and relatively recent in their formation. The latter may indicate that the problem is no more serious than one of insufficient time having elapsed to permit a build up of reserves.

Somewhat of a surprise is the decline in the reserve ratio between 1991 and 1994. The average reserve ratio for all credit unions in 1991 was 10.04%, marginally above the requirement of the Registry of Friendly Societies. Given that, as earlier highlighted, the average dividend rate paid by credit unions fell by around 1% over the same period it is unlikely that they would have distributed an increasing share of their surplus as dividend payments to the detriment of reserve accumulation. Rather, the problem appears to be one of credit unions as victims of their own success. Over the period 1991 to 1994, UK credit unions experienced a growth in their assets of 96.7% (157.68% for those in Great Britain and 82.45% for those in Northern Ireland). The decline in the reserve ratio, therefore, suggests that reserve accumulation failed to keep pace with asset growth. For example, if a credit union found its reserve ratio beneath 10% and it adopted the minimum guidance of the 1979 Act of transferring 20% of its surplus to reserves, and that credit union's asset base was growing at the UK average, then it would experience a drop in its reserve ratio.

A low reserve ratio only becomes a problem for a credit union when it is coupled with a significant level of loan default. The existence of such a twin combination then indicates that the institution in question is subject to a pronounced risk of failure. Information on the bad-debt position is also documented in Table 5.4. Two measures are employed. The first is bad-debt write-offs/total assets. Other things being equal, an increase in this ratio indicates a decline in the quality of the credit union's loan book and a greater exposure to credit risk. The second ratio is bad-debt provision/total assets, which gives an insight into how the credit union perceives the future quality of its loan book and the likely impact of market conditions on that loan book. An increase in this ratio, all other things being equal, suggests that the credit union is adopting a more pessimistic stance.

Taking the bad-debt ratio first, the figures for 1994 and 1991 highlight the fact that the credit union industry faces a negligible bad-debt problem. This result is somewhat of a surprise in that credit unions are generally viewed as institutions that provide finance for low-income communities, where, for many, credit requirements tend essentially to be a response to financial difficulty. In such circumstances, the expectation would be one of significant bad-debt problems. That this is not the case may be a consequence of the fact that credit unions serve a membership that is characterised by a common bond. Black and Duggar (1981) suggest that the common bond restriction on membership reduces the cost of gathering credit information and, of course, bad-debt losses. It also emerges from the write-off figures that there are no substantive differences between large and small credit unions. In this instance, if the Black and Duggar (1981) argument is to be accepted, the expectation might have been that small credit unions would have a lower incidence of bad debt than their larger counterparts. The rationale for this statement is that the common bond is somewhat better defined in the case of most small credit unions.

In addition, it appears that the economy impacts on credit union bad-debt only in a very marginal manner. The bad-debt write-off ratios for the respective credit union categories in 1991, when the economy was in the depths of the most recent recession, are of a similar magnitude to those in 1994, when economic conditions were of a much more favourable nature.

The picture as described for the bad-debt write-off ratio very much mirrors that which emerges *vis-à-vis* the bad-debt provision ratio. Again, the provision figures are extremely small, there is little difference in the 1991 and 1994 figures and very little difference between the provision levels of small and large credit unions. Perhaps the only additional noteworthy point is that credit unions appear extremely cautious in the setting of provision levels, with provisions over 10 times the magnitude of bad-debt write-offs.

Omitted from Table 5.4 is a risk profile of credit unions in terms of their affiliation to the respective trade organisations. Such information would not have added much to the picture as currently portrayed in that credit unions classified under the banner of their respective umbrella organisations behaved, in both 1991 and 1994, in a very similar fashion to the industry as a whole. Only one point of note emerges when the figures are broken down in terms of trade classification. It is that ILCU credit unions have a somewhat superior reserve ratio. This, in all probability, relates to the fact that NFCU and ABCUL affiliates are, on average, of a more recent origin and, consequently, are more likely to be in the early stages of reserve accumulation.

CONCLUDING COMMENTS

In this chapter, emphasis has been placed on the identification of the viability of the UK credit union movement, on an assessment of the quality of service on offer from credit unions and on testing whether it is the larger organisations that offer the superior service.

Viability, it was argued, can be defined and interpreted in many ways. If, in the context of this discussion, the most robust definition is employed, that of self-sufficiency, it transpires that, out of the 611 registered credit unions in the United Kingdom, only 122 make the grade. That is, the latter have achieved a critical mass that allows them to offer a good return on members' savings, have in place adequate reserves and generate income to cover their operating expenditures, including salaried staff, without the necessity of recourse to outside funding sources. Some commentators might view the fact that only 20% of credit unions make the self-sufficiency grade as an indictment on the UK movement. We, in contrast, would prefer to couch this more in terms of a significant achievement, in that no further back than 35 years ago the credit union movement did not exist in the United Kingdom. This significant achievement has been made possible because of the industrial setting within which credit unions operate in the United Kingdom which, as we have argued in earlier chapters, gives full rein to the in-built logic that encourages their development into full-scale and main-line financial institutions.

Equally encouraging is the rapid asset growth experienced by credit unions (between 1991 and 1994 total assets grew by 157.68% for credit unions in Great Britain and 82.45% for those in Northern Ireland). Such strong performance by the industry necessarily implies that in the coming years many more credit unions will achieve self-sufficiency.

Of further importance for the movement as it is currently constituted, and, indeed, for its future development, is the price-competitive service on offer and the relatively low-risk environment within which the service is provided. This service, in terms of the return on members' savings and the interest rate charged on loans to members, compares favourably with the deposit rates on offer and interest rates charged on personal loans by the retail banks. This price-competitive service is available from all credit unions classed as self-sufficient, as well as from most of them in the stage immediately prior to self sufficiency.

Having adopted an upbeat approach, it is perhaps judicious to also reiterate the downside, which is that there are a number of small-asset-volume credit unions that provide no dividend to their members and have an almost non-existent capital base. For a sizeable proportion of these credit unions, their weakness stems from the fact that they are newly established; consequently, the passage of time is likely to rectify any present deficiencies. For the remainder, the expectation must be, as in the case of any other industry in an industrialised and market-driven economy, that failure is just around the corner. Such failures should not be viewed as unduly problematic, particularly if a deposit insurance mechanism is introduced to provide a safety net for the movement (see Chapter 9 for more details on this issue), as it is simply part of the natural process in the growth of an industry.

6

The Operational Efficiency of UK Credit Unions

INTRODUCTION

In Chapter 4 we noted a difference in emphasis between credit unions affiliated to the NFCU, on the one hand, and those affiliated to ABCUL and the ILCU, on the other. The primary focus of the NFCU is on community development, self-help and small units. While the NFCU encourages its members to become economically viable, it, nevertheless, prefers them not to exceed a few hundred members. Expansion, where it occurs, should be in the development of new credit unions. ABCUL and the ILCU, in contrast, are in favour of individual credit unions achieving significant critical mass, which is supposed to result in the generation of business efficiency and scale economies.

Consequently, for a sizeable component of the UK credit union industry, growth and the achievement of cost efficiency have become issues of considerable importance. Indeed, it could also be argued that as NFCU credit unions have shared with others in the unprecedented growth in loans outstanding, assets under control and membership, the effect of size increases on the operational efficiency of NFCU members is of equal importance to its impact on the operational efficiency of either ABCUL or ILCU affiliates.

In more general terms, the achievement of economies of scale may be considered to be of much more importance for credit unions than for other forms of retail financial institution. The argument for this centres upon the fact that credit unions are prone to membership bias and this potential conflict between borrowers and savers may be exacerbated as the credit union increases in size. Koot (1978), citing Taylor (1971), elaborates on this point. Growth, if it, for example, caused an increase in the demand for loans by new members, could lead to a rise in loan rates (until the maximum of 1% per month), which would adversely impact on existing borrowing members. If, in contrast, growth resulted in an increase in deposits by new members, a drop in deposit rates might occur, which, in this instance, would be to the detriment of existing depositors. In addition, it should be noted that even if the introduction of new members resulted in an unchanged balance between borrowers and savers, if diseconomies of scale emerged, then the likely consequence is a fall in net returns for all existing members. Of course, if increasing returns to scale were to emerge, membership conflict would be less likely to surface, with a possible outcome of an increase in net returns for all existing members.

The purpose of this chapter is, therefore, to examine UK credit unions for the existence of economies of scale. While the industry in aggregate is the main focus of the investigation, the opportunity will also be taken to subdivide the industry in terms of the trade organisations to which credit unions belong and to then examine whether similar patterns of scale efficiency hold across the respective subgroups. This part of the discussion will enable us to determine whether the current growth objectives of the respective trade organisations conform to their identified scale-efficiency characteristics.

In terms of the format of the discussion, the analysis commences with an overview of the literature pertaining to scale efficiency in credit unions. Emphasis is placed on studies that focus on the US industry, not least because little research has been undertaken on scale efficiency in other countries. The cost structure of UK credit unions is then examined. This part of the analysis highlights the fact that, as most credit unions depend on donated labour, subsidised office supplies and office space, a divergence occurs between the reported cost of operation and the true opportunity cost of operation. This result raises serious implications for our investigation of scale economies in UK credit unions. The methodology employed to obtain the returns-to-scale measures is then detailed, with the discussion completed by an analysis of the findings.

LITERATURE REVIEW

In that the credit union movement in the United States is at a much more advanced stage of development than that in the United Kingdom, it may be of little surprise to note that most of the literature on scale efficiency in credit unions focuses upon US institutions. Although, even in the United States, Berger, Hunter and Timme (1993) do suggest that unlike other US financial groups:

> The efficiency of thrift institutions, such as savings and loans (S&L) and credit unions (CUs), has not been studied extensively in the literature to date.

Most early studies (see, for example, Taylor, 1971; Flannery, 1974; and Cargill, 1975), argue that credit unions offer a significant advantage over other financial institutions for investigating cost functions in that they produce a homogeneous product, primarily short-term consumer loans. They are also viewed to present a unique difficulty, since many credit unions depend on donated labour, subsidised office supplies and office space, which results in a divergence between the actual reported cost of operation and the true opportunity cost of operation. The true cost of operation exceeds the actual cost to a greater extent for smaller credit unions than for larger ones, because the latter are more likely to aspire to being managed on the same professional basis as other financial institutions and purchase their labour, office supplies and office space in the marketplace.

Cargill (1976), in a review article, argues that at first reading the three above-noted studies of scale efficiency in US credit unions all lead to apparently different conclusions. However, when the divergence between actual and true operating costs is taken into account, the results are broadly similar.

Taylor (1971) found that there existed small economies of scale to be achieved for a sample of large credit unions. Cargill (1975) discovered large and statistically significant economies of scale for a sample of very large credit unions. (In this paper he also cites an unpublished paper by Cargill and Vincell, 1969, which found economies of scale for a heterogeneous group of Californian state-chartered credit unions for the year 1965.) Flannery (1974) employed a much less homogeneous sample set than the other two studies in that it was based on a representative sample of 1000 drawn from all federal credit unions in 1972. In the case of Flannery's study, the weight of evidence suggested the existence of constant returns to scale. Cargill (1976) suggests that, since there is a much wider variation in the divergence between actual and true operating costs in Flannery's sample, the finding of constant returns to scale may imply that real economies of operation are offset by the tendency for large credit unions to rely less on donated labour and materials. Consequently, Cargill (1976) argues that all three studies, at a minimum, support the existence of constant cost conditions facing a credit union. However, it is much more likely to be the case that US credit unions in the early 1970s were characterised by increasing returns to scale; that is, as size increased, per unit costs declined.

The estimation procedures adopted by these early studies were very much relevant for US credit unions prior to 1977, when most credit unions were single-product intermediaries. Radical institutional changes during the late 1970s and 1980s have, however, reshaped the industry and, in consequence, the early 1970s model no longer applies. US credit unions are now multi-product institutions very similar in form to other retail financial intermediaries. Where the early 1970s US model does have relevance is to UK credit unions today. This relates to the fact that, as has been highlighted in earlier chapters, the credit union industry in the United Kingdom still depends to a large part on donated labour and premises, with member unions still very much single product intermediaries.

In the late 1970s and 1980s, those studies that investigated scale economies in credit unions employed the Benston–Bell–Murphy cost specification (see, for example, Koot, 1978; and Wolken and Navratil, 1980a). The Benston–Bell–Murphy model derives a Cobb–Douglas cost function under the assumption of constrained cost minimisation, with emphasis placed on deriving all relevant variables that affect cost. The database on which the Koot (1978) study was based was that of a special survey conducted by the Credit Union National Association (CUNA), the major trade association in the United States. This study was carried out in 1976 and collected data for the 1972–1975 operations of credit unions. This database enabled Koot (1978) to incorporate a measure for the subsidies granted to credit unions and, hence, allow for the fact that the degree of subsidisation declines with increasing size. At variance with previous studies, Koot (1978) found that the US credit union industry was subject to decreasing returns to scale. Wolken and Navratil (1980a) take exception to the Koot analysis. They argue that he incorrectly incorporated labour subsidies and they demonstrate that, when subsidies are correctly included, the estimated scale economies increase consistently. Wolken and Navratil conclude that credit unions reap small, but statistically significant, economies of scale.

One limitation of these studies is that the Cobb–Douglas cost function imposes a constant scale elasticity of cost that is not consistent with a U-shaped average cost curve. Consequently, recent investigations of the cost efficiency and structure of credit unions have employed the translog cost function (see, for example, Murray and White, 1983; Kim, 1986; and Tripp and Cole, 1994). The translog cost function originates from the work of Christensen, Jorgensen and Lau (1971). It is from the family of flexible functional forms. It places no restriction on the elasticity of substitution between inputs, and is non-homothetic in that the ratio of cost-minimising input demands can vary with the level of output. Again, primary emphasis in this approach is directed towards deriving all relevant variables that affect costs.

The Murray and White (1983) and Kim (1986) studies both focus on credit unions in British Columbia and, as with the previous studies that focused on the United States, find that the credit union industry is characterised by mild overall economies of scale. The study by Tripp and Cole (1994) examines 528 US credit unions. The authors find that average total operating costs decrease as the size of the credit union increases up to $100 million in assets. They also indicate that economies of scale are most significant for those credit unions between $20 million and $50 million in total assets. Furthermore, the authors tentatively suggest that credit unions with total assets in excess of $100 million show slight signs of diseconomies of scale. The authors consequently conclude that, for average operating costs, bigger is better up to a point, then bigger becomes worse. The deciding point is about $100 million in assets.

Another methodology employed to investigate for the existence of scale economies relates to an examination of the operational efficiency of credit unions. Cox and Whigham (1984), Kohers and Mullis (1988) and McKillop, Ferguson and Nesbitt (1995a) are examples where such a methodology is utilised. The first two studies employ this methodology to examine for the existence of operational efficiency gains in US credit unions, while the latter study conducts a similar analysis for the United Kingdom. These authors argue that cost minimisation is synonymous with operational efficiency and, consequently, if operational efficiency were to increase as the size of the financial institution increased, then this would be indicative of the existence of scale economies. An institution's cost per transaction and its operating expenses to operating income are the measures most generally employed to assess operational efficiency.

Both US studies found that large credit unions operate more efficiently than their smaller counterparts. The Kohers and Mullis (1988) study was the more comprehensive in that it considered 5676 federal-chartered and 2469 state-chartered credit unions for the year 1984. They found a sizeable dichotomy between large and small credit unions. Those institutions with assets between $50 million and $100 million had, on average, an operating cost/operating income ratio of 0.285 compared with 0.481 for credit unions with assets less than $50,000.

McKillop, Ferguson and Nesbitt (1995a) considered 519 UK credit unions for the year 1992. The authors concluded that significant efficiency gains were available through credit unions adopting a policy of asset growth. The analysis was also conducted with credit unions grouped in terms of their affiliation to the respective trade organisations. Again, the analysis revealed that larger credit unions were more efficient than their smaller counterparts, although it did transpire that the opportunity for efficiency gains was not as pronounced in the case of NFCU members.

A further insight obtained from the analysis was that a break in the steady improvement in operational efficiency occurred at an asset level between £500,000 and £999,999. The explanation put forward for the break rested with the fact that, at this asset level, credit unions were no longer able to rely solely on donated labour and, hence, faced a more burdensome array of input costs than their smaller counterparts. What, however, also emerged from the analysis was that, although larger credit unions found it necessary to employ full-time staff and this initially impacted adversely upon cost efficiency, once they achieved significant critical mass, assets in excess of £1 million, further and much-enhanced levels of operational efficiency were achieved.

From this literature review, which, although primarily focusing on US credit unions, has also provided supporting material on the Canadian and UK industries, the clear picture that emerges is one of an industry characterised by increasing returns to scale. Consequently, the idealistic view held by many proponents of the credit union movement, i.e. of small organisations offering share savings and consumer loans and serving a membership forgotten by main-line financial institutions, comes under threat if larger credit unions are markedly more cost effective. Before we address this issue for the UK credit union industry in 1994, consider first an overview of the current cost structure of the UK movement.

THE COST STRUCTURE OF UK CREDIT UNIONS

As has been indicated, an analysis of the cost structure is, to some extent, blurred, in that while large credit unions are faced with the need to hire staff and rent or lease premises to cover their higher volume of business, small credit unions can, in contrast, cover their obligations with volunteer staff and the use of community premises, free of charge. In addition, given that smaller credit unions are more likely to have been formed more recently, it is probable that they can avail more readily of grants and subsidies from both charities and local authorities. Consequently, the implication is that the true cost of operation will exceed the actual cost to a greater extent for smaller credit unions than for larger credit unions.

To examine this facet of credit union behaviour, the opportunity is taken, in Table 6.1, to decompose the expense incurred in operation for both asset ranges and trade bodies.

The remuneration values documented in Table 6.1 are defined to include salaries, wages, national insurance plus the treasurer's honorarium. Salaries as a proportion of total expenses for the subcategory 'all credit unions' declines, almost in linear fashion, from 34% for those with assets over £1 million to marginally less than 3% for credit unions with an asset level between £613 and £49,999. It is, perhaps, in this category of expenditure that the most visible demonstration of the subsidised nature of the operation of small credit unions emerges and, of course, by implication, the inherent difficulty in attempting to test for the existence of scale economies. In addition, although the operation of larger credit unions is on a much more market-orientated basis, they also rely on unpaid volunteers, which introduces a bias into their relative expenditure on salaries.

In terms of credit unions affiliated to the respective trade organisations, the relative remuneration to employees for ILCU and ABCUL credit unions mirrors that previously documented for the industry as a whole, accepting, of course, that ILCU affiliates occupy the upper-range asset categories. In contrast, the relative share attributed to remuneration in the cost expenditure of NFCU credit unions is much lower. The relative expenditure on remuneration for the upper-bracket NFCU credit unions, £500,000 to £999,999, is 14% compared with 25% for ILCU and ABCUL organisations in this size class. The

Table 6.1 UK credit unions cost structure, 1994

Asset range (£)	Remuneration (£)	Occupancy costs (£)	Other expenses (£)	Total expenses (£)
All credit unions				
Over £1,000,000	2,413,702	644,055	3,982,815	7,040,572
£500,000 to £999,999	395,843	231,621	978,160	1,605,624
£250,000 to £499,999	120,547	81,720	450,542	652,809
£100,000 to £249,999	54,284	52,678	391,455	498,418
£50,000 to £99,999	7796	19,635	178,041	205,472
£613 to £49,999	11,444	33,982	375,198	420,624
Total	3,003,616	1,063,691	6,356,211	10,423,518
ABCUL credit unions				
Over £1,000,000	586,805	98,940	828,753	1,514,498
£500,000 to £999,999	74,064	33,762	184,545	292,371
£250,000 to £499,999	94,248	31,550	174,674	300,472
£100,000 to £249,999	16,605	11,034	219,573	247,212
£50,000 to £99,999	4446	8176	126,183	138,805
£613 to £49,999	10,545	24,560	257,884	292,990
NFCU credit unions				
Over £1,000,000	—	—	—	—
£500,000 to £999,999	15,622	32,139	57,354	105,115
£250,000 to £499,999	1900	7895	79,698	89,493
£100,000 to £249,999	5018	15,478	76,482	96,978
£50,000 to £99,999	2900	7441	37,350	47,691
£613 to £49,999	699	8819	103,936	113,453
ILCU credit unions				
Over £1,000,000	1,810,242	525,256	3,118,687	5,454,185
£500,000 to £999,999	289,893	165,336	696,434	1,151,663
£250,000 to £499,999	23,329	36,920	162,051	222,300
£100,000 to £249,999	3150	5571	41,544	50,265
£50,000 to £99,999	—	—	—	—
£613 to £49,999	0	73	850	923

relative share drops to less than 1% for NFCU credit unions in the smallest asset range. The dichotomy that has emerged between the latter and those affiliated to the other trade organisations no doubt rests with the more overt emphasis placed on self-help by the NFCU.

Occupancy costs are defined to include: rents and rates; heating, lighting and cleaning; repairs and renewals to premises, fixtures and fittings; and depreciation.

Occupancy costs, on average, account for approximately 10% of operating expenditures. At the trade organisation level, a pattern for this ratio is difficult to discern. However, the picture becomes somewhat less blurred when the industry as a whole is considered. A straight-line increase from 8% to 14% occurs as the asset-size category increases to the size range £500,000 to £999,999, with the ratio then falling back to 9% for the top asset category, over £1 million. Again, the picture is likely to be clouded because of the higher incidence of subsidies for smaller credit unions, although, in this instance, there is much less scope for divergence between the true and the reported figures. Credit unions, with perhaps the exception of employer-based ones, are likely to be subject to most of the components of occupancy costs shortly after their formation. The dip in occupancy costs to 9% for credit unions in excess of £1 million may centre on the fact that once they achieve this critical mass, membership and asset size experience significant increases. This, in turn, gives rise to a sizeable increase in expenditure, but this increase is perhaps not as marked in the case of occupancy costs, as the credit union will continue to operate out of one office. Consequently, in this area of cost expenditure, scale economies may emerge.

The final cost category detailed in Table 6.1 is headed 'other expenses'. These encompass expenditure on postage, printing and travel; accountancy and audit charges; loan and share insurance; general insurance; plus miscellaneous related expenses. For smaller credit unions, this class of expenditure makes up the bulk of their reported costs. This is no surprise, in that most unions from the outset are liable for almost all the respective cost components of 'other expenses'. In terms of the percentage weights, 89% of operating expenditures goes on 'other expenses' for credit unions in the asset class £613 to £49,999. This percentage weight steadily drops as the asset size increases. For credit unions with assets over £1 million, the comparable relative weight is 57%. While the decline in this expense category's share is dictated by the increased expenditure on staff remunerations, the pronounced nature of the decline may suggest that in this category of expenditure there is another potential source for the achievement of scale economies.

In Table 6.1 there is no mention of interest expenses, with the emphasis focused completely on non-interest operating costs. The exclusion of interest expenses from Table 6.1, and, indeed, from the later calculation of operating efficiency, rests with two facts. First, a significant proportion of credit unions, owing, in the main, to their recent formation, do not as yet pay a dividend to shareholders (279 out of the 611 registered UK credit unions did not pay a dividend in 1994). Consequently, the inclusion of interest expenses would result in considerable bias in the calculation of operational efficiency. Secondly, for those that do pay a dividend to shareholders there is only a limited scope for variation. This centres on the fact that, to some extent, the setting of interest rates by individual credit unions is influenced by market conditions outside their control.

METHODOLOGY

From the literature overview, it appears that a cost-function approach is the most accepted methodology to examine for the existence, or otherwise, of scale economies. Unfortunately, for a number of reasons it is not possible to pursue a cost-function methodology in this study of UK credit unions. First, as indicated, a significant proportion of UK credit unions depend totally upon donated capital and labour and, consequently, their input costs relate solely to 'other expenses'—printing and stationery, loan and share insurance, etc. Secondly, for those unions that report capital and labour expenditure in their annual accounts, the problem still remains as to the determination of appropriate input prices. With respect to the labour input, the problem rests with the fact that individual credit unions do not publish statistics on employee numbers, making it impossible to compute an input price. With regard to the capital input price, varied theoretical and practical problems make it difficult to compute a representative input price irrespective of the form of the financial organisation (see for example, Glass and McKillop, 1992, for an analysis of capital input price problems).

The second best alternative, as in the work of Cox and Whigham (1984), Kohers and Mullis (1988) and McKillop, Ferguson and Nesbitt (1995a) is to examine the operational efficiency of credit unions. In this current study, the income statement measure, operating costs to operating income, is employed as the key measure of efficiency. For the reasons earlier elucidated, operational expenses do not include interest expense. This contrasts with the study by McKillop, Ferguson and Nesbitt (1995a), where operating costs were defined to include interest expense. This necessarily implies that caution must be exercised in any direct comparison between the results reported in that paper and those in this chapter.

A number of alternative proxies could be employed in the measurement of operational efficiency. The majority of these measures are, however, strongly positively correlated with operating costs to operating income and would, therefore, be unlikely to yield additional information, an example being that of operating expenses to total assets. One measure less likely to be positively correlated is that of cost per transaction. The problem, in this instance, is more methodological in nature. It relates to the fact that, in the case of credit unions, many small loans translate into two transactions—a small deposit to establish membership and a second transaction for the loan—while, in contrast, one large loan might just be one transaction. Such a situation could lead to the erroneous conclusion that a credit union with small multi-transaction loans is more efficient than one specialising in large loans. Accepting this methodological problem, we nevertheless employ, as a back-up to the efficiency measure, operating cost to operating income, operating income to total loans made. This latter measure is calculated relative to loans made rather than to the

number of transactions, because UK credit unions do not publish information
on the number of deposit transactions in any one year. In addition, it must be
stressed that this efficiency measure very much suffers from the aforementioned methodological problem. For example, the average loan made by credit
unions in the top and next-to-top asset classes for 1994 were, respectively,
£1050 and £1044. This compares with an average loan of £330 and £540 for
the bottom and next-to-bottom asset ranges.

As a precursor to the statistical analysis, the opportunity is taken in Table 6.2
to set out the operational efficiency measures at industry level. Reworked
figures are also presented in Table 6.2, with remuneration being excluded from
operating costs. The objective, in this instance, is to remove that component of
cost that is most likely to be subject to understatement. Adopting this
procedure, then, gives a feel for the size of potential efficiency gains, if it were
possible to generate true operating cost figures.

If the initial focus is on the industry in aggregate and on operating costs to
total income, it is clear that, as credit union size increases, there is a marked
improvement in the efficiency measure. A temporary break does, however,
occur at the asset class £500,000 to £999,999. As earlier indicated, this credit
union class faces a much broader and more comprehensive range of input costs
than the other classifications, costs that are not offset as a consequence of
achieving increased operational efficiency through scale. Only when credit
unions enter the asset range greater than £1 million does it appear that the scale
effect outweighs the broader portfolio of input costs and causes a further
improvement in operational efficiency. This point is no better highlighted than
by the reworked operational efficiency measure that is computed with staff
remuneration excluded from operating costs. The picture that then emerges is
one of an unambiguous and pronounced improvement in efficiency as the
average credit union size increases. Furthermore, the fact that the reworked
ratio relative to the original ratio improves more rapidly, and to a much greater
degree, provides some indication of the cost advantage that smaller credit

Table 6.2   Efficiency measures, 1994

Asset Range (£)	Operating costs/total income	Operating costs/no. of loans	(Operating costs − remuneration)/ total income	(Operating costs − remuneration)/ no. of loans
Over £1,000,000	0.4351	43.00	0.2879	28.45
£500,000 to £999,999	0.5070	48.20	0.3934	37.40
£250,000 to £499,999	0.5049	42.39	0.4203	35.29
£100,000 to £249,999	0.6263	40.86	0.5683	37.07
£50,000 to £99,999	0.6714	31.38	0.6465	30.22
£613 to £49,999	0.7215	23.76	0.7024	23.13
Total	0.4669	41.88	0.3363	30.16

unions have through being able to rely almost exclusively on donated labour for their staffing needs. The reworked ratio declines from 0.7024 for credit unions with assets between £613 and £49,999 to 0.2879 for those with assets in excess of £1 million. Comparable values for the original and unadjusted efficiency ratios are 0.7215 and 0.4351.

What was emerging as a clear picture of efficiency improvements with credit union size increases is thrown into question when the second efficiency ratio detailed in Table 6.2, that of operating costs to the number of loans, is examined. Indeed, with this ratio, the picture is actually reversed. Smaller credit unions are much more efficient than their larger counterparts. For credit unions with an asset base between £613 and £49,999, operating costs to the number of loans stands at 23.76 but rises to 43.00 for those with an asset base greater than £1 million. There is one positive development, which is that this efficiency ratio, as in the case of the first measure, reaches its peak at the asset range £500,000 to £999,999 and then falls back, indicating a relative efficiency gain for credit unions with assets greater than £1 million. When staff remuneration is stripped from this ratio, the efficiency differential between the top two categories becomes even more pronounced. The removal of staff remuneration also considerably weakens the efficiency advantage that small credit unions have over their larger counterparts, although it by no means completely eliminates the differential.

The problems inherent in this analysis of scale efficiency are no better highlighted than in the conflicting results presented for these two relatively simple measures of efficiency. As earlier indicated, the confusion centres on the methodological problems. The main difficulty is that the average loan made by the top credit union group is some three times greater than that made by those at the other end of the asset spectrum. Indeed, as initial groundwork for this chapter, numerical adjustments were made to equate the average size of loan with the efficiency measure recomputed on this basis. The removal of the loan-size differential led to larger credit unions being classed as much more efficient than smaller ones. Accepting the documented problems, let us now proceed to detail the statistical technique employed to determine whether there are statistically significant scale economies to be achieved in the operation of UK credit unions.

To test for the existence of scale economies, credit unions were paired on the basis of size differences. The six size categories employed in the previous tables were again utilised in this aspect of the analysis, with the data again obtained from 1994 annual accounts. Credit unions in each size category were compared with those in the other size categories, which allowed, in total, for 15 size-category comparisons. The mean differences in the operational efficiency measure employed were then tested for statistical significance. The null hypothesis for a test of the comparison of sample means with paired observations is $\bar{d} = 0$, where $\bar{d}$ is the population mean difference in the efficiency measure between paired observations. The test statistic is distributed as Student's t and may be expressed as follows:

$$t = \bar{d}/S_{\bar{d}},$$

where

$$\bar{d} = \sum_{i=1}^{n} (x_{1j} - x_{2j})/n = \text{sample mean difference}$$

x_{1j} = the measure of efficiency for the jth credit union in the first category, e.g. small credit unions,

x_{2j} = the measure of efficiency for the jth credit union in the second category, e.g. large credit unions,

n = the total number of pairs,

and

$$S_{\bar{d}} = \sqrt{\frac{\sum_{j=1}^{n} (x_{1j} - x_{2j})^2 - \left[\sum_{j=1}^{n} (x_{1j} - x_{2j})\right]^{2/n}}{n(n-1)}}.$$

In that the sector may not be strictly homogeneous, given that, as argued, the respective umbrella organisations have been seen to have differing growth aspirations, paired difference analysis is also undertaken from the perspective of the individual trade organisations. This aspect of the analysis will allow us to determine whether similar patterns of scale efficiency hold across the respective subgroups. It will also provide answers to other questions, for example, as to whether the NFCU is justified from a cost efficiency stance in encouraging their member unions to remain small-scale in size.

The paired difference methodology, in that it is based on the efficiency ratios, suffers from the fact that smaller credit unions rely more heavily upon donated inputs and, in particular, donated labour. The implication of this, as earlier stressed, is that operating costs are distorted, with a bias introduced against finding scale economies. This, in turn, implies that any scale economies that survive this bias should be treated all the more seriously.

RESULTS AND INTERPRETATION

Documented in Table 6.3 are the size category comparisons, the number of paired observations per category compared and the computed mean differences and associated standard errors for the efficiency measures, operating costs/operating income and (operating costs – staff remuneration)/operating income.

Table 6.3 Paired difference analysis of size economies, 1994

Credit union size category comparison[a]	Pairs of observations	Operating costs/ operating income (mean difference)[b]	(Operating costs − remuneration)/operating income (mean difference)[b]
C6 with C5	49	0.1677* (0.0627)	0.1930* (0.0603)
C6 with C4	59	0.2805* (0.0555)	0.2889* (0.0578)
C6 with C3	42	0.3609* (0.0755)	0.3996* (0.0789)
C6 with C2	49	0.4487* (0.0865)	0.5682* (0.1011)
C6 with C1	59	0.4018* (0.0586)	0.5526* (0.0771)
C5 with C4	49	0.1388* (0.0488)	0.1513* (0.0489)
C5 with C3	42	0.1261* (0.0598)	0.1597* (0.0518)
C5 with C2	49	0.2312* (0.0537)	0.3098* (0.0543)
C5 with C1	49	0.1835* (0.0511)	0.3084* (0.0577)
C4 with C3	42	0.1595* (0.0497)	0.1521* (0.0370)
C4 with C2	49	0.0679* (0.0276)	0.1428* (0.0331)
C4 with C1	59	0.1047* (0.025)	0.2121* (0.0335)
C3 with C2	42	−0.0102 (0.0600)	0.0111 (0.0218)
C3 with C1	42	0.1030** (0.0539)	0.1280* (0.0272)
C2 with C1	49	0.0648* (0.0240)	0.0853* (0.0146)

[a] C1 = £1 million or more; C2 = £0.5 million to £999,999; C3 = £0.25 million to £499,999; C4 = £100,000 to £249,999; C5 = £50,000 to £99,999; C6 = £613 to £49,999.
[b] Standard errors are in parentheses.
* Statistically significant at the 5% level of significance.
** Statistically significant at the 10% level of significance.

It is clear from the mean difference values set out in Table 6.3 that, for the most part, smaller credit unions have significantly higher operating costs to operating income ratios. Indeed, a pronounced pattern emerges when the C6 group of credit unions, those with an asset base between £613 and £49,999, are compared with the other credit union classifications. The pattern is one of a staged increase in the mean difference of the efficiency variable as the size difference compared increases. The fact that the C6 group is so markedly inefficient from an operational perspective has significant implications for the movement as a whole, in that some 57% of all credit unions fall into this asset categorisation. The inefficiency of the C5 group, those with assets between £50,000 and £99,999, relative to the other larger-asset-size groupings is also apparent from Table 6.3, as, indeed, is the inefficiency of the C4 group, those with assets between £100,000 and £249,999, relative to larger-scale credit unions.

The uniform picture of increasing operational efficiency then appears to break down somewhat when the C3 group is employed as the control in the pairing process. The problem, in the main, relates to the pairing of C3 (assets between £250,000 and £499,999) with the C2 group (assets between £500,000 and £999,999). The paired mean difference estimate suggests greater operational efficiency for the smaller-scale credit union group. This apparent dichotomy in the findings relates to the broader and more comprehensive range of input costs faced by the C2 group, which are not offset as a consequence of achieving increased operational efficiency through scale. Only when credit unions enter the C1 category, assets greater than £1 million, does the scale effect outweigh the broader portfolio of input costs and cause a further significant upward movement in operational efficiency. This point is high-lighted by the fact that the paired mean difference values between C1 credit unions and the other groups, C2 to C6, are indicative of C1 unions having, in each case, a significantly lower operating costs to operating income ratio. It might, of course, be argued that the finding of scale economies is indicative of scale-related factors distorting operating income. For example, if large credit unions tend to have market power, they would have disproportionately large operating income, which would reduce the observed cost-to-income ratios and lead to a spurious appearance of economies of scale. This is not the case for the UK credit union movement. There are, for example, few barriers to entry in the establishment of new institutions. Indicative of this is the fact that, as the 1979 Act currently stands, only 21 members are required before a credit union can be established. In addition, existing credit unions have little or no sway in determining whether new unions may, or may not, establish. This decision is made by the Registry of Friendly Societies, which operates independently of both individual credit unions and their trade organisations.

Also reported in Table 6.3 are the mean difference values for the ratio operating costs minus staff remuneration divided by operating income. These reported figures and their associated standard errors add little new information. The trends identified mirror completely those identified in the mean difference analysis on the basis of the unadjusted measure of operational efficiency. The only difference of any real substance relates to the magnitude of the reported values. As would be expected, excluding remuneration expenses results in an increase in the reported mean difference values. This relates to the fact that credit unions in the larger-asset-size categories are more liable to pay salary expenses; hence, its removal from operating expenditure widens the cost ratio gap with those of a smaller asset size.

To date, and very much conspicuous by its absence, is any mention of mean difference values computed on the basis of the second operational efficiency measure, operating costs to the number of loans made. The lack of emphasis rests with the fact that each of the calculated mean difference values for the original and, indeed, the adjusted ratio (remuneration removed from total expenditure) yielded values that were insignificantly different from zero. This meant that we could not identify a statistically significant improvement, or, for that matter, deterioration, in operational efficiency with increases in credit union size. That is, constant returns to scale in the operation of UK credit unions could not be ruled out. This result may be of some surprise because the values documented in Table 6.2 for the unadjusted version of this ratio would indicate that efficiency declined as credit union size increased. The fact that this *a priori* perspective proved to be wrong centres on the extreme variability in the value of this measure between credit unions. This extreme variability results in large standard deviations, which, in turn, leads to high standard errors that render the reported mean difference values insignificant.

To complete the discussion, the paired difference analysis is repeated with, in this instance, credit unions matched with regard to the trade organisations under which they had membership. The mean difference results are presented in Table 6.4. Information is provided only for the unadjusted efficiency measure, operating costs to operating income. The previous discussion has already demonstrated that adjusting this measure by deleting remunerations increases the probability of credit unions exhibiting increasing returns to scale, while the alternative measure, operating costs to the number of loans, yields results that are insignificantly different from constant returns to scale. Another point of note is that the trade organisations do not have the same mix of credit unions in the various asset categories. From Table 6.4 it can be seen that the mean difference analysis for ILCU credit unions concentrates on the top three asset categories. It would have been impossible and, in one instance, statistically unfair to perform the mean difference analysis for the C4, C5 and C6 groups, as only 10 of the 104 ILCU members fell into these asset groupings. In the case of the NFCU, the focus is on smaller credit unions, while with ABCUL the full asset-size range is scrutinised.

ABCUL and the NFCU have the monopoly of small-asset-scale credit unions and it is again clear that the pattern of the small-asset-range category being

Table 6.4 Paired difference analysis of size economies: trade organisations, 1994

Credit union size category comparisons	Pairs of observations	Operating costs/ operating income (mean difference)[a]	
ILCU			
C3 with C2	16	0.0050	(0.0061)
C3 with C1	16	0.0702	(0.0512)
C2 with C1	35	0.0646[**]	(0.0322)
ABCUL			
C6 with C5	29	0.1749[*]	(0.0619)
C6 with C4	30	0.2961[*]	(0.0874)
C6 with C3	14	0.3041[*]	(0.0715)
C6 with C2	9	0.3198[*]	(0.0169)
C6 with C1	14	0.3132[*]	(0.0803)
C5 with C4	29	0.1643[*]	(0.0632)
C5 with C3	14	0.2232[*]	(0.0862)
C5 with C2	9	0.3033[*]	(0.0137)
C5 with C1	14	0.2449[*]	(0.0818)
C4 with C3	14	0.0427	(0.0594)
C4 with C2	9	0.0977[*]	(0.0475)
C4 with C1	14	0.0953[*]	(0.0175)
C3 with C2	9	0.0696	(0.0743)
C3 with C1	14	0.0203	(0.0630)
C2 with C1	9	0.3757	(0.0515)
NFCU			
C6 with C5	14	0.4466[*]	(0.1353)
C6 with C4	13	0.0932	(0.0913)
C6 with C3	8	0.2714[**]	(0.1458)
C5 with C4	13	0.1386	(0.1539)
C5 with C3	8	0.3263	(0.2098)
C4 with C3	8	0.2601[*]	(0.0398)

[a] Standard errors in parentheses.
[*] Statistically significant at the 5% level.
[**] Statistically significant at the 10% level.

identified as less efficient holds true. If, initially, we concentrate on the C6, C5 and C4 groups for ABCUL and the NFCU, all bar two of the mean difference values are significant at the 5% level, indicating the existence of increasing returns to scale. Both of the insignificant mean difference values are for NFCU credit unions, which suggests that there is less opportunity for the achievement of scale economies for credit unions affiliated to this trade organisation. A part explanation for this difference between ABCUL and NFCU unions relates to the fact that the members of NFCU focus to a somewhat greater extent on the promotion of self-help and community development, particularly in areas of economic disadvantage. Such a focus is unlikely to manifest itself in enhanced operational efficiency.

Turning attention to the larger-asset-size credit union groups, a number of points of interest emerge. First, the ambiguous picture identified for NFCU-affiliated credit unions continues. The largest asset group to which NFCU credit unions belong is C3, and while C3 credit unions are significantly more efficient than either C4 or C6 classes, the comparison with C5 yields a mean difference value insignificantly different from zero. Secondly, ABCUL credit unions tend to be characterised by increasing returns to scale. Indeed, the pattern that emerges for ABCUL-affiliated unions matches that for the industry in aggregate, with a breakdown in the increasing returns to scale pattern only emerging when the C3 group is employed as the control in the pairing process. The mean difference values for C3 credit unions with C4, C2 and C1 are all insignificantly different from zero. Finally, shifting the focus to the ILCU, the analysis detailed in Table 6.4 indicates that the majority of ILCU credit unions occupy the upper-range groups and that a problem again emerges when the C3 group is used in the pairing process. Values insignificantly different from zero emerge in the comparison of the C1 and C2 groups with C3. Note, however, that the C1 group of ILCU credit unions is significantly more efficient than the C2 group. This reaffirms the phenomenon noted earlier for the industry in aggregate, which is that when credit unions enter the asset range greater than £1 million, the scale effect outweighs the broader portfolio of input costs and leads to an improvement in operational efficiency.

CONCLUDING COMMENTS

This analysis has proved somewhat problematic to undertake in that credit unions do not report the full costs of their operations, relying heavily on donated capital and labour. The problem is further compounded in that these hidden costs are not uniformly spread across credit unions of differing asset sizes. In an effort to get some measure of the magnitude of the problem, the operational efficiency measures were recomputed with staff remuneration deleted from operating costs. As expected, this tended to enhance the operational efficiency of the larger credit unions relative to their smaller counterparts.

Ambiguity was also a feature of the analysis, primarily because the two main efficiency measures did not provide similar results. The mean difference analysis conducted in terms of the measure, operating costs to operating income, provided support for the existence of increasing returns to scale within the industry. Unfortunately, this was contradicted by the measure, operating costs to the number of loans, where constant returns were mainly in evidence. In the body of the discussion we hypothesised that the contradictory results stemmed from differentials in the average size of loan made by small and large credit unions. Significant bias was introduced into the latter measure owing to the fact that, for example, the average loan made by the top credit union group was some three times that made by small credit unions. When numerical adjustments were made to equate the average size of loan, larger credit unions were again classified as more efficient than their smaller counterparts.

We are confident in the analysis, and in the validity of our finding that the UK credit union industry is characterised by increasing returns to scale. Nevertheless, we still feel that it has been important to have begun this summing-up by reiterating the problems encountered by the analysis to ensure that caution is exercised if, for example, our findings are employed as a basis for future policy developments.

What then of our findings and potential policy measures on the back of them? The discussion highlighted that significant efficiency gains are available through credit unions adopting a policy of asset growth—a finding that is very much in line with that documented in scale efficiency studies carried out on both US and Canadian credit unions. If the history of the movement in the United States and Canada points the future for UK credit unions, then the idealistic view of the UK movement, held by the NFCU, as one of small-scale credit unions offering share savings and consumer loans to a membership forgotten by main-line financial institutions, comes under threat. The attraction of cost efficiency gains is likely to drive credit unions continually towards the goal of asset growth.

Although the result of increasing returns to scale holds good irrespective of the umbrella organisation to which credit unions belong, it also transpired that the opportunity for efficiency gains is perhaps not as pronounced in the case of NFCU members. This latter finding was to be expected, given the NFCU's emphasis on self-help and community development, particularly in areas of economic disadvantage.

A further insight obtained from the analysis was that for the credit union industry in aggregate, a break in the improving operational efficiency occurred at an asset level between £500,000 and £999,999. The explanation put forward for the break rested with the fact that, at this asset level, credit unions face a more burdensome array of input costs than their smaller counterparts. What, however, also emerged from the analysis was that although larger credit unions found it necessary to employ more full-time and part-time staff, and this initially impacted adversely upon cost efficiency, once they achieved significant critical mass, i.e. assets in excess of £1 million, further and much-enhanced levels of operational efficiency were achieved.

From a cost-efficiency perspective, this analysis would, therefore, tend to support the achievement of continued asset growth by credit unions. The current policy shift towards relaxing borrowing and savings limits, plus the relaxation of the upper ceiling on credit union members, will help in the achievement of this asset growth. Indeed, such policy adjustments find considerable support in this environment, characterised as it is by increasing returns to scale.

Equally constraining in the achievement of asset growth and, consequently, increasing returns to scale, appears to be the concept of a narrowly defined common bond. Relaxation of the criteria on which the common bond is determined, in that it provides individual credit unions with a much wider potential membership, would open up the opportunity for the achievement of scale economies and the accompanying cost-efficiency effect through merger activity.

Finally, as argued in the introduction to this chapter, the finding of increasing returns to scale is likely to dampen any potential for membership conflict. Increasing returns to scale can translate into higher returns for shareholding members and lower loan costs for borrowing members, although it should be stressed that if a membership bias does exist, the direction of the bias is likely to dictate which group benefits most from increasing returns to scale. If the bias is in favour of savers, the enhanced operational efficiency is more likely to translate into higher dividend rates. In contrast, if the directional bias is borrower orientated, the benefits are likely to take the form of lower loan rates. Membership bias is the subject under investigation in the next chapter.

7
Member-Group Orientation

INTRODUCTION

The fundamental motivation of a credit union is to provide financial services for its membership; in particular, a depository for savings and an access to consumer credit. In practice, there are, however, a number of reasons why a credit union may achieve a less-than-perfect balance in the treatment of borrowers and savers. More specifically, maintaining low loan rates may reduce the credit union's ability to offer high dividend rates, while the maintenance of high dividend rates may require higher loan rates. Consequently, the competing pull of these two objectives may result in the emergence of conflict between those members who, on the one hand, are net savers and those who, on the other hand, are net borrowers. Given that the members are, in turn, the owners, the member-group conflict could potentially result in preferential treatment for one particular member group (borrower-orientated or saver-orientated behaviour), rather than balanced or neutral treatment.

In some countries, credit unions have open or community-based membership policies. This leads to them competing with each other for members, with the net effect that loan and dividend rates will tend to standardise across the industry. In such an environment, and assuming that the industry has a significant proportion of the savings and loan market, it is also likely that credit union interest rates will be dictated by market rates. The open approach to membership is at odds with the present situation in the United Kingdom, where the membership of individual unions is defined in terms of a relatively narrow and restrictive common bond. All other things being equal, the restrictive common bond, in that it insulates credit unions from competition with each other, provides a greater latitude for the emergence of preferential treatment in the form of either borrower-orientated or saver-orientated behaviour.

A further factor that is likely to exacerbate the situation vis à vis the UK movement, rests with the regulatory framework. Currently, UK credit unions are subject to a ceiling rate on both dividend payments and loan charges. They are prohibited from paying a dividend on members' shares that exceeds 8% per annum and are restricted from charging in excess of 1% per month (12.68 APR) for loans to members. Under such circumstances, it is not difficult to envisage how a bias might emerge, although, in this instance, the bias, if it emerges, will be borrower orientated in form. For example, if market interest rates are high, as they were in the early 1990s (the base rate in the United Kingdom touched 14% on 8 October 1990), credit unions would be entitled, through the dictates of market forces, to offer higher dividends than the 8% maximum and charge higher loan rates than the 1% per month ceiling. Regulation in such a situation, therefore, automatically encourages the emergence of a borrower-orientated bias. The contrasting situation of low market interest rates does not, however, result in a pro-saver bias, given that there is no regulatory floor in the setting of dividend and loan rates. An additional characteristic of the UK industry, which accentuates the pro-borrower bias, is the convention of paying, from the year-end surplus, not only dividends, but also interest rebates.

On a more positive tack, the finding, in the previous chapter, that the UK industry is characterised by increasing returns to scale implies that, as credit unions grow, the destructive effect on the membership cohesiveness of a borrower-orientated, or, for that matter, a saver-orientated bias, is less likely to manifest. While the membership bias, if it exists, is likely to continue, the decline in per-unit costs can be divided between both member groups. Even if there is a further bias in the division of the benefits from the fall in per-unit costs, the fact that the non-dominant group also benefits is likely, at least in the short term, to keep membership conflict in check.

The focus of attention in this chapter is, therefore, on membership bias and on whether the regulatory environment leads to a biased allocation of the benefits of membership. To investigate these issues, we adopt the methodology put forward by Walker and Chandler (1977) and Patin and McNeil (1991a, b). These authors developed the concept of the net monetary benefits of credit union membership and established the conditions for the equitable allocation of such benefits. The authors employed this methodology to examine for the existence of non-neutral behaviour in US credit unions and, in addition, whether neutral behaviour provides greater benefits than borrower-orientated or saver-orientated behaviour.

In terms of the discussion format, the analysis commences with a formal treatment of the potential conflict that arises between the interests of members who are primarily savers and those who are primarily borrowers. The next step is an outline sketch of the key literature in this area. As with most material on credit unions, research on membership bias concentrates almost exclusively on the United States. The methodology employed in both the calculation of the benefits from membership and the identification of bias towards a particular member group is then detailed. An application of this methodology to UK credit unions is then undertaken. The analysis concludes with an overview of the salient findings and discussion of whether it is in the interest of credit unions to pursue policies that promote an equal treatment of members.

AN ECONOMIC MODEL OF THE INHERENT CONFLICT WITHIN CREDIT UNIONS

The potential dynamic of conflict can be demonstrated in the following simple economic model of credit union behaviour. In this model, first detailed by Taylor (1971), it is assumed that assets comprise solely of loans to members and that the liabilities comprise solely of members' savings.

The key elements of the model are shown in Figure 7.1. Output, which can be considered as loans to members (assets) or as savings of members (liabilities), is measured along the horizontal axis. Per-unit costs and revenue are represented on the vertical axis. The average cost curve, AC, stands for the joint costs of production which are assumed to be long-run optimal. The long-run savings function, S, is that level of savings forthcoming at each level of average return if all individuals within the potential membership are permitted to join. Similarly, the loan demand function, L, constitutes the quantity of loans demanded by all potential members at each level of the loan interest rate.

In Figure 7.1, the equilibrium output is at X. Here, the price for borrowers is RX, the return to savers is LX, and the joint cost of the credit union's operations is CX.

The model can accommodate the special cases of saver-dominated behaviour and borrower-dominated behaviour. The former is depicted in Figure 7.2.

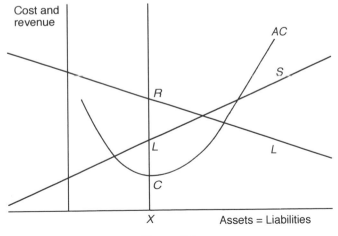

Figure 7.1

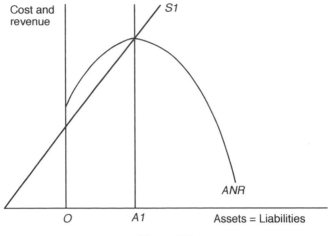

Figure 7.2

When the credit union is saver dominated the objective of the dominant group is the maximisation of average net return (loan demand – average operating costs). Entry by new borrowing members will be regarded by the dominant saver-orientated group as being complementary to their own interests since additional borrowers give an enhanced capacity to pay dividends. However, conflict develops after *A*1, as any increase in savings by new members will reduce dividend rates for all members, including current savers.

Within a borrower-orientated context, as depicted in Figure 7.3, the objective is to minimise the average net cost, *ANC*, of securing funds (joint

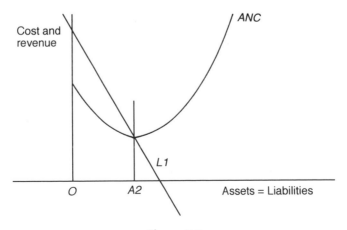

Figure 7.3

production costs plus long-run savings). In this situation it is in the interest of the dominant borrower group to allow all savers within the potential membership access to the savings facility of the credit union, because they represent the lowest cost source of borrowed funds. The interests of the borrowing members are complementary with those of saving members. In terms of the diagrammatic representation in Figure 7.3, $L1$ denotes the short-run loan demand by the optimal number of borrowing members, since it intersects the ANC curve at its minimum point, at output level $A2$. Up to $A2$ it is in the interests of current borrowers to accept new borrowers, as this permits existing borrowers to operate at a level of output that results in a lower average net cost (the decline in average net cost occurs because the decline in operating costs exceeds the associated increase in savings costs). Conflict becomes evident after $A2$, as any further loan demand by new members will have a detrimental effect on the borrowing charges faced by existing borrowers.

Credit unions do, however, possess certain characteristics that may help to soothe and ameliorate the conflict situation. In the first instance, although the diagrammatic presentation suggests that conflicts may emerge between current borrowers and new borrowers, and current savers and new savers, it also highlights the complementary nature of the relationship between, on the one hand, current borrowers and new savers and on the other, between current savers and new borrowers. Secondly, in that members, for the most part, do not exclusively belong to one group or the other, this in itself is likely to be a major factor in dampening the fires of conflict.

The Taylor (1971) model, as a description of credit union behaviour, is somewhat basic in form. For example, this model has no role for reserves or reserve accumulation. Taylor (1979) corrects for this by explicitly introducing reserves into the analysis and demonstrates that a credit union with higher reserves can support a higher loan portfolio at a lower dividend cost. It is, therefore, noted that higher initial reserves are beneficial to current borrowing members. Spencer (1996) develops the analysis further. He argues that while the later work of Taylor allows for the effect of accumulated reserves in the balance sheet, it does not allow for growth and the current accumulation of reserves in the analysis of current period behaviour. Spencer demonstrates that this omission leads to systematic error, such as an underprediction of asset growth and too high a prediction of the loan interest rate.

LITERATURE REVIEW: AN EMPIRICAL EMPHASIS

Taylor (1971) was one of the first authors to note theoretically the inherent source of conflict between borrowers and savers within co-operative organisations. Almost all subsequent work has recognised that member-group conflict could affect the manner in which credit unions are operated.

Quantitative information on the member-group breakdown was first presented by Flannery (1974). From an examination of 951 US credit unions, the author found that a plausible categorisation was possible for 589— borrower dominated (143); saver dominated (233); and neutral (213).

Walker and Chandler (1977) shift the focus somewhat and assess the impact of US regulatory constraints (loan rate and dividend rate ceilings) upon the equitable distribution of the benefits accruing from membership. The authors divide the benefits of membership into monetary and non-monetary benefits, where the latter includes financial counselling, convenience of saving and loan repayments by pay-roll deduction, free life assurance and share insurance. Walker and Chandler (1977) postulate that these non-monetary benefits are distributed evenly amongst members, and, consequently, emphasis in their analysis is placed upon the allocation of the net monetary benefits. The authors define the net monetary benefits of membership as the increase in the interest rate earned on savings and the decrease in the interest rate paid on loans that a member receives as a result of dealing with the credit union rather than the next best alternative. Walker and Chandler formalise the potential conflict between member groups and then, from a theoretical perspective, demonstrate that the legal restrictions on dividend rates and loan interest charges result in strong pro-borrower bias. Other early studies that have focused on the impact of deposit and loan rate ceilings include those by Goudzwaard (1968), Long (1976) and Wolken and Navratil (1980b).

Walker and Chandler (1978) develop an approach to resolve the member-group conflict, which they incorporate into a goal-programming model. This work again explores the concept of the net monetary benefits of membership as the appropriate measure of the benefits received by a credit union member. A goal-programming model is developed that incorporates the regulatory and environmental constraints and has as its objective the equal allocation of net member benefits between the member groups. The authors, in the course of this study, highlight that, as a result of the US legislative ceiling on the dividend rate, a balanced distribution of monetary benefits is unattainable, and employ simulation exercises to highlight a pro-borrower bias.

Smith, Cargill and Meyer (1981) combine many of the earlier theoretical perspectives on credit unions into a much more versatile framework. Their main contribution is the construction of a generalised objective function that allows explicit weights to be attached to saver welfare versus borrower welfare. The authors' analysis and policy discussion emphasise the impact of regulation and taxation on a saver-dominated credit union. In such a situation, the savers act as profit maximisers *vis à vis* borrowing members, then distribute the surplus amongst themselves. The authors claim that a deposit rate ceiling prohibits the saver-dominated credit union from distributing its earnings to the saving members. Furthermore, Smith, Cargill and Meyer argue that a saver-orientated union would respond to binding deposit rate ceilings by retaining an excessive amount of earnings in the form of reserves. The rationale in this instance being that, since savers' current dividend rates cannot be raised, the second-best alternative is to increase reserves to ensure that future dividend payments are made safer. The authors suggest that a policy of taxing these additions to reserves should result in saver-orientated credit unions taking a more neutral or borrower-orientated stance.

Flannery (1981), in a response to this paper, questions whether the primary response of a saver-orientated union to a dividend rate ceiling would be that of increasing its reserves. He argues that most credit unions, at least in the United States, should be able to distribute their earnings via a combination of implicit interest payments and the introduction of higher yielding certificate accounts.

Navratil (1981) constructs a six-equation simultaneous model to estimate aggregate flows within the US credit union industry. Navratil concludes that credit unions are loyal to their historical goal of providing members with low-cost consumer credit, even if some potential revenues are sacrificed in the process. Loans are granted to members at a rate high enough to cover dividend and operating expenses. The author further suggests that the willingness of US credit unions to forego some potential profitability in order to benefit borrower members results in a misallocation of resources into the consumer credit sector. As a consequence of this resource misallocation, Navratil argues that future legislative change may be unfavourable towards the industry — a supposition very much borne out by the facts in later years.

Smith (1984) retraces much of the analysis presented in Walker and Chandler (1977) and Smith, Cargill and Meyer (1981). Once again, market rate comparisons are utilised in order to gauge the pecuniary gains accruing to members. However, many of the essential features of the previous models are recast in order to accommodate the intertemporal nature of transactions. The author examines the major implications of his model using comparative static analysis and underlines the factors impacting most significantly upon the optimal loan and dividend rates. These factors include operating costs, regulatory constraints (which are suggested to induce a pro-borrower bias), inherited balance sheet portfolios and potential borrower–saver bias. Smith (1984) demonstrates with the aid of the comparative static framework that whereas neutral credit unions vary both their dividend and loan rates to militate against fluctuations in operating costs, those that discriminate in favour of borrowers (savers) will opt to adjust solely the loan (dividend) rate in order to accommodate the disturbances.

Smith (1986) translates his earlier theoretical models into an estimable framework capable of detecting variant objective functions — the idea being that the borrower-saver conflict, and the resolution of this conflict, could lead to a variety of credit union types, ranging from complete borrower or saver preference at the extremes to some sense of neutrality as the intermediate position. The author hypothesises that credit unions may reasonably be categorised depending upon whether their observed loan and dividend rates fall below or above overall sample averages. However, because member-group bias may not be the only influence to impact upon observed loan and dividend rates, the comparison on the basis of means is incomplete. Smith (1986) therefore augments the system by regressing observed loan and dividend rates on a set of appropriate institutional geographical and loan heterogeneity variables. Credit unions are then classified in comparison with predicted rates. Applying the scheme to a sample of 951 federally insured credit unions for each of the years 1976 to 1979, Smith (1986) found that 10% manifested a borrower preference and 22% a saver preference.

Credit unions categorised as having either an extreme borrower, or extreme saver, preference were then employed to test empirically the variant objective function hypothesis. The test employed was a regression of the loan rate on variables from the balance sheet—capital reserves, average cost of operations and the periodic transfer from revenue to reserves. A similar regression was carried out with the dividend rate as the dependent variable. Smith (1986) indicates that the sign of the coefficient from the regressions would depend on behavioural preference—the essence of the test being to determine whether the parameters for the respective member groups differ in a significant way. Importantly, Smith (1986) found that the pattern of results did not provide sufficient evidence of the variant objective function hypothesis. Consequently, the author concludes that a neutral objective function is a reasonable and workable description of credit union behaviour.

Patin and McNeil (1991a) return to the topic of member imbalances and employ a methodology similar in form to that of Walker and Chandler (1977). The authors conduct their analysis for 9660 US credit unions for the year 1984. By the mid-1980s considerable deregulation had occurred in the United States. For example, on the asset side of the balance sheet the lending powers were significantly enlarged with credit unions permitted to make residential mortgage loans of any size or maturity, but, perhaps more importantly, the NCUA was empowered to raise the interest rate ceiling on loans if warranted by economic conditions. Regulatory changes also increased the ability of credit unions to attract deposits. They were permitted to offer members a wide variety of share accounts with, importantly, no restrictions on the interest rate they could pay (for more details see Pearce, 1984). Consequently, the equations employed by Walker and Chandler (1977) to estimate monetary benefits to member groups were reworked by Patin and McNeil (1991a) to reflect the enhanced product freedom on offer. Employing somewhat *ad hoc* boundary conditions, the authors concluded that 2.7% of the sample could be classified as extreme borrower orientated; 12.9% although viewed as unclassifiable, were considered to exhibit the characteristics of weak borrower-orientated behaviour; 45.1% were categorised as neutral; 29.7% although for all intents and purposes unclassifiable, were ranked as weakly saver orientated; and, finally, 9.6% were considered to be strongly saver dominated.

The authors indicate that the conventional wisdom that neutral behaviour generates more benefits for members than credit unions that are orientated towards a particular member group appears to be inaccurate. They found that members of extreme saver-orientated credit unions receive significantly larger total net monetary benefits than the members of neutral ones and, in addition, the difference in the benefits received by members of those classified as neutral and extreme borrower orientated is of questionable statistical significance. In addition, the authors found that when benefits per member, benefits per dollar of loans and shares, and benefits per dollar of assets were considered, neutral credit unions provide substantially fewer benefits to members than either extreme saver-orientated or extreme borrower-orientated credit unions. Patin and McNeil (1991a) conclude that while it is possible that the total benefits to members could be increased by regulations designed to discourage extreme borrower-orientated behaviour and encourage neutral behaviour, discouraging extreme saver-orientated behaviour would produce undesirable member-benefit effects.

A subsequent paper by Patin and McNeil (1991b) based on the same data set and utilising the same methodology raises further important points. In the first instance, occupational credit unions were discovered to have a stronger saver orientation than other common-bond types. Secondly, extreme borrower-orientated credit unions and, to a lesser extent, extreme saver-orientated ones, were found to restrict membership and size (non-price rationing) in order to increase benefits per member. The empirical evidence provided by the authors suggests that US credit unions that are orientated towards a particular member group tend to be more concerned with maximising benefits per member, whereas neutral credit unions are more concerned with maximising the total benefits of the group. Patin and McNeil (1991b) suggest that the finding, i.e. credit unions subject to member-group bias restrict membership size, is consistent with the theoretical model documented by Taylor (1971), which hypothesised that for those subject to membership bias a conflict of interest emerges between existing and potential new members.

The literature under consideration has been exclusively US-based. Many of the papers did, however, adopt a theoretical stance and, in consequence, have relevance for movements in other countries. As the regulatory environment within the United Kingdom is similar in form to that in the United States preregulation, it is the pre-1980 literature on membership bias that is most pertinent to the UK movement. In the prederegulation period, US credit unions were restricted in their provision of savings and lending services and were subject to dividend and loan rate ceilings. The prederegulation structural environment within which US credit unions operated therefore mirrors that now in place in the United Kingdom. The expectation must, therefore, be that the pro-borrower bias identified in prederegulation studies as the probable outcome for those that adhere to dividend and loan rate ceilings, will be the dominant result for UK credit unions. Attention is now turned to the methodological approach to be adopted in the investigation of member-group orientation.

METHODOLOGY UTILISED TO ESTIMATE MONETARY BENEFITS TO MEMBER GROUPS

The methodology followed in this chapter to both calculate the benefits from membership and identify biases towards a particular member group is found in the work of Walker and Chandler (1977) and Patin and McNeil (1991a, b). As indicated, the latter studies by Patin and McNeil were employed to address the issue of membership bias post-deregulation in the United States. The studies are, however, important to this investigation as they go further than the earlier work of Walker and Chandler (1977) and explore issues such as the relationship between member-group orientation and common bond and whether asset size is an influence in member orientation.

The net monetary benefits of membership are the increase in the interest rate earned on savings and the decrease in the interest rate paid on loans that a member receives as a result of dealing with the credit union rather than the next best alternative. In equation form, the net monetary benefit received by the credit union saver (NMB_S) is defined as

$$(NMB_S) = (D_C - S_O) \cdot TS, \tag{1}$$

where,

(NMB_S) = the net monetary benefits received by credit union savers,

D_C = the dividend rate paid on savings by the credit union,

S_O = the best alternative interest rate on savings available to credit union members

TS = the total volume of member savings balances.

Equation (1) measures the monetary benefits accruing to saving members net of the opportunity costs associated with their decisions:

$$(NMB_B) = (L_O \cdot (1 - R)) \cdot TL, \tag{2}$$

where

(NMB_B) = the net monetary benefits received by credit union borrowers,

L_O = the effective loan interest rate available at the lowest cost non-credit-union lender,

L_C = the interest rate charged on a credit union loan,

R = the proportion of interest income on loans refunded to credit union borrowers,

TL = the total volume of loans to credit union members.

Equation (2) measures the monetary benefits accruing to borrowing members net of the opportunity cost of their decision to obtain funds from the credit union rather than their best alternative source of funds. The next step in the process is to compare empirically the benefits received by each member group, consequently the difference (D) between NMB_S and NMB_B is calculated for each union, that is,

$$D = NMB_S - NMB_B. \tag{3}$$

A particular credit union generates more net monetary benefits for saving members than for borrowing members if $D > 0$. In contrast, if $D < 0$ the credit union generates more net monetary benefits for borrowing members, while, if $D = 0$, the credit union provides equal benefits for both member groups.

Patin and McNeil (1991a, b) suggest that employing D to classify credit unions as borrower orientated, saver orientated or neutral presents two major problems. The first relates to the fact that D may be subject to size bias. The authors give the example—a credit union with \$100 million in assets and a D value of \$320,000 is not necessarily 100 times more saver orientated than one with assets of \$1 million and a D value of \$3200. The second problem centres on the fact that, as an absolute measure, D is not suitable for comparisons on the basis of the relative extent to which credit unions generate benefits for one member group versus the other.

To adjust for the potential problem of size bias, the member-group benefit imbalances are weighted by the total asset size of the credit union, that is,

$$DR = (NMB_S - NMB_B)/TA, \tag{4}$$

where

TA = the credit union's total assets.

To introduce a relative measure of member imbalances, an index of benefit imbalances (DI) is computed by standardising DR relative to $DR = 0$,

$$DI = (DR - 0)/STD_0, \tag{5}$$

where

STD_0 = the standard deviation of DR about zero.

An idea of the total monetary benefits (TB) that accrue to the members of a credit union can also be calculated and is given by,

$$TB = NMB_S + NMB_B \tag{6}$$

DATA AND RESULTS

In that a significant component of the UK movement is recently formed, spurious results would be likely to emerge if all 597 credit unions were included in the analysis of member-group orientation. This rests with the fact that a sizeable section pay either no dividends or simply a token dividend in the first few years after formation. These credit unions, in that at best they pay only a marginal dividend, would automatically be classified as borrower orientated. Consequently, those that paid a dividend of less than 1% in 1994 were removed from the data set. This resulted in the omission of 314 from the database, leaving 283 on which to base the analysis.

The next stage in the analysis was the determination of the best alternative market loan rate and savings rate on offer outside the industry. Scrutiny of savings and loan rates available from other financial institutions revealed that the best alternative rates were offered by building societies. A problem that did, however, emerge was that within this financial grouping it was not the large national players that provided the best interest rate package but rather the smaller regional or local societies. By definition, this latter group do not have a national exposure through a branch network system and hence choosing one of these institutions would be unfair in that the majority of credit union members would not be able to avail of its services. As a second-best alternative, the building society offering the best savings rate and the best loan rate in each of the 12 regions of the United Kingdom was identified. The best regional rates were then employed to compute an average savings rate and an average loan rate and it was these rates that were used as proxies for the rates on offer outside credit unions.

There were, however, a number of further complications in the calculation of the monetary benefits to the member groups. Most members who save with a credit union are able to access their savings on demand, and for the vast majority their savings are somewhere between £500 and £1000. There are a wide variety of savings products on offer at building societies. To match the characteristics of savings in credit unions, we opted for a building society instant access account with the interest rate on offer that for an account with a minimum balance of £500. The alternative savings rate was calculated at an average rate of 2.374% for 1994.

A second problem relates to the fact that, on the loan side of the balance sheet, credit unions make secured and unsecured loans. Approximately 78% of loans are unsecured, with the residual 22% secured. While a standardised loan rate is charged irrespective of whether the loan is secured or unsecured, this is not the case with other UK financial institutions, including building societies. It was therefore necessary to compute a weighted loan rate. In this instance, the hypothetical loan portfolio was viewed to consist of a personal loan for between £500 and £5000 of which 78% was unsecured. The average annual percentage loan rate (APR) for 1994 was calculated to be 19.971%.

The final complicating factor is that a number of credit unions in 1994 provided loan rebates to their members. Of the 283 under scrutiny, 35 provided an interest rebate. As detailed in an earlier chapter, the board of directors of a credit union may recommend a loan rebate to members who have received loans from the credit union, with such a rebate being proportional to the interest paid by, or due from, such members during that year of account. For the 35 providing loan rebates, the effective loan interest rate was reduced, on average, by marginally in excess of 1%.

MEMBER-GROUP ORIENTATION

The member-group orientation is determined by the sign of DI. A value of $DI > 0$ suggests that the credit union tends towards saver-orientated behaviour, while a value of $DI < 0$ is indicative of it adopting a pro-borrower stance. When DI values were calculated, it transpired that the degree of member-group benefit imbalances ranged on a continuum from extreme borrower orientation (minimum value of $DI = -3.4083$) to marginal saver-orientated behaviour (maximum value of $DI = +0.2991$). For the sample set, the mean value of DI was estimated to be -0.8927. This value indicates that for 1994 the average credit union was characterised as borrower dominated. Indeed, in that only three had a positive value of DI, the vast majority could, at least nominally, be classified as being subject to borrower-orientated behaviour.

Patin and McNeil (1991a, b), while arguing that boundary lines between saver-orientated, neutral and borrower-orientated credit unions cannot be drawn with any great precision, nevertheless adopt the following classification scheme. Credit unions with a DI value ≤ -1.5 are categorised as extreme borrower dominated, while those with $-1.5 < DI < -0.5$ are viewed as borrower orientated, but are, in all probability, unclassifiable. Those credit unions with $-0.5 \leq DI \leq +0.5$ are considered to be neutral in their behaviour. To be characterised as saver orientated, although, again, probably unclassifiable, $+0.5 < DI < +1.5$, while to be ranked as extreme saver dominated, $DI \geq +1.5$. On the basis of this classification scheme, no UK credit unions were classified as exhibiting either weak or extreme saver-orientated behaviour, 40 were classed as neutral in the treatment of their members, 223 were viewed to be weakly borrower orientated, with the remaining 20 classed as extreme borrower dominated.

Patin and McNeil (1991a, b) stress that classification as borrower orientated, neutral or saver orientated obviously depends on how liberally or restrictively balanced and unbalanced behaviour is defined. Indeed, it could be argued that the classification scheme employed by Patin and McNeil and adopted in this study underplays extreme behaviour. In the case of this present study, many commentators are, for example, likely to argue that a distinction should not be drawn between those credit unions with $-1.5 < DI < -0.5$ and those with $DI \leq -1.5$. Both subgroups should be considered as borrower dominated. Irrespective of where the demarcation lines are drawn, it is very clear that the UK industry in

1994 is heavily borrower dominated with no evidence of saver-dominated behaviour and little evidence of the neutral treatment of member groups.

It is possible to calculate the excess allocation of benefits to borrowers on an individual credit union basis. As an example, if the DI value for the average credit union ($DI = -0.8927$) is taken in conjunction with the computed standard deviation of DR about zero (2.69 pence per £1 of total assets), the excess allocation of benefits to borrowers by the average credit union was 24 pence (-0.8927×2.69) per £1 of assets. With 47.5% having a value of $DI < -0.8927$, it is evident that an excess allocation of benefit to borrowers permeates the industry at this point in time.

Should we be surprised at the strength of the pro-borrower stance of the movement? The answer must clearly be in the negative. The regulatory environment, manifested in terms of dividend and borrowing rate ceilings, almost dictates that a bias emerges in favour of borrowers. This point can be highlighted by returning to the early work of Walker and Chandler (1977) and recasting it in terms of the behavioral characteristics of UK credit unions.

The condition for the equitable distribution of the benefits from membership is given as

$$NMB_S = NMB_B \tag{7}$$

which, in terms of Equations (1) and (2) may be rewritten as

$$(D_C - S_O) \cdot TS = (L_O - L_C \cdot (1 - R)) \cdot TL. \tag{8}$$

For all intents and purposes, the credit union has direct control only over D_C, L_C and R. To some extent, through the setting of D_C and L_C, it exercises a degree of control over TS and TL. The remaining variables, S_O and L_O are, however, determined outside the system and must be treated as exogenous.

In the analysis of the UK industry, the best alternative savings rate, S_O, was 2.374% and the best alternative loan rate, L_O, was 19.971%. Share capital, TS, was some 1.132 times as large as loans to members, TL, for the average credit union. Importantly for attempts to establish equity in the distribution of the net monetary benefits of credit union membership, this ratio of 1.132 is relatively stable across all credit unions, not only during 1994 but also in each of the years from 1991 onwards. Under these conditions, even a credit union that levies the maximum loan interest rate (12.68 APR) on its members, and in addition offers no interest loan rebates, will necessarily be characterised as adopting a pro-borrower stance. This becomes clear on substituting the above noted values into Equation (8), with the additional assumption being made that loan rebates are not paid. Equation (8) becomes

$$(D_C - 2.374) \cdot 1.132 = (19.971 - 12.68 \cdot (1 - 0)).$$

Solving for D_C yields a value of 8.81%. In the context of the United Kingdom such a solution is not possible, as credit unions may not pay a dividend on members' shares that exceeds 8% per annum. Therefore, at present, they are locked into borrower-orientated behaviour. It should also be noted that loan interest rates in 1994 were at their lowest level since October 1977. Consequently, in each of the last 17 years, industry must also have been characterised as borrower dominated.

At present, the situation persists where the net monetary benefits to savers are less than the net monetary benefits that accrue to borrowers, that is,

$$NMB_S < NMB_B, \tag{9}$$

which may be rewritten as

$$(D_C - S_O) \cdot TS < (L_O - L_C \cdot (1 - R)) \cdot TL, \tag{10}$$

which can in turn be written as

$$(D_C \cdot (TS/TL)) + (L_C \cdot (1 - R)) < L_O + (S_O \cdot (TS/TL)). \tag{11}$$

Again, assume that savings continue to run at 1.132 times loans to members and that credit unions do not offer interest rebates. In addition, assume that they adopt a policy of paying the maximum dividend rate possible, 8%. Under such circumstances, the right-hand side of the inequality in (11), $L_O + (S_O \cdot (TS/TL))$, would need to fall to 21.736% before the pro-borrower bias is eliminated and there is equity in the treatment of borrowers and savers. On the assumption that the savings-to-loan ratio remains constant, the fall in $L_O + (S_O \cdot (TS/TL))$ must occur through a fall in either L_O or S_O. A change in the former would lower the monetary benefits to savers, while a fall in the latter would cause the benefits to borrowers to decline. If credit unions were to operate at their loan and dividend rate ceilings, equity in the treatment of membership groups could be achieved with a net fall in $L_O + (S_O \cdot (TS/TL))$ of only 0.922% (given the present best alternative savings rate of 2.374% and the best alternative loan rate of 19.971%, $L_O + (S_O \cdot (TS/TL))$ is calculated at 22.658%). While this net fall is relatively small, it must be remembered that nominal interest rates are, at present, extremely low, and, in fact, have not been this low, on a consistent basis, since the mid-1960s. It must, therefore, be concluded that if the dividend and interest rate ceilings continue in place, then there is little prospect of achieving a balanced treatment of member groups.

Assuming that an equal distribution of net monetary benefits is desirable, what are the necessary steps that must be taken to reduce the biases in the distribution of benefits? There are, in fact, two steps that could be taken. One is to raise or eliminate the maximum dividend rate, while the second is to raise or eliminate the maximum loan rate. It is, of course, also possible to opt for some combination of the two steps. In the analysis by Walker and Chandler (1977), a similar dilemma was faced in the United States. Walker and Chandler made the point that if the maxims of welfare economics are followed, then the choice must be to raise the dividend rate. Such a measure would seek to reduce the pro-borrower bias without reducing the welfare of either group. The problem for UK credit unions in adopting this proposal is that the loan rate ceiling at 12.68 APR is relatively low, and as the dividend rates would need to exceed 8% to generate equity of treatment of member groups, this might result in too narrow a margin to permit the credit union to operate efficiently. This is likely to be particularly the case when the credit union achieves a size where it becomes necessary to employ full-time staff.

Increasing the maximum loan rate thus becomes a more viable alternative, although such an action will reduce the welfare of borrowers. Of course, raising the maximum loan rate does not automatically force higher loan rates to be charged. What it does do, however, is to create the potential for equality in the treatment of borrowers and savers. It is then a decision for the membership of individual unions as to whether a balanced or unbalanced treatment of member groups should be pursued.

MEMBER BENEFITS AND GROUP ORIENTATION

The implicit assumption throughout the discussion has been that a balanced treatment of members is desirable. To investigate whether this is the case, a correlation analysis was undertaken between total benefits, TB, given by Equation (6) and the degree of member imbalance as given by DI in Equation (5). A correlation of 0.1024 was obtained, which suggests that there is a weak positive correlation between total benefits and the degree of member imbalance. Of course, one of the problems with this analysis is that most of the credit unions in the sample are borrower orientated (there are no saver-orientated credit unions and only 40 are classified as neutral). Therefore, with the correlation analysis, we are only really addressing whether different magnitudes of borrower orientation confer differential total benefits on members. Nevertheless, a positive correlation coefficient, albeit weakly positive, was obtained, which indicates that the less the degree of pro-borrower bias, the greater the total benefits to members. This, at least, provides a tentative indication that as we continue to move along the continuum of member orientation towards the neutral position, total benefits to membership should increase.

This latter hypothesis is, to some extent, confirmed by an examination of average total benefits per credit union and total benefits per member for the earlier member-group classifications. For the 40 unions classed as neutral in the treatment of their members, average total benefits (benefits per member) were £71,000 (£42.86); for the 223 viewed to be weakly borrower orientated, the average total benefits value (benefits per member) was £66,685 (£40.33); while for the remaining 20 classed as extreme borrower-dominated, the mean total benefits value (benefits per member) was £10,326 (£33.57). While nominally the calculated values could be considered to provide strong support for the theoretical argument that neutral behaviour maximises total benefits and, indeed, benefits per member, it should be noted that the respective values had high associated standard deviations and hence a difference between means analysis did not yield significant results.

Affiliation could also be a determining factor in both member-group orientation and in the benefits that accrue as a consequence of membership. The degree of pro-borrower bias for ILCU affiliates was calculated at -0.7074. Comparable values for ABCUL- and NFCU-affiliated credit unions were respectively -1.0512 and -0.9319. The inference to be taken is that ILCU unions have a lower degree of pro-borrower emphasis than those affiliated to the other two trade organisations. In this instance, the differential has little to do with differences in the ethos of the trade organisations. Rather, it is a function of the fact that the ILCU represents a more mature, longer established group of credit unions, with this longevity and greater maturity manifesting itself in the form of higher dividend rates to savers relative to those paid by credit unions more recently formed. This automatically results in longer established credit unions generating higher monetary benefits for savers, leading to a reduced borrower-orientated bias. Credit unions in their formative years, such as many of those affiliated to the NFCU and ABCUL, traditionally pay only a token dividend. This is because of the fact that any surplus generated through operations is initially reinvested in premises, equipment and staff training. Only after they have been in existence for a number of years does the dividend rate begin to creep up towards the notional average for the industry. This contrasts with rates charged on loans, where credit unions immediately levy a rate close to, or at, the loan rate ceiling.

Consequently, it is likely to be the case that the present differential in the index of borrower orientation between ILCU credit unions and those affiliated to the NFCU and ABCUL is, in all probability, transitory. This is also true for the mean total benefit value per member, which for ILCU members was calculated at £70.13, compared with £52.28 for ABCUL members and £31.56 for NFCU members. What, however, should be stressed is that while maturity will reduce the degree of borrower imbalance and raise benefits per member for both NFCU and ABCUL credit unions, the regulatory environment, if it remains, will ensure that borrowers are the dominant member group.

CONCLUDING COMMENTS

The results documented in this chapter indicate that almost all credit unions in 1994 exhibited borrower-dominated behaviour. It was also stressed, on the basis of an examination of market rates of interest, that the industry was likely to have been characterised as pro-borrower in each of the prior 17 years. This result was, in part, almost a foregone conclusion, given that the 1979 Credit

Union Act requires credit unions not to pay dividends above a stipulated maximum of 8% per annum, nor charge loan interest rates in excess of 1% per month.

It was also argued that further falls in market interest rates would aid the reduction of the pro-borrower bias. However, it is our view that, irrespective of the degree of further interest rate falls, credit unions will not be able to achieve a neutral treatment of their members. Given the present dividend and loan rate ceilings, the achievement of a balanced treatment of borrowers and savers would require that credit unions operate off relatively narrow margins, with the required interest rate spread probably too narrow even for financial institutions that pay only a fraction of their true operating costs.

On a more positive front, the analysis also highlighted that ILCU affiliates were less borrower orientated than those affiliated to either the NFCU or ABCUL. This finding was taken to suggest that, as credit unions become longer established, the average dividend paid tends to rise, which reduces the degree of borrower orientation. If this finding is coupled with the fact that the UK industry has been shown to be characterised by increasing returns to scale, then the long-run 'equilibrium' position of weak borrower orientation may not lead to membership conflict and hence a threatening of the co-operative principles on which credit unions are based. Indeed, we can proceed a step further and argue that membership conflict may not emerge because individual members, over time, are likely to enjoy some periods as net savers and other periods as net borrowers.

The theoretical debate has always centred on the first-best position being that of a neutral treatment of borrowers and savers. In this discussion we have shown that the achievement of this objective in the context of the regulatory environment under which UK credit unions operate is impossible. In the body of the analysis it was suggested that if credit unions were to achieve a balanced treatment of their membership, then it was necessary to remove the interest and dividend rate ceilings to which they must adhere. However, if we abstract from the theoretical debate and refocus on the fact that credit unions are invariably based in low-income communities, where access to cheap loan funds alleviates a degree of the hardship faced by many families, then it may, in fact, be a retrograde step to create an environment where there is not an upper loan rate ceiling. Indeed, it may be the case that the UK situation of weakly borrower-orientated behaviour, while not theoretically optimal, is, nevertheless, socially optimal. Given the unique and positive role played by credit unions in low-income communities, it is, therefore, our view that weak borrower domination is an insufficient reason for a revision of the dividend and loan rate ceilings.

8

The Growth and Development of Community-Based and Employer-Based Credit Unions

INTRODUCTION

This chapter investigates the role played by both employer-based and community-based credit unions in fostering the growth of the movement in the United Kingdom. Community-based credit unions dominate. A total of 537 unions have a common bond that is community in form compared with 60 with an employer/occupational common bond. In consequence, it could be argued that the discussion in preceding chapters has, to all intents and purposes, been about community credit unions (indeed a subsection of Chapter 4 was devoted specifically to local government support of community credit unions). In recognition of this, a more overt emphasis is placed in this chapter on employer-based credit unions.

Although the number of employer-based credit unions is small, it will be argued that increased penetration of the workplace is likely to enhance the standing of the movement by offering a significant new pool of membership beyond the traditional clientele within disadvantaged communities. The emergence of more employer unions will provide the demonstration effect that the movement has the capabilities to move up-market and that the image of credit unions being specifically the 'poor man's bank' does not necessarily apply to all unions in the movement. In addition, we are also interested in the current drivers and restrainers affecting the take up and growth of both community- and employer-based credit unions and whether differences emerge as a consequence of the setting in which the credit union is based. To examine these issues, this chapter adopts the following organisational format. The analysis commences with an examination of a range of ratios, which it is expected will present a picture of significant differences in the operational structure of community and employer credit unions. In part, the expectation that differences exist centres upon the clientele served by these two subgroups, with employer-based unions having a membership with a higher net worth than their community counterparts. A further important influence is, of course, the setting in which the credit union is located and the size of the potential market it can serve. The second part of the discussion pursues a case study methodology. In this instance, two recently formed credit unions are scrutinised; one community-based, the other employer-focused. The pace of growth of both is charted, as are the factors instrumental in the achievement of this growth. In particular, the initiatives that they have pursued to promote themselves, and the obstacles that they faced in their formative period, are examined. The anticipation is that the case study will help to locate the conditions necessary for sustainable growth in both credit union subgroups. The chapter is completed with a consideration of the prospects for employer and community credit unions in view of anticipated legislative change and the shift towards a more embracing concept of the common bond.

AGGREGATE STATISTICS

In numerical terms, employer-focused unions are dwarfed by their community counterparts. As indicated, there are at present 60 employer-based unions (a further three are listed by the Registry of Friendly Societies, although they have not filed returns and in consequence are not included as part of the statistical overview). For the most part, they are firmly located in the public sector. Local authorities have the largest incidence of employer credit union establishment, followed by the police service.

In Chapter 4 it was noted that local authorities are strong supporters of the establishment of, in particular, community credit unions. Thomas and Balloch (1994) were cited, in which they advanced four main reasons for the establishment of credit unions in local communities:

1. Credit unions prevent and counter indebtedness by providing a source of reasonably priced credit to disadvantaged groups not usually eligible for other forms of credit,

2. Credit unions help combat poverty and financial distress amongst the unemployed and ethnic groups,

3. They provide training for the unemployed and low waged through the actual establishment process,

4. Credit unions are run by local people, which exerts a social pressure on members to save regularly and clear their borrowings, which, in turn, enables families and individuals to weather more easily unexpected financial crises.

Given this array of arguments put forward by local authorities for the establishment of community credit unions, and the evident importance they attach to credit unions as an input into economic regeneration, it would, therefore, be somewhat of a surprise if they did not use their own organisations as demonstration models for credit unions. Promotion of a concept is always made much easier if the promoter has experience of the concept in action. Of course, a further reason for the relatively heavy incidence of credit unions within local authorities relates to the fact that council workers tend to occupy the lower salary scales and the four reasons documented for establishment in low-income communities would, therefore, find equal justification within this employment segment.

In Chapter 4 it was noted that 12 credit unions were linked to the police service. The rationale for the establishment in constabularies is not to be found in low-income-centred arguments but rather rests with the demands placed upon members within the police service. There is an onus on members of the police force to behave prudently in the management of their financial affairs, to stay out of the grasps of money lenders, and, at all costs, to ensure that any debts that they might have are not known about within the public domain. The latter requirement centres on the fact that the knowledge of such debt might potentially be exploited by unscrupulous individuals. Under such circumstances, the workplace credit union has an important role to play, not just in terms of the provision of cheap loan facilities, but also in terms of providing a financial planning service to members.

The remaining public-service-focused credit unions do not have, perhaps, such pertinent reasons for establishment as those within the local authorities and police service. The remainder are small in number and scattered across a range of organisations, including postal workers, the fire service, a transport body, employees of the Open University, the commonwealth secretariat and a health authority. The largest of the remaining credit unions is Strathclyde transport employees with some 2809 members and £1.8 million in assets (1994 figures). Most of them, however, have both less than 200 members and less than £150,000 in assets.

Credit unions in the private sector are also very much in the minority. Only 14 could be classified as truly privately-based. In this instance, the transport business appears to be the common denominator. There are three bus companies with credit unions, two taxi companies, plus British Aerospace, British Airways and First Shipbuilders in Scotland. There is no obvious reason for credit union establishment within the transport industry, with perhaps the exception that employees within many companies in this area are relatively poorly paid. Again, it should be noted that most of these credit unions are relatively small in size. The largest of all the private sector unions is Merseyside Passenger with 1590 members and £1.4 million in assets (1994 figures).

Although direct information is difficult to obtain, there is the expectation that a distinction can be made within the employer-based credit union group between those that are essentially demand led and those that are supply led. For the most part, local authority credit unions could, for example, be viewed as demand-led institutions in that they are actively encouraged and supported by the local authorities themselves. This support is forthcoming because of the demonstration effect already highlighted and the fact that the credit union philosophy blends with the political philosophy of these authorities. Thomas and Balloch (1994) point to examples such as the metropolitan authorities of Wirral, Calderdale, Salford and, more recently, Liverpool, which have actively encouraged their staff to set up workplace unions. This encouragement has been complemented by a range of support measures from the local authorities including:

● start-up loans to help with the study group stage and to cover registration fees

● grants, usually between £500 and £2000, again to help cover start-up costs

● subsidised accommodation

● assistance with publicity

This very much contrasts with the experience particularly of many private sector workplace unions which, as with most credit unions, are supply led, receiving, at least in the conception and embryonic stages, little or no support from the employer. Employers in the United Kingdom, unlike their counterparts in many other countries, have, as yet, failed to recognise the significant potential of workplace credit unions. In many other countries they are viewed as a means of retaining employee loyalty, in that members see the workplace credit union almost as a form of fringe benefit. The establishment of workplace unions in the United Kingdom appears to be very much employee led and dependent upon the drive and commitment of individuals within the firm. In that the United Kingdom has no significant track record of private sector workplace credit unions, those committed to the ideal find it very much an uphill battle to obtain the requisite support from their employer. Again, the support required would include office accommodation and equipment, assistance with printing and promotional material, and, at least in the initial stages, a freeing-up of some staff time to enable involvement in the business of the credit union. Later in this chapter, when the two case studies are developed, emphasis will again focus on the problems involved during the establishment of private sector workplace credit unions.

The opportunity is now taken in Table 8.1 to compare a selection of size statistics for credit unions classified as workplace-based (Emp.) as well as for those classed as community organisations (Comm.). The database on which the table is based relates to the 1994 reports filed by credit unions.

Table 8.1 Size characteristics of community and workplace credit unions, 1994

Asset range (£)	Number		Assets of group as a percentage of the total		Number of members		Assets per member (£)	
	Emp.	Comm.	Emp.	Comm.	Emp.	Comm.	Emp.	Comm.
Over £1,000,000	11	48	67.90	72.22	39,332	151,3C6	689	977
£500,000 to £999,999	9	40	14.93	14.68	9831	46,069	607	652
£250,000 to £499,999	12	30	10.58	5.18	7761	19,883	544	533
£100,000 to £249,999	12	47	4.79	3.72	4377	19,475	437	391
£50,000 to £99,999	5	44	1.07	1.51	936	12,064	458	256
£613 to £49,999	11	328	0.73	2.69	1305	35,797	220	154
Total	50	537	100	100	63,542	284,594	628	719

As in previous chapters, the tabular information is presented for credit unions on the basis of asset size. The first part of the table documents the actual number of credit unions that fall into the respective size classes. As already stated, it is clear that community credit unions are more abundant than workplace unions. From the table it does, however, appear that the size distribution of employer unions is much more evenly spread across the respective classes; 11 workplace credit unions (18%) have assets over £1 million while a similar number have assets between £613 and £49,999. The comparable statistics for community credit organisations are 48 (9%) in the top asset range and 328 (61%) in the bottom asset class. Thus, there is a much heavier incidence of community unions in the bottom asset range relative to employer unions and while, numerically, there, is also more in the top asset category, the relative percentage weights tell a different story. Perhaps the reason for the relatively greater percentage of workplace unions in the top asset range centres on the fact that once such a credit union is established, it can progress much more rapidly. This centres on the fact that its common bond is extremely well defined and publicity material promoting the union can be targeted easily at all potential members within the common bond. The fact that the potential membership work together must also result in word of mouth being a highly effective tool in the promotion of the credit union. In addition, convenience is also likely to play a role, in that access to savings and loan facilities are provided within the employee's own work environment. Community credit unions face a much more uphill battle in the promotion stakes. The common bond, although still quite well defined, will embrace a much more disparate membership, making it more difficult to promote the credit union, with the locational choice for premises also likely to result in inconvenience for a section of the potential membership.

Reported also in Table 8.1 is the aggregate membership of credit unions within the respective classes. However, perhaps a more interesting statistic is the average number of members in credit unions within the various asset categories, and here little difference emerges between workplace and community credit unions. For workplace unions with assets in excess of £1 million the average number of members is 3575. The comparable figure for community-focused unions is 3152. For the asset range £613 to £49,999, the figures for employer and community unions are respectively 118 and 109. Even within the top asset range it is clear that credit unions, irrespective of their common bond, are small-scale organisations. Furthermore, it should be recognised that workplace credit unions, much more so than community-based organisations, are likely to face difficulty recruiting members once the formative years of the credit union have passed. This is because most work-based common bonds are located within the confines of a relatively small workforce, subject to only marginal year-on-year change. Contrast this with a common bond based on a community where the potential membership is likely to be much larger, with considerably more movement in and out of the community. Therefore, from a scale-efficiency perspective, the proposed change to Section 1(4) of the 1979 Act, permitting, in the future, residents and employees to join the same credit union, is likely to be of particular benefit to employer-based unions.

The final set of statistics detailed in Table 8.1 refers to assets per member. In this instance, the larger community credit unions, those with assets in excess of £500,000, are more wealthy per member than their employer counterparts. The opposite is the case however, when credit unions of a smaller size are examined. Employer-based unions, up to an asset size of £499,999, have a higher assets-to-member ratio than community unions. Such a trend is difficult to explain and may, at one level, be no more than a statistical quirk. Indeed, on an a priori basis, it is possible to design a competing hypothesis with respect to which subgroup should have the higher assets-to-member ratio. It could, for example, be argued that members of workplace unions, in that, by definition, they are all in work, will, on average, have higher disposable incomes than the membership of community unions and should, therefore, have higher wealth ratios. A competing argument would be that the members of workplace unions are more likely to use other financial institutions, not least because salary cheques are now, almost as a matter of course, paid direct into the employee's 'bank' account. Workplace credit union members are therefore likely to belong to two or more financial firms, which automatically reduces their reliance on the credit union. Even with this latter hypothesis, caution is required. McArthur, McGregor and Stewart (1993), in a survey-based analysis of credit unions and low-income communities, found that most members, 70%, also had either a bank, building society or post office account. In this sense, they argued that there appeared to be a broad similarity with the population as a whole, citing that, in 1987, 53% of adults in Great Britain had a building society account, 22% had an interest-bearing bank account and 10% a post office savings account. The authors then concluded that members of credit unions located in low-income communities are not typically 'unbanked' or completely cut off from mainstream financial services.

Table 8.1 fails to capture any regional dimension to the debate. Examination of the data on a regional basis reveals one point of major note, which is that there are no employer-based credit unions in Northern Ireland. As indicated in Chapter 4, this should be of little surprise, given that Northern Ireland is already well covered by established and relatively successful community credit unions. This then raises the question, if Northern Ireland-registered credit unions were removed from the data base, what would be the comparative profile of community and workplace unions? The answer is that the community subgroup would be significantly weakened. Take, for example, the asset category over £1 million. Only three credit unions would now be placed in this category; their share of the asset base would fall to 24.26%; the average number of members would fall to 2211, as would assets per member, dropping to £762. Again, this emphasises the weakness of the movement in Great Britain. However, what it also highlights is that although workplace unions are in an overall minority numerically, they are much more evident in the top asset class than their community counterparts and, in a Great Britain context, it may, in fact, be workplace unions that are the demonstration models for the future of the movement. This is an issue that will be pursued further in the case study.

Attention now turns to Table 8.2 in which a selection of performance ratios are compared.

The first ratio detailed is that of bad-debt write offs as a percentage of total assets. In general, write offs are not a significant problem for credit unions, with this particularly true for workplace credit unions. The fact that work-place unions face an almost non-existent bad-debt problem centres on two factors. The first is that the majority of the membership is in full-time employment and in consequence will have a steady stream of income from which outstanding loans can be repaid. The second relates to the manner in which the workplace union organises the loan repayment. Many, for example, simply set up repayment through a pay-roll deduction mechanism, which guarantees the outstanding loan as long as the employee remains in employment with the company. In addition, many credit unions have an agreement with the employer where, in instances of loan default, a member's pay may be sequestrated.

Set against the above portrayal of a low-risk environment for workplace unions must, of course, be the disastrous consequences for the credit union if the sponsoring company gets into difficulty. At present, workplace unions are comprised almost entirely of the employees of a single employer. Consequently, the financial lives of the members, as well as the existence of the credit union, are almost totally dependent upon the financial fortunes of the parent organisation. There is little diversification of occupational or income risk among depositors or borrowers. If a company collapses, the primary source of income of the credit union member disappears. Indeed, the catastrophic effect of such an event is accentuated for the employee with share capital invested in the credit union in that the movement in the United Kingdom has not as yet adopted a share insurance mechanism. Share insurance as a concept is considered further in Chapter 9.

Reserves as a proportion of total assets are also detailed in Table 8.2. The Registry of Friendly Societies stipulates that a credit union should maintain a general reserve of 10% of total assets. If the general reserve is less than 10% the credit union is obliged to transfer to general reserve not less than 20% of its profits for that year or such lesser sum as is required to bring reserves up to the 10% level. Workplace credit unions clearly operate on a much lower reserve ratio than community unions. The reserve ratio of workplace credit unions trends around 5% compared with ratios of mostly 7% and above for community unions. Low surpluses, resulting in an inability to build up reserves, could

Table 8.2 Performance ratios for community and workplace credit unions

Asset range (£)	Bad-debt write-offs/total assets		Reserves/total assets		Cash in hand + in bank/total assets		Loans to members /share capital	
	Emp.	Comm.	Emp.	Comm.	Emp.	Comm.	Emp.	Comm.
Over £1,000,000	0.0016	0.0031	0.0607	0.0928	0.0933	0.1304	0.992	0.888
£500,000 to £999,999	0.0018	0.0041	0.0522	0.0967	0.0993	0.1853	0.994	0.804
£250,000 to £499,999	0.0000	0.0039	0.0561	0.1019	0.1394	0.2117	0.960	0.808
£100,000 to £249,999	0.0002	0.0028	0.0530	0.0701	0.2909	0.2521	0.864	0.886
£50,000 to £99,999	0.0000	0.0041	0.0502	0.0749	0.1525	0.2362	0.891	0.870
£613 to £49,999	0.0007	0.0025	0.0487	0.0642	0.4223	0.3751	0.640	0.682
Total	0.0014	0.0032	0.0584	0.0920	0.1115	0.1516	0.974	0.865

potentially be the cause of the reserve shortfall experienced by workplace unions. An examination of surplus after tax as a percentage of total assets, however, reveals broadly similar patterns between the two subgroups. Workplace and community credit unions in each of the top three size categories have surplus ratios of approximately 5%, while in the bottom three asset classes the surplus ratio for community unions is only marginally higher than that of employer unions, 2.5% compared with 3%.

The reserve ratio differential between the two groups might also be explained if workplace unions experienced relatively stronger asset growth. Under such circumstances, reserve build-up, in terms of achieving a ratio that is itself scaled on the basis of asset size, becomes akin to being required to achieve an ever-increasing target. In that employer-based unions occupy, at least in relative terms, a disproportionately larger share of the top asset range, it is clear that they have grown faster than credit unions within the community subgroup and hence differences in the pace of asset growth do have some explanatory power.

Of course, a more cynical view might be that the Registry of Friendly Societies recognises that employer-based credit unions have a much lower delinquency rate, as seen in their write-off ratios, and in theory these unions require lower provisions for loan losses. Under such circumstances, the Registry may not be just as rigorous in the enforcement of the 10% minimum reserve requirement.

The next ratio detailed in Table 8.2 is that of cash in hand plus cash in the bank expressed as a percentage of total assets. This ratio is employed as a measure of liquidity. In this instance, it is hypothesised that credit unions that operate in an unstable environment have a greater need for maintaining liquidity compared with stable credit unions. This liquidity need results essentially from more volatile deposit accounts. Again, the expectation is that the workplace credit union with the continuity of a membership in employment is likely to be much more stable than a credit union located within a low-income community. The computed ratio in Table 8.2 supports this hypothesis. In particular, workplace credit unions within the top three asset classes operate on much lower liquidity ratios than their community counterparts.

The final measure set out in Table 8.2 is that of the loans-to-savings ratio, which is calculated as loans to members as a proportion of share capital. Credit unions that face a more uncertain environment would be expected to operate on a somewhat lower ratio. A credit union that faces uncertainty, given the profile of its membership, would, in all probability, make smaller value loans, with a relatively greater proportion of these being on a secured basis. In addition, the credit union would be likely to retain a larger percentage of its share capital either in the form of reserves or in liquid assets. In the prior discussion it was noted that community-based credit unions operate on higher reserve and liquidity ratios, consequently the fact that their loan-to-share capital ratio is considerably lower than workplace unions should be of little surprise. On average, the loan-to-share ratio for community credit unions is some 10 percentage points lower than employer-based unions, with this differential most pronounced for credit unions within the top three asset categories.

From the data analysis, it appears that the subdivision of the industry into the constituent parts of community and employer unions yields tangible differences in behavioural characteristics. To explore these differences further it is now proposed to present an even more disaggregate analysis in the form of a detailed consideration of the operational structure and *modus operandi* of one workplace credit union and one community union.

A TALE OF TWO CREDIT UNIONS

A case study methodology is adopted in this section. It is proposed to examine two credit unions—British Airways UK Employees, which is classed as a workplace union and Drumchapel, which is categorised as a community union. Both credit unions have a membership base approximately equal in size (end 1994 figures) but they differ considerably in terms of their history, the type of support that has been made available to them, their membership profile, and their ambitions. Through an exploration of these differences it is hoped that a clearer picture should emerge of the future challenges that face both credit union forms, as well the prospects for both.

British Airways UK Employees

In June 1993, British Airways launched the first credit union for a blue-chip company in the United Kingdom. Its common bond embraces all British Airways 48,000 UK staff and all have been invited to join the union. While the launch date was in 1993, the credit union had been in the planning stage over the three previous years. Most of this planning took the form of trying to convince management that British Airways staff actually wanted a credit union. This was despite the fact that, in the United States, British Airways already ran a credit union that now has an asset base of over $23 million and is approaching 4000 in membership. Graham Tomlin, chairman of the British Airways UK union and the main driving force in its establishment, argues that once management got over its initial suspicions it became extremely supportive. This support included: the provision of office accommodation and meeting facilities during normal office hours for the conduct of credit union business; providing general office equipment including furniture, a personal computer and printer, some software and a telephone; the use of a photocopier and the internal communications system; some assistance with printing and promotional material and up to 30 hours per week of staff time. Tomlin, however, indicates that the most beneficial help from management to the growth and success of the credit union has been the granting of permission for pay-roll deductions on a monthly basis for both share savings and loan repayments. (Members, for example, can save a minimum of £3 per week, which is deducted from their wages.) The fact that, in the case of loan repayments, the authorisation is irrevocable eliminates almost all potential for bad debt.

The data analysis in this text is primarily on the basis of 1994 figures. At the end of 1994, 18 months after introduction, the British Airways employee union had a membership of 1000 and assets of around £300,000. Calling a halt to the statistical analysis at 1994, however, fails to do full justice to the rapid progress made. Examination of the most recent available data, June 1996, reveals that there has been a further marked growth in both membership and assets, which now stand at 1800 and £1.05 million, respectively.

Publicity has been the key to the rapid growth in membership. The initial launch was heralded in a blaze of publicity and obtained national coverage through, for example, articles in the *The Guardian*, 26 June 1993, *The Observer*, 25 July 1993 and *The Financial Times*, 26 July 1993. In each of these months new membership applications approached 120. The next major recruitment drive was in September 1994. A stall at the open day for engineering at British Airways was taken in order to promote the credit union. This resulted in 70 new applications during that month. November 1995 witnessed the most effective method of recruitment. The credit union advertised on the back of the company's pay-slip. The highlight points of this advertisement were that: all British Airways staff, their close family members and retired staff were eligible to join the union; there was no penalty for early redemption of a credit union loan; all accounts were covered by free loan protection and life savings insurance; the union was managed by British Airways staff; for the month of November only, the joining fee was reduced from £5 to £2; for November only, all new members would be entered into a free prize draw for a flight on Concorde; and, finally, information on the monthly prize money paid out by the union's member lottery was detailed. The net outcome was that in November 1995 there was a total of 315 applications for membership. Indeed, the statistics also reveal something of a ripple effect. Prior to this advertisement, applications per month trended around 45 but from November 1995 to April 1996 the monthly average rose to 65. The latest recruitment drive was in May 1996 when a full-page advertisement, similar in form to that on the pay-slip, was taken in *British Airways News*. This led to 100 new applicants in that month.

Such speed in membership growth is exceptional and highlights the benefit of targeted and highly focused publicity. The credit union has also introduced incentives as a recruitment mechanism. These have included a reduction in the joining fee during specified periods, as well as a lottery that pays out £600 per month in prizes. The lottery is itself a significant revenue generator for the union.

For example, the union's budget for 1995 to 1996, reported on 31 May 1996, projected income from the lottery of £10,000, which compares relatively favourably with its other reported income sources—£3000 from membership fees and £101,000 from loans.

Three years into operation, the credit union employs two full-time staff members and is in the process of recruiting two more. Staff costs at £39,000 for 1995 to 1996 take up the largest share of the credit union's expenditure. Other sizeable expenditures are—insurance at £12,500, equipment at £6400, marketing at £5000 and then training at £4000. The only real difference between this expenditure profile and that of others relates to the extent of the marketing budget. Although this particular component of expenditure is larger than for most other unions it is money well spent, as evidenced by the pace of membership growth. The first dividend to shareholders was paid in 1995 and was calculated at approximately 2%. In line with most other workplace unions, the reserve ratio for 1995, at approximately 5%, was significantly lower than the 10% stipulated by the registrar. Tomlin (chairman of the credit union), argues that the 10% ratio is excessive for workplace unions and points to the negligible risks faced by his own union, where loan repayments are made from pay-roll deductions with authorisation irrevocable.

Future ambition is perhaps what most sets apart the British Airways credit union from others. Its membership profile is dominated by medium- and high-income earners who are generally better informed as to the range of financial products available in the marketplace. This awareness then creates a demand for the credit union itself to offer a broader product portfolio. British Airways has already responded and is to offer its members an affinity Visa card. ABCUL, to which British Airways belongs, has an agency agreement with the US banking group MBNA International Bank Ltd for the issue of these cards. British Airways plans to overprint its logo on the generic ABCUL card and, in the tradition of the affinity scheme, will receive a percentage commission on the cards taken up by its members. Tomlin is also on record as wanting significant liberalisation of the constraints placed on credit unions. Mortgage provision, larger secured loans, as well as a more comprehensive loan service, are all areas that he feels should be open to credit unions.

The establishment of a credit union for employees of British Airways can be viewed as a positive development for the overall UK credit union movement. At the most basic level there is the free national publicity for the credit union ideal that came with the launch. This publicity is not only a good recruitment agency for existing unions but it may also be instrumental in the establishment of new unions. On this latter count, Lloyds banking group trade union is reputed to be about to launch its own credit union. Secondly, the establishment of the British Airways union highlighted that credit unions were not simply a savings and loans vehicle appropriate only for low-income communities. This broader view of the credit union role was succinctly encapsulated by Garrett (1993):

> When British Airways launched its own credit union—dubbed Plane Saver—last month, among the first to sign up were a handful of the airline's pilots. The participation of these high-flyers, with their airborne salaries, did not go unnoticed. It was proof that the image of credit unions as the 'poor man's bank' no longer applies to all such organisations (A. Garrett, *The Observer*, 25 July 1993).

Finally, the fact that with the introduction of the British Airways union the movement in the United Kingdom is being seen to embrace a more financially sophisticated membership base, must provide the present militation for enhanced credit union freedoms with an increased probability of success.

Drumchapel Community Credit Union

This credit union, established in 1979, is one of the oldest community-based credit unions in Scotland. It is located on the outskirts of Glasgow and services a sprawling housing estate, built in the 1950s. The housing estate has one of the highest levels of unemployment in Scotland. Approximately 70% of the adult population are on state benefit. This, in turn, dictates the membership profile of the credit union. Although accurate statistics are not available, it is estimated that 60% of the credit union's membership are also unemployed, with the remaining 40% mostly manual workers and shop, office and factory workers.

As of June 1996, Drumchapel credit union had an asset base of £543,000 and a membership of 1300. It has three full-time staff, a development worker and a clerical officer, both funded through the urban aid programme, plus another clerical officer funded directly by the credit union. Drumchapel credit union operates out of shared premises provided by the council. A rent is paid for these premises. This rent is paid out of the grant received through the Urban Aid Programme. Consequently, in a circuitous manner, it is the council that pays the rent. (The Urban Aid Programme is financed by the Scottish Office, which puts up 75% of the funds, with the local authority making up the residual 25%.) The credit union is open four days per week, Monday, Tuesday, Thursday and Friday, from 10.00 a.m. to 4.00 p.m., and again on Thursday only from 7.00 p.m. to 8.30 p.m. Although opening hours are designed for members' convenience, the location of the credit union is somewhat out of the way. Therefore, at present, members are examining the feasibility of constructing their own centrally located and purpose-built premises. The credit union has the resources to construct and equip the premises, although the economics of the project would be on a more secure footing if the local council were to supply the site free of charge, or at least for a nominal sum.

To attract new members, Drumchapel advertises in the local health magazine and the local free-sheet newspaper. Membership growth has not, however, been significant in recent years, remaining static at about 1300. For this reason, the board of Drumchapel view positively the government's deregulation initiatives. They highlight, in particular, the extension of the common bond to include those who live and work in the same area. Factories and offices in Drumchapel have a significant share of their employees living outside the area. With deregulation, these employees become a further catchment of potential members for the credit union. A further aspect of deregulation positively received by Drumchapel is the amendment to permit those who move from the area to still remain as members of the union. Again, this amendment is viewed as easing pressure on the credit union's membership base.

Stepping away from the impact of deregulation on membership size, the Drumchapel credit union is of the opinion that deregulation offers other benefits. Perhaps the most significant is the extension of the loan repayment period. The maximum repayment periods of two years for unsecured loans and five years for secured loans increases to four years and ten years, respectively. (Although this applies only to credit unions that have general reserves amounting to at least 10% of total assets at the last balance sheet date). One tangible benefit of the loan extension period for Drumchapel members is that it now gives many more the opportunity to purchase their houses from the council. The council pitches house prices at around £7000. Previously, the monthly loan repayments would have been outside the means of most of the credit union's members. This is no longer the case with the increase to 10 years in the repayment period for a secured loan.

As with many credit unions, Drumchapel is of the opinion that the deregulation measures do not go far enough. The credit union points to services such as bill-paying and lending to groups, as opposed solely to individuals, as two new freedoms that would be of significant benefit to the membership of their union. The idea behind the group-lending centres on the provision of finance to small businesses, perhaps in their start-up phase, which would have neither the status nor the guarantees to obtain traditional bank finance. The credit union would lend, at any one time, to no more than two members within the group. The group itself would probably consist of about six members and their respective businesses. The expectation would then be that peer pressure within the group would ensure that loans were repaid.

Drumchapel credit union is affiliated to ABCUL and through the Strathclyde Chapter some of the union's training needs are serviced. The impression we obtained, however, was that the service provided by ABCUL as a trade organisation did not meet the needs of Drumchapel—a community-based credit union located in a housing estate. The ambitions of ABCUL were viewed to have grown faster than the UK movement, with these ambitions not in tune with the realities faced by community credit unions. Indeed, Drumchapel's level of disillusionment was such that, in the near future, they will listen to the 'sales pitch' of the SLCU. A comfort factor for ABCUL is that CUNA Mutual only recognises one trade body in its provision of life assurance and loan protection. ABCUL is the recognised intermediary. It is this factor that may well militate against Drumchapel and, indeed, other community-based unions leaving the ABCUL fold.

CONCLUDING COMMENTS

Although the legislative framework makes no distinction between workplace and community credit unions the data overview in this chapter revealed certain differences in their behavioural characteristics. Workplace unions appear to have grown at a much faster pace, occupying in relative terms a greater share of the top asset range. In addition, they hold less reserves, they have a lower percentage of their asset base in the form of liquid assets, they on-lend a greater proportion of members' share capital, and they have a negligible bad-debt problem. Set against this relatively positive profile is the fact that employer credit unions are susceptible to the additional risk of host company failure. If the sponsoring company should fail, then there is little or no prospect of survival for the linked credit union. In the United Kingdom there is, however, a low probability of host company failure as most sponsoring organisations are located in the public sector, which to some extent is insulated from cyclical movements in the economy.

The difference between community and workplace credit unions was reinforced by the two unions chosen as case studies. Differences again emerged in where they obtained support and the form of that support. There was also a marked difference in their speed of establishment. Primarily through targeted marketing, the workplace union achieved in three years an asset size and membership level that the community union took 17 years to generate. The most revealing difference, however, centred on the aspirations unlocked by recent legislative change. Drumchapel—the community credit union—wants additional freedoms to permit it to introduce new services such as bill-paying and group-lending. The emphasis on the latter relates to the fact that Drumchapel wishes to become involved in the provision of start-up finance to small businesses, most of which do not have the status or guarantees to obtain traditional bank finance. In contrast, British Airways, the workplace union, wishes to provide a much more comprehensive loan service, dare it be said, along similar lines to that provided by mainstream financial institutions. This non-uniformity of aspirations is essentially dictated by the membership profile of the respective unions. The members of British Airways are medium to high earners who are generally well informed as to the range of financial products available in the marketplace. Contrast this with Drumchapel's membership—60% are unemployed with the remainder manual, office, shop and factory workers.

Going by the lessons of mature industries, such as those in the United States, Canada and Australia, employer-based credit unions appear to be the catalyst that generates significant overall expansion in the movement. Indeed, the rapid growth of British Airways, in only a three-year period, is a further demonstration of the critical role to be played by workplace unions. It is our view that the take-off potential of the UK industry is crucially contingent upon mobilising increased support for employer-based credit unions in both the public and private sectors. However, we also firmly hold the view that this must not be at the expense of community-based unions. The traditional role embraced by credit unions of serving disadvantaged communities should be neither placed in jeopardy nor diminished by an expansion programme driven by workplace unions. Overall expansion by the movement at the expense of service provision to low-income communities would not be a price worth paying.

9

The Design of an Optimal Deposit Insurance Mechanism

INTRODUCTION

From the analysis to date it is clear that UK credit unions have successfully made the case both for an upward revision in the deposit and borrowing ceilings and a liberalisation of the common bond. The expectation is that, having achieved this additional flexibility, they are likely to press, in the coming years, for even greater freedoms. The obvious area where pressure is likely to focus is in the range of financial products that credit unions can provide.

If the changes that have occurred to date are coupled with enhanced product freedom this may result in significant changes in credit union operating characteristics and performance. In particular, the risk profile will alter with credit unions subject to more pronounced levels of business risk. For example, information cost advantage on new loan applicants may decrease and default rates may rise as the common bond widens.

It is, therefore, perhaps somewhat incongruous that the UK credit union movement is, at this juncture, seeking enhanced flexibility and freedoms, with obvious implications for its risk profile, without as yet having in place a depositor/shareholder protection scheme. (Legally a credit union does not accept deposits but issues shares to its members: in that shares are so similar to deposits, all references in this chapter will be to deposits and deposit insurance.) Although, under Section 15(1) of the Credit Unions Act 1979, UK credit unions are required to be insured against loss to their members from fraud, such insurance does not cover all forms of loss, notably failure of administration or failure of borrowers to repay their loans. While the respective umbrella organisations have agreed to the principle of establishing a mutual protection scheme, there appears to be a reluctance to progress the matter speedily, much to the frustration of the Registrar of Friendly

Societies:

> It is with disappointment that I have to report again that no scheme for the protection of members' funds has yet been set up. Section 16 of the Credit Unions Act 1979 enables credit unions to make arrangements for making funds available to meet losses incurred by members. Whilst a scheme should not be seen as a substitute for a credit union establishing and maintaining adequate reserves and systems of control the Registry has continued to impress upon the two national promoting bodies the desirability of establishing an industry wide scheme for the benefit of their member credit unions and the good of the credit union movement as a whole. Both bodies have expressed their commitment to setting up appropriate schemes (Registry of Friendly Societies, Annual Report, 1991/1992).

The purpose of this chapter is, therefore, to examine whether a depositor protection scheme is necessary for the UK credit union movement as it currently stands and, if so, are certain operational forms of such a mechanism more appropriate than others. This latter aspect of the discussion is deemed particularly important in that the introduction of legislation in 1970 providing federal deposit insurance for US credit unions is viewed by many commentators to have induced greater risk-taking, which, in turn, led to higher levels of delinquent loans and, indeed, bankruptcy rates within the industry. The problem, as will be demonstrated, can be viewed within a moral hazard framework in that insuring the deposits of the institution causes the institution to act in a riskier manner. The opportunity will also be taken in this chapter to examine the Savings Protection Mechanism that is operated by the ILCU for its members in Ireland. Although, importantly, it should be noted that participation in the scheme does not confer any legal right on a credit union to receive any financial assistance under the scheme.

THE HISTORY OF DEPOSIT INSURANCE FOR US CREDIT UNIONS

Credit unions in the United States can trace their roots back to 1909. However, it was not until 60 years later that a system of federal deposit insurance was established for the US credit union movement (see Clair, 1984). More specifically, legislation providing federal deposit insurance was enacted, which created the National Credit Union Share Insurance Fund, NCUSIF. Implementation of the insurance program began in 1971. To qualify for entry into the scheme, credit unions had to satisfy certain minimum financial standards. Those credit unions that did not meet the required standards were issued a temporary insurance certificate that provided insurance cover for a two-year period. At the end of this period, these substandard institutions were required either to have satisfied the requisite financial conditions, to have merged with another credit union, to have switched to a state charter or to have liquidated. During this two-year transition period, a sizeable number of credit unions availed of one of the latter three options, with the number of cancellations of federal charters rising from an average annual rate of 300 to around 700 in both 1972 and 1973. By the end of 1973, all federal credit unions were insured and the transitory effects had significantly reduced with federal registered cancellations falling back to between 300 and 400.

Under the 1970 legislation state-chartered credit unions can themselves elect to have NCUSIF coverage. For those that do not opt for the federal scheme, insurance coverage is provided by a state agency. Kaushik and Lopez (1994), however, indicate that, at present, some 93% of all credit unions are covered by federal deposit insurance and that, in total, they control approximately 88% of the industry's assets. Credit unions in the United States can be subdivided into three categories—federally chartered, federally insured; state chartered, federally insured; and state chartered, privately insured. The statistics reveal that the proportion of credit unions in the latter category has declined steadily since the early 1980s, falling from 19% in 1980 to 7% in 1994. Kaushik and Lopez suggest that the decline in state chartered, privately insured has been primarily due to 'event risk-related' activities. These 'events' have been shocks to the perceived solvency of the private insurers, with one of the latest examples being the Rhode Island problems of 1990–1991. The difficulties that emerged in Rhode Island were caused by the failure of a savings bank that was assured by the same private company that insured credit unions. Given that there have been other examples of private insurance companies getting into difficulty, the decline in state-chartered privately insured credit unions should be of no surprise. In Rhode Island, many of the privately insured credit unions applied for, and received, federal insurance while keeping their state-chartered status, while in other states, where private insurance was prevalent, the state legislators changed their insurance requirements and many credit unions converted to federal coverage.

Federal deposit insurance currently covers individual deposits up to a level of $100,000, the same level as for other US depository institutions. In the case of federal credit unions, the insurance coverage is extensive in that it covers almost 100% of total deposits, with deposits making up some 90% of credit unions' liabilities. The insurance premium is the same percentage of insured deposits for all credit unions regardless of risk. Initially, the premium was set at 0.083% of the total amount of deposits in insured accounts. However, this was revised to 0.15% of total deposits in insured accounts by the Financial Institutions Reform, Recovery and Enforcement Act of 1989.

MORAL HAZARD AND ADVERSE SELECTION

The basic ideas

Whenever one side of a trading relationship has superior information over the other, post-contractual performance becomes difficult to enforce. In many cases it may be difficult to distinguish the contribution of a particular agent to a particular outcome from the contribution of nature. For example, was a bad loan the fault of a careless small businessman or simply the consequences of some unforeseen business downturn? If, in the above example, both the bank and the businessman were privy to the same level of information, there would be no problem in the bank and the businessman being able to price the risk of the loan and, thereafter, each deciding to accept or reject the offer. In contrast, if one of the contracting parties, realistically here the businessman, *ex post* is able to distinguish his contribution to the loan default from the contribution of nature, then he/she has superior information over the bank. As a consequence, the bank, in this instance, has difficulty in assuring the businessman's level of effort after the contract is signed. Such a situation as described is known as a moral-hazard problem and it arises whenever one of the contracting parties has superior information as to a particular outcome over the other parties to the agreement. The parties who have the inferior information are known as the principals, while those with superior information are known as the agents. The agents may have superior information either because they get the information first, or, as in the above example, it is difficult for the principal to disaggregate the agent's effort from acts of nature.

We might assume that, under this situation of asymmetric information, the agent is better off than he/she would be if both parties were as equally well informed. This, however, is generally not the case. Returning to the previous example, if it is assumed that: the bank recognises that *ex post* opportunistic behaviour by the borrower is likely; there are high-risk and low-risk borrowers, with a sufficient percentage of borrowers high risk; the bank cannot distinguish a high-risk borrower from a low-risk one; and the bank knows the mean and variance of borrowers' riskiness, then it can be demonstrated that the bank will price all borrowers as if they were high risk. This, in turn, implies that if the bank sets the rate of interest at the risk mean, then only those with a higher risk will borrow. This, then, has a ratchet effect, causing the bank to increase the rate of interest continually until it reaches the rate that it would charge the highest-risk borrower. It is, therefore, clear that both borrowers and lenders would be better off with some contractual arrangement that would limit the ability of the agent to engage in *ex post* contractual behaviour.

Another environment within which severe moral hazard and adverse selection problems can occur is in the area of insurance contracts. Here, the insurer is the principal, while the insured is the agent. From a moral-hazard perspective the agent, *ex ante*, bears all the cost of his/her risk-taking behaviour, but once the insurance contract is signed, in the case of 100% insurance, the agent shifts the cost of his/her risk-taking behaviour entirely on to the insurance fund. Moreover, given asymmetric information, the insurer finds it difficult to determine how much of the circumstance that led to the claim was the fault of the insuree as distinct from an act of nature. For example, when a bank runs into insolvency problems, how much fault can be assigned to poor judgement by the bank management and how much can be assigned to factors outside the control of the latter?

Examples of post-contractual opportunistic behaviour are often extended to analyse firm structure as essentially being the result of a conflict between bond-holders and shareholders, on the one hand, and shareholders and management, on the other. The source of the potential conflict between bond-holders and shareholders rests with the fact that the latter hold residual claims on a firm's earnings and hence their interests may at times diverge from those of the former. Because their liability is limited to the amount of their investment, shareholders have incentives to invest in risky assets if the increase in the firm's variance of returns from investing in these assets is sufficiently increased. Indeed, the lower the equity proportion of a firm's total assets, the lower the downside risk of the shareholders and the more gain from upside risk. On the other hand, bond-holders incur only downside risk. This basic conflict, combined with the fact that shareholders, because they control the firm, have superior information, leads to a serious agency problem. This argument is all the more powerful the lower the fraction of equity in a firm's total assets. Thus, this analysis is particularly important for analysing the structure of privately owned banks, where the equity proportion of total assets is typically small relative to other types of firms.

Moral hazard, adverse selection and deposit insurance

The incentive for shareholders to invest in risky assets exists with or without deposit insurance. Without deposit insurance, depositors would, however, impose market discipline on the use of their funds either by requiring a higher return on their funds for bearing increased risk, or by reducing the availability of funds to perceived riskier institutions. The net outcome is that the firm's desire to invest in risky assets is counterbalanced by the concern of depositors for the safety of their funds.

Deposit insurance schemes, in that they are designed to protect depositors' funds, can, somewhat paradoxically, create a framework that encourages excessive risk-taking by firms. As with any insurance contract, the insured firm, in that it is shielded from the consequences of its actions, has an incentive to operate in a way that increases the insurer's exposure to risk. In essence, the cost of the insured firm's risk-taking is shifted on to the insurance fund. The danger that the insured party may act in this manner is, of course, another example of moral hazard. As will be highlighted later, when the design of an optimal system of deposit insurance for UK credit unions is considered, poorly constructed deposit insurance schemes, such as those that do not discriminate between high- and low-risk firms, can exacerbate the moral hazard problem even further.

Deposit insurance funds also create adverse-selection problems. Assuming that membership in the insurance fund is voluntary and noting the fact that the insurance fund now bears risk in return for some particular premium, only those insurees who have *ex ante* costs of risk-taking greater than that premium, will accept the insurance contract, and the higher the insurer sets the premium, the higher will be the average riskiness of his/her insurees. To get around such problems, insurers are reduced to identifying risk classes of potential insurees through observable characteristics, and then to price-discriminate across these classes, although, within such classes, the insurer still faces not only a moral-hazard problem, but, again, the same adverse-selection problem.

DEPOSIT INSURANCE AND CREDIT UNIONS

It should by now be clear that there are both costs and benefits in the establishment of a deposit protection scheme, with the key cost that a deposit insurance mechanism reduces the incentive for depositors to impose market discipline on the use of their funds. Accepting that such costs are involved in the establishment of a protection scheme, the case for its introduction may be viewed to be even further weakened in the case of credit unions in that they differ in many important respects from other financial services organisations.

The first point of distinction relates to the fact that depositors in most other financial institutions can be considered bond-holders who are assigned no voting rights. This is not the case in credit unions, where the deposit base, for the most part, consists of members' shares. The 'depositors' in credit unions are the shareholders, who have broadly the same rights as shareholders in other privately owned financial institutions. Thus, if the credit union were to take a more risky posture, then the gains and losses are fully borne by the shareholders, who stand to gain according to their share position, which must be proportional to the extent of their exposure. Even without the above argument of risk matching return, it should be noted that there is little incentive for shareholders of UK credit unions to engage in such behaviour, as there is not only a limit on the maximum number of shares a member can hold but also, more importantly, in line with credit union principles, there is a limit placed on the return on share capital.

There are also, of course, members who hold net debt positions, in the sense that their borrowings exceed their shareholdings. Net debtors, in that they are shareholders, also have voting rights within the credit union. (The democratic nature of control is enshrined within credit unions, as all members enjoy equal voting rights, irrespective of the extent of their shareholding.) There is also no reason for shareholders who are in a net debt position to vote for risk-taking behaviour. One argument is that, in the case of credit union bankruptcy, the debtor depositors are still liable as before. A second argument centres upon the fact that credit unions are not in a position to engage in risk-taking behaviour with the objective of increasing the expected return. In excess of 80% of credit unions' assets in the United Kingdom are tied up in loans to members that are subject to an interest rate ceiling of no more than 1% per month. It is, therefore, clear that credit unions are not susceptible to post-contractual opportunistic behaviour by their membership, irrespective of whether the membership occupies a net debt or net equity position.

Turning now to the question of whether credit union managers display traces of post-contractual opportunistic behaviour in the form of greater risk-taking, again, the adoption of such behaviour is unlikely in that for the majority of UK credit unions, managerial-type decisions are made by a board of directors, which is elected by the membership and which receives no remuneration. Consequently, there is no incentive for board members to engage in post-contractual opportunistic behaviour.

The board of directors has specific powers and functions in the operation of the credit union. These specific powers and functions of board members include: making decisions on membership applications; determining the rate of interest charged on loans to members and payable on members' deposits; making decisions on the investment of surplus funds; making decisions on property purchasing, leasing, etc.; authorising borrowing; and employing persons necessary for the day-to-day running of the organisation. (Salaried staff are employed by larger credit unions for jobs such as cashier or office manager.) It might potentially be argued that if the office manager has carved out a pivotal position within the credit union this may offer the opportunity and incentive to engage in post-contractual opportunistic behaviour. This is highly unlikely for two reasons. First, the control of the credit union is very much with the elected board of directors, which, to a large degree removes the opportunity to engage in post-contractual opportunistic behaviour. Secondly, most credit union managers receive a flat wage, which negates any incentive to operate in a post-contractual opportunistic fashion.

The above analysis suggests that a system of deposit insurance may prove to be unnecessary for credit unions, given the organisational structure and ethos. Such a conclusion may, however, abstract from the realities of the UK credit union movement. In earlier chapters it was demonstrated that a considerable dichotomy exists between the larger-asset-size credit unions and those of a more modest asset base. In particular, the following points of note emerged. First, larger credit unions are more cost efficient in their operations. Secondly, larger credit unions are considerably wealthier than smaller unions. Indeed, it transpired that a strong inverse relationship existed in that, for the top credit union group, assets per member in 1994 stood at £902, while, for the smallest group the comparable figure was a mere £157. Thirdly, smaller credit unions had much lower reserve ratios than their larger counterparts, with this being particularly pronounced for the three smallest groupings (see

Chapter 5). Fourthly, larger credit unions also had a much superior surplus performance to that of the smaller ones. The implication drawn from this was that those credit unions most in need of reserve accumulation would have the most difficulty in its generation, given their low surplus levels. Finally, when low reserve levels are taken in conjunction with bad debt provisions, it is clear that currently there are a number of credit unions, particularly small credit unions, that face serious financial difficulties. Figures 9.1(a) and (b) diagrammatically depict the problem on an individual credit union basis, which is perhaps more informative than the subgroup mean ratio analysis adopted in previous chapters.

Figure 9.1(a) provides information on bad-debt provisions/total assets and total reserves/total assets for those credit unions with an asset base in 1994 greater than, or equal to, £500,000. Comparable information is provided in Figure 9.1(b) for those credit unions with assets less than £500,000. While there are no more than four unions with assets in excess of £500,000 that commit the twin crimes of low reserves and high bad-debt provision (Figure 9.1(a)), the occurrence is much more frequent for credit unions with assets below £500,000. From Figure 9.1(b) it emerges that approximately 70 credit unions find themselves in this highly disadvantageous situation.

If this scenario, as described, is accepted and if we add to this that the loan portfolio is highly concentrated and hence subject to greater risk, plus the fact that most UK credit unions are run and operated by volunteers with only limited financial expertise, then under such circumstances there must be a significant probability of failure, although, as intimated, this is more likely for the smaller-asset-size credit unions. Indeed, in a somewhat similar vein, Flood (1993) suggests that the cause of bank failures in the United States has been misidentified. He states that the traditional explanation is based on moral hazard, where, as we have elaborated, bank failure is the result of management responding to financial incentives to take increased risks. Flood proposes the alternative explanation that incompetent managers were unable to evaluate the risks they were taking, with this problem compounded by deregulation during the 1980s.

Irrespective of the cause, in a situation where there is a significant chance of insolvency, and without a system of deposit insurance, there is always an incentive for depositors to withdraw funds at the first hint of financial difficulty, be it real or imaginary. Furthermore, if a run on one credit union shakes depositors' confidence in the industry as a whole, contagious runs may emerge that may drive solvent ones insolvent if, to restore liquidity, they have to sell assets at knock-down prices. In that the UK credit union movement is still very much in its formative stages, the occurrence of a contagious run would, in all probability, lead to its demise. Consequently, the establishment of an appropriate deposit insurance mechanism may prove to yield significant benefits.

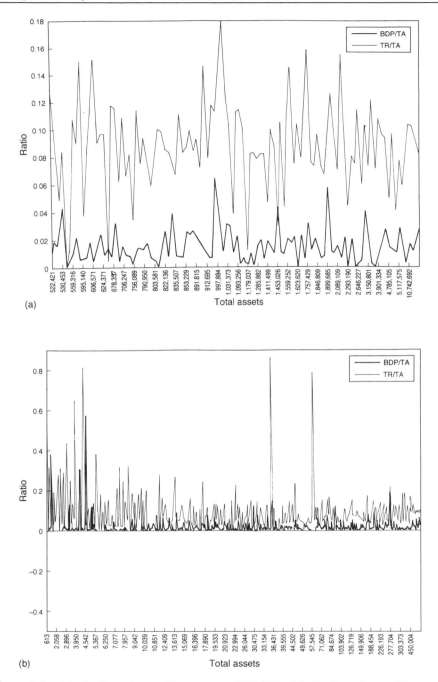

Figure 9.1 (a) Credit unions with assets ≥ £500,000; (b) Credit unions with assets < £500,000

AN APPROPRIATE DEPOSIT INSURANCE MECHANISM FOR UK CREDIT UNIONS

The question that now looms large is: What are the key characteristics of an optimal deposit insurance system? An obvious starting point in the construction of an answer is the identification of those aspects of deposit insurance in the United States that brought that system into disrepute. Under the US federal deposit insurance system, each credit institution pays a flat rate for insurance regardless of the riskiness of its portfolio. Under this flat-rate system, the riskiness of an institution's portfolio is not controlled by differential risk premiums and therefore institutions may take on more risk than is best for society. As insured deposits are guaranteed irrespective of whether or not the institution remains solvent, depositors have no incentive to place a brake on an institution's risk-taking behaviour through the demand of higher rates on deposits. Under the flat-rate system, regulations and examinations are the methods employed to control a financial institution's risk-taking behaviour. In the United States these control procedures have proved increasingly ineffective although Mester (1990) points out that this, in part, was the result of the twin combination in the early 1980s of expanded product freedom and relaxed net worth requirements.

The main problems with US federal deposit insurance therefore appears to centre on the flat-rate nature of the system; its total protection of depositors; plus the ineffective nature of legislation designed to reduce an institution's risk-taking behaviour. Mester argues that the central problem is that neither the regulators nor the insured depositors demand that the institution pays more for taking on more risk. As the financial firm gets closer to bankruptcy there is a tendency for depositors to bet the financial firm because they have everything to gain and little to lose. If the risk does not pay off, the deposit insurer takes the loss.

Private insurance

Suggested reforms of the system have been many and varied. The most radical suggested reform has been to replace federal insurance by private insurance. Mester, however, documents a selection of arguments why it is unlikely that deposit insurance can be totally private-based. Two arguments stand out as particularly important. First, private insurance lacks the credibility of federal insurance in that, unlike private insurers, government can impose taxes to maintain the solvency of the fund. Secondly, as the social benefits of a stable financial system do not accrue to individual institutions, a totally private insurance system would probably provide too little insurance for the system.

For these reasons, coupled with the fact that the majority of UK credit unions are small-scale, inadequately resourced units, which would face considerable difficulty in generating the requisite insurance premiums, private insurance must also be viewed as an unrealistic option.

A lender-of-last-resort facility

Another radical reform of the US system is the replacement of federal deposit insurance by a lender-of-last-resort facility. The argument, in this instance, is that runs on institutions, particularly when they cause solvent ones to fail, are costly, as they disrupt efficient intermediation between savers and borrowers. Therefore, during a run, rather than having 'good' institutions liquidate assets at below market value, a preferable option is to allow the institution to pledge these assets as collateral for loans from the Federal Reserve. The loans would solve the temporary liquidity problems and prevent runs resulting in the insolvency of 'good' institutions. The key argument against a lender-of-last-resort facility is that it may also result in institutions taking on too much risk, cushioned by the fact that, if they get into difficulty, a borrowing facility will be extended by the Federal Reserve. To surmount this problem it would be necessary for the latter to adopt a strict policy of extending loans to only 'good' institutions. Such a judgement could only be made if the Federal Reserve had detailed information on the quality of the institution's assets. Largely on account of the extensive information set required, the lender-of-last-resort facility has been ruled out as a viable option for the United States.

With regard to UK credit unions, although similar problems to those detailed above might emerge, a lender-of-last-resort facility, particularly if it were combined with a very much scaled-down private deposit insurance scheme, may prove both workable and a suitable compromise to those concerned—workable in that the information required in order to make informed lender-of-last-resort decisions is not overly extensive. The number of credit unions involved is relatively small and even in the future, with additional opportunities for portfolio diversification, their asset range is likely to remain highly restricted. The combination of a lender-of-last-resort facility, plus scaled-down private insurance, may be viewed as a compromise position as, in part, it meets the Registrar of Friendly Societies' continual call for an industry-led deposit protection scheme, with the small-scale nature of the deposit insurance scheme also likely to be affordable to all but the smallest of credit unions.

Depositor discipline

Another much-voiced reform of US deposit insurance is to lower the ceiling for insured deposits to as low as $10,000 from the current level of $100,000. Another version of this reform is the imposition of co-insurance, where only a certain percentage of a saver's deposits are insured. Both reforms are intended to encourage depositors to discipline institutions by demanding a risk premium for placing deposits in riskier institutions. Mester (1990) also puts the argument that the ceiling should be lowered on the grounds that depositors with $100,000 are not the small depositors that deposit insurance was designed to protect. The primary problem with this option is that it is not clear whether small depositors can, in fact, differentiate between high-risk and low-risk institutions. Indeed, what might happen with the introduction of such an amendment is that, instead of trying to assess the financial condition of an institution, savers might simply find it easier to remove their funds at the first hint of trouble, real or fictional. The net outcome might, therefore, be an increase in runs as opposed to a decline.

It is unlikely that either co-insurance, or a ceiling on the volume of funds insured, would be a high priority in the design of a deposit insurance scheme for UK credit unions, particularly in that depositors are currently constrained to an upper savings limit of only £5000. Even substantive upward revision of this savings limit would, in all probability, still leave the limit too low for an insurance ceiling to be expected to influence depositor behaviour. Furthermore, as is the case with US credit unions, it is not immediately obvious that depositors with UK credit unions would have the available information, or the ability to obtain that information, in order to discipline effectively the operational behaviour of their savings institution.

Differential premiums

At present with the flat-rate payment under federal deposit insurance, it is necessary for regulators to control risk-taking by way of supervision and regulation rather than price. From a theoretical perspective it could, of course, be argued that if the more risky financial institutions had to pay more for their insurance cover, then this would eliminate excessive risk-taking. In consequence, a further suggested reform of federal deposit insurance is the replacement of flat-rate insurance with a differential system, where premiums are determined by the relative riskiness of the institution's portfolio. Flood (1993) details the risk-based premium system that has recently been adopted by the Federal Deposit Insurance Corporation. Under this new system, a financial institution's insurance premium is jointly determined by its level of capitalisation and an evaluation of its financial health provided by regulators. The most important element in this evaluation is the capital adequacy, asset quality, management, earnings and liquidity (CAMEL) rating—a five-point summary ranking of its overall soundness. Flood identifies two potential problems with the Federal Deposit Insurance Corporation proposals. First, it may be possible for people to use an institution's risk premium to infer its confidential CAMEL rating. This might lead to runs on those institutions with low CAMEL ratings. Secondly, institutions may endeavour to mask potential problem areas from regulators through creative accounting.

More generally, the problem that emerges with a differential premium system is that subdividing assets into risk classes and levying higher premiums on those institutions with more high-risk assets does not correctly measure the institution's asset-portfolio risk. Even if this problem is overcome, there still remains the difficulty of establishing premiums that will induce, from society's perspective, optimal levels of risk-taking by the institutions involved.

The costs produced in establishing sophisticated procedures for measuring portfolio risk, and then translating the risk assessment into individually tailored premiums, are obviously high. In that a large section of the UK credit union movement has been identified as small scale in nature, the cost of the resultant premiums might prove overly prohibitive. Furthermore, levels of portfolio risk may not be markedly different across the majority of UK credit unions in that they are very much restricted in the activities that can be undertaken and future legislation, at least in the short to medium term, is unlikely to offer much greater product freedom. Consequently, it could be argued that the costs of establishing a sophisticated assessment system that may highlight differences between only a limited number of credit unions far outweighs the potential benefits.

A Regulatory alternative

A further suggested amendment of federal deposit insurance centres not on alterations to the scheme itself but rather on increasing regulation and the supervision of those institutions party to the scheme; see, for example, Nakamura (1990). The key point is that while it is important to change the incentives faced by both the depositors and the management of institutions, it is also important that adequate levels of regulation and supervision are in place and that regulators can close loss-making institutions quickly. The importance of this latter point rests with the fact that the largest claims on US insurance funds have arisen from fraud and from risky gambles made by institutions allowed to remain open for business, although technically insolvent.

For UK credit unions, increased regulation and supervision are not required. In terms of regulation it is clear that, if anything, the industry suffers from too much regulation in terms of borrowing and saving limits and constraints on product range, while, with regard to supervision, the 1979 Credit Union Act already provides the Registry of Friendly Societies with all the necessary powers. Under this Act, the registry is empowered to monitor credit unions by requiring the completion of a quarterly return from each in order to provide an early warning system for those in difficulties. It can appoint an inspector to investigate the affairs of a credit union or suspend it from accepting savings or making loans. It can also cancel a union's registration or wind it up by court order. In addition, under the Act credit unions are required to provide sufficient information prior to registration to satisfy the registrar of an adequate basic management capability and system of control.

The in-house alternative

In this instance, experience can be drawn from the credit union movement in Ireland where, following discussions between the registrar and the ILCU, a savings protection scheme was launched in 1989. This scheme is funded by a pool of money set aside by the ILCU with the sum being no less than 1% of the movement's total savings. Initially, £9 million was provided for the savings protection scheme from reserves accumulated over time in the ILCU's stabilisation fund, with individual members' savings protected up to a maximum figure of £10,000. All affiliates of the ILCU are entitled, if they are experiencing financial difficulties, to be considered for support under the scheme. Particularly important in terms of its operational nature is that continued participation in the scheme is subject to compliance with the ILCU's requirements on, for example, ratios and other operational standards. More specifically, the ILCU, as part of this protection scheme, monitors the annual accounts and returns of member credit unions. They employ the CAMEL scoring system to rate the relative performance of the respective institutions. The ILCU sends reports back to individual credit unions about their performance, which are expected to be studied by their board and supervisory committees with a view to taking remedial action, if necessary. The trade organisation may also send field officers to credit unions experiencing problems, with the task of the field officer being to advise on appropriate corrective measures.

In some ways, the system operated by the ILCU is along the same lines as the mutual guarantee systems operated by a number of states in the United States in the pre-Civil War period. The underlying principle of the mutual guarantee system was that liabilities of failed banks, not covered by liquidated assets, were redeemable by surviving banks. Take, for example, the mutual guarantee system operated in Indiana. At its height at the end of the nineteenth century over half the state's banks, and 75% of their liabilities, were in this system. The system's president and board of directors were appointed by the individual banks. Thus, control of the supervisory authority was in the hands of member banks, which was important because it gave regulatory authority to those with a strong interest in monitoring the behaviour of members. The board of directors carried out an examination of member banks each six months and had the power to limit risk-taking by restricting loans relative to capital or, in extreme cases, by closing the bank (for details of the operation of mutual guarantee systems in other states, see Calomiris, 1989).

Similarities between the mutual guarantee system and the savings protection scheme centre on the fact that both are controlled by those that have the most interest in ensuring the industry's prosperity, both are operationalised in broadly the same way and both are essentially self-financed. There are two main differences. First, unlike the mutual guarantee system, the savings protection scheme has limited liability and, secondly, participation in the protection scheme does not confer any legal right on a credit union to actually receive financial assistance.

What then of the relevance of such a scheme for the United Kingdom? The first point of note is that this system is not a deposit insurance mechanism but rather, in the Irish context, as stated by Quinn (1994), it is a means of copper-fastening various existing levels of support for protecting members' savings. Therefore, if UK credit unions were to adopt such a system it could not be seen as the introduction of a self-financed deposit insurance scheme. It would, nevertheless, be a significant improvement over the current status quo. There are, however, problems for UK credit unions in the establishment of even this intermediate scheme. The main problem centres on the fact that the trade organisations in the United Kingdom, unlike the ILCU, have not accumulated reserves with which to both jump start and provide a safety net for individual savings protection schemes. The only feasible option is, therefore, to establish a scheme to which credit unions can belong, irrespective of their affiliation. At this juncture, it is difficult, for two reasons, to envisage such co-operation. First, the respective trade organisations are in the business of competition with each other for membership. Secondly, they each have a different ethos, which is likely to result in the respective trade organisations viewing the others' members as more risky and hence a potentially greater drain on the resources of the scheme.

THE CORRECT OPTION FOR UK CREDIT UNIONS

From this overview of both the suggested structural revisions to the US system of deposit insurance and their relevance or otherwise to the United Kingdom, we are now in a position to identify the probable key characteristics of deposit insurance for this country. As a start position, it is perhaps best to begin by reiterating the characteristics viewed to be either unnecessary or impractical. Such features include the incorporation of co-insurance or a mechanism that encompasses an upper ceiling on the volume of funds insured. Differential premiums, based on an assessment of the portfolio risk to which individual credit unions are subject, was also considered inappropriate. Additional regulatory and supervisory power for the Registrar of Friendly Societies, instead of a deposit insurance mechanism was also viewed as unnecessary in that more than ample powers are already in place. Finally, a system, be it a deposit insurance mechanism or a savings protection scheme, where success hinges on co-operation between the trade organisations, is unlikely to get past the design stage.

The future design of a deposit insurance scheme for credit unions is, therefore, likely to adopt a flat-rate payment approach. Although this then necessitates that regulators control risk-taking by way of supervision and regulation rather than price, this does not create a problem in that unlike the US situation adequate controls already operate under the legislation. In terms of who provides the requisite insurance cover, two options are available. The first is for the insurance cover to be provided by government. From the perspective of credit unions and their depositors this would be the first-best option, primarily because private insurance costs may prove prohibitive, particularly for smaller organisations, but also because government insurance, backed as it is by tax-payers' funds, offers more credibility than private schemes. This latter point is reinforced by the savings and loan crisis in the United States that reached epidemic proportions in the 1980s and resulted in the bankruptcy of the Federal Savings and Loan Insurance Corporation, which had then to be bailed out by the federal government. The second option is the introduction of private-based insurance, but with the government also providing a lender-of-last-resort facility. The importance of including a lender-of-last-resort facility rests with the fact that it would provide additional assurance for the private insurance backers, which, in turn, would allow premiums to be set at an affordable level for all but the smallest of credit unions. In addition, as earlier indicated, such a scheme may prove to be a suitable compromise position between the Registry of Friendly Societies, which wants an industry-led deposit insurance scheme, and a sizeable section of the credit union industry that views private insurance as an unaffordable extra.

As an intermediate position, a savings protection scheme was also mooted. The downside, in this instance, was the competitive stance that the respective trade organisations currently take towards each other. This places in question features such as self-supervision and control, which are the cornerstones of the scheme operated by the ILCU in Ireland. Nevertheless, such a scheme might work if it were pump primed by government to create an initial reserve of funds. This pump priming would have two benefits. First, it would reduce the level of contributions from member credit unions, which would mean that a greater number of smaller institutions would find the scheme affordable. Secondly, it would provide a strong incentive for the trade organisations to co-operate in the establishment of the protection scheme and in the supervision of members of the scheme. As in the case of the protection mechanism operated by the ILCU, it would be useful to stipulate that participation in the scheme does not confer any legal right on a credit union to receive any financial assistance from it. This would then place additional onus on individual credit unions to ensure that they met the stipulated ratios and prudential requirements and, in addition, it would significantly raise the importance and relevance of the supervisory role of the trade organisations. If conflict were to emerge between the umbrella organisations as to whether a particular credit union should receive financial support, then the Registrar of Friendly Societies could be called in to adjudicate. Finally, a secondary benefit of the scheme would be to create a habit of working together between the trade organisations, which in itself must occur if the movement is to continue to prosper in the United Kingdom.

Irrespective of the type of deposit insurance system introduced or, indeed, whether a savings protection mechanism is deemed more appropriate, a necessary prerequisite before a credit union is permitted entry is that it should satisfy certain minimum financial standards. Credit unions, by meeting these minimum standards, then limit the riskiness of the mechanism. The obvious minimum financial standard would be that of the current stipulated reserve asset ratio of 10% as set out in the1979 Act. As with the establishment of the National Credit Union Share Insurance Fund in the United States, credit unions that, at present, do not satisfy the required standard could be allowed entry for a provisional two-year period. At the end of this period, those that had still not met the requisite financial conditions would either merge with another credit union, achievable now, given the relaxation of the common-bond requirement, or liquidate.

The establishment of the insurance fund may entice existing credit unions to undertake more risk-orientated business and also encourage the formation and entry into the industry of high-risk unions (this is less likely with a savings protection scheme). In both instances, the risks faced by these institutions would be borne by the insurance fund. It is, therefore, important that the Registry of Friendly Societies not only maintains, but is also willing to exercise, its current wide-ranging supervisory powers. These powers, as indicated, include the quarterly monitoring of credit unions; the ability to suspend or terminate poorly managed or loss-making ones; plus the necessity that, prior to registration, the registrar is satisfied that adequate basic manage ment capabilities and a system of control are in position.

CONCLUDING COMMENTS

Adverse selection and moral hazard are more than theoretical constructs. The US experience has demonstrated that deposit insurance schemes that fail to deal effectively with these problems can be undone by them. The analysis, however, also revealed that adverse selection and moral hazard are not likely to be pronounced problems for credit unions. The constituent nature of these bodies is such that the incentive for both members and management to engage in opportunistic behaviour is eroded, a fact that weakens significantly the case for the introduction of deposit insurance.

Credit union officials will, however, continue to press for greater regulatory freedom and if the institutions continue to be run by essentially volunteer staff, most of whom have little financial expertise, then it becomes much more important to have a deposit insurance mechanism in place. As argued, the importance centres not just on the fact that insurance protects the depositors of individual credit unions but, more crucially, that it eliminates the possibility of contagious runs. As credit unions increasingly venture into the financial marketplace, the case for comparable safeguards for their depositors, akin to those in place for depositors with other institutions, becomes more pronounced. Banks, building societies, insurance companies and friendly societies each operate protection schemes for their members.

Although it is important not to be overly prescriptive, the analysis revealed that the future design of a deposit insurance scheme for credit unions was likely to adopt a flat-rate payment approach backed by stringent regulatory and supervisory control. In terms of who provides the requisite insurance cover, two options were viewed as possible. The first was for the insurance cover to be provided by government. From the perspective of credit unions and their depositors, this would be the first-best option, primarily because private insurance costs may prove prohibitive, particularly for smaller bodies, but also because government insurance, backed as it is by tax-payers' funds, offers more credibility than private schemes. The second option was the introduction of private-based insurance but with the government also providing a lender-of-last-resort facility. The importance of this last point rests with the fact that it would provide additional assurance for the private insurance backers, which, in turn, would allow premiums to be set at an affordable level for all but the smallest of credit unions.

Finally, in the course of the discussion an alternative surfaced, which was that of a savings protection scheme. Given that such a scheme may be viewed as an intermediate position before full deposit insurance, in that it places an in-built constraint on members, it may be the best option for UK credit unions at this point in time. The key components of this scheme were that it was administered by the trade organisations themselves; they would monitor the financial soundness of member credit unions; participation did not confer a legal right for assistance; and the government would provide an initial cash injection to the scheme. The fact that participants were not assured of protection under this mechanism necessarily meant that its operation did not negate the need for self-discipline by credit unions in their business activities. This, in turn, would be likely to ameliorate claims on the protection scheme's resources. Another positive feature was that it required the trade organisations to work together not only in the administration of the scheme but also in assessing the financial health of their member credit unions. We feel that if this latter outcome were a feature of a savings protection scheme, then it would be a significant secondary benefit, not least because the future growth of the credit union movement in the United Kingdom depends, among other things, on a concerted, co-ordinated and united approach by the trade organisations.

10
A Vision for the Future

INTRODUCTION

The discussion in the preceding six chapters has had as its common denominator the UK credit union movement. The issues under scrutiny have been diverse, ranging from structural specifics, such as profit performance, capital adequacy, scale efficiency and membership orientation, to those couched in a much more general framework. Reference on this latter count is to that of legislative change, the pros and cons of a deposit insurance mechanism and the demands placed on credit unions in their different settings—employer, occupational and community. The objective in this present chapter is to employ the stock of knowledge now amassed to, on the one hand, identify potential blockages to the future development of credit unions and, on the other, to sketch out how we see this development taking place.

From the outset we must, however, stress that it is our perception that the economic climate in the United Kingdom coupled with recent changes in the composition of the financial services sector, make the present most advantageous for significant and pronounced expansion by UK credit unions. On the economic front, perhaps the biggest factor relates to the recent sustained period of low inflation. This has resulted in a steady fall in market interest rates, which, in turn, has made dividend rates paid by credit unions much more attractive. The importance of compositional changes in the financial services sector centres on the increasing demutualisation of building societies. As this process monthly gathers pace (the number of building societies has fallen from 253 in 1980 to 70 at the start of 1996) an ever-widening gap in the marketplace is emerging for credit unions. Gosling (1995) quotes the chief executive of the Halifax building society, the largest society in the United Kingdom, as urging the general public:

> ...not to mourn the demutualisation of building societies, but to recognise instead that credit unions were the modern face of relevant mutuality.

Indeed, this particular chief executive even identifies a specific niche in the building society backyard, pointing out that housing associations are likely to become strong advocates of credit unions for their tenants.

Although this latter point is as an aside, the key fact to grasp is that through the natural cycle of evolution, institutions maturing and moving on to compete in other arenas, a widening gap is being created in the UK financial services sector that credit unions appear almost destined to fill. Credit unions have the opportunity to move forward, and some commentators would argue that they are now in a position to take over the mantle of community banks. In contrast, others might argue that the pursuit of such a strategy would be a retrograde step in that it may result in credit unions becoming increasingly distant from their anti-poverty work. However, we would not be advocates of such an argument. Credit unions should not abandon the role they occupy in providing a financial and advice service within low-income communities but, at the same time, they should take the opportunity to embrace a much wider and diverse membership base. Indeed, it should be noted that Thomas and Balloch (1994) see significant advantage in such a development for low-income communities. They argue that the benefit to the low-income community relates to credit unions having a mechanism for recycling resources from relatively wealthy areas to those that are more deprived.

In terms of progressing the discussion, the start point in this chapter is an examination of the changing social, demographic and technological trends in the United Kingdom. The rationale for such a discussion is that it presents a backdrop to the opportunities and challenges now faced by credit unions. Next, a summary of the salient issues that have emerged in earlier chapters is outlined, with this summary position then used to benchmark the UK movement in terms of the typology detailed in Chapter 2. The next stage in the discussion is to consider problems and issues that must be addressed at the individual credit union level if credit unions are to grasp the opportunity now presented. This is followed by a similar analysis conducted from the perspective of the movement as a whole. The discussion then switches to an analysis of 'new freedoms' for credit unions. Concluding comments are then presented.

CHANGING UK SOCIAL, DEMOGRAPHIC AND TECHNOLOGICAL TRENDS

Before considering in detail the future prospects for UK credit unions, it is first useful to consider some broad social, demographic and technological features that are likely to impinge on the environment affecting the provision of financial services, and assess the consequences of this for credit unions. In Chapter 3, the importance of social, demographic and technological change was alluded to when considering the pressures that built up in the United States for reforms that enabled credit unions to better deal with new demands created in their operating environment. Equally, changing social, demographic and technological trends in the United Kingdom will, no doubt, similarly influence the future shape of credit unions, particularly where these trends affect the nature of the financial services market.

The changing demographic composition of the UK population is a factor that has been uncovered by recent census data. Comparative data relating to the decade 1981 to 1991 reveals that there has been a lowering of the birth rate and a decrease in the death rate. The net effect of this is, of course, an ageing population. Similarly, there has been a fall in the proportion of traditional nuclear families, a fall in household size and a rise in single living. Associated with this has been a change in patterns of household leadership, with a slight increase in female heads of family from 24% in 1981 to 28% in 1991. Additionally, there has also been a trend towards increasing age at marriage.

These demographic changes hold their own opportunities and threats for providers of financial services. For instance, a lower birth rate implies a reduced-size market for the financial services industry in the future, although an ageing population offers the opportunity posed by an expansion in the wealthier segment of the population who are renowned for their propensity to save. The rising proportion of female heads of family and the increase in single living also requires responsiveness from financial institutions, including credit unions. The increasing age at marriage (plus a 50% increase in the number of separated couples) has increased the total number of private households from 0.976 million in 1986 to 1.029 million in 1991. When the fall in population during this period is taken into account, this rise in private households is an even more remarkable phenomenon.

There has been much debate, as a consequence of the effects of continuing economic depression in the United Kingdom, about the growth of social deprivation, where the social and economic disparity between the 'haves' and 'have nots' is held to be increasing. Given the traditional role of credit unions in serving disadvantaged individuals and communities, the need for access to financial services, particularly by those most likely to be refused service by mainstream institutions or, worse still, those most likely to fall under the grasp of moneylenders and loan sharks, is likely to remain a primary objective for credit unions. The effects of the recession have not, however, been restricted to disadvantaged communities. Many middle-class families have suffered detriment because of their high credit spending in the late 1980s and from speculation on the housing market, where house prices were assumed to be permanently rising. The United Kingdom has witnessed a period of house repossessions and has seen the growth of 'negative equity' in properties, particularly in the south-east of England. That many middle-class families are disillusioned and possibly receptive to alternative ways of managing their financial affairs on the basis of the more prudent and thrifty precepts of credit union principles offers a major opportunity for the UK industry. When this is tied in with the growth of employer-based credit unions, the opportunity to attract middle-class salaried members can be seen to be all the more realisable. The importance of employer-based credit unions in the transition UK industry is discussed more fully in Chapter 8.

That the financial services market is currently being driven by a 'technological imperative' was stressed in our appraisal of the US industry. The significance of technological innovation in the United Kingdom financial services market is no less important. The financial services industry in the UK has traditionally been at the forefront of the application of information technology, although this early lead has proved not to provide an enduring advantage as the first account-based mainframe database applications are now being (expensively) replaced by customer-relational databases. This reinvestment in technology mirrors a transition in the use of information technology within the financial services industry away from purely 'efficiency' data processing to a more strategic, long-term use of information technology aimed at more effective marketing of financial services through cross-selling.

The competitive forces within the UK financial services market are intense, with all the major institutions being forced to reduce their cost–income ratios and deliver services on a more efficient basis. Information technology developments have been seized as a means of doing this, especially in revolutionising delivery channels for products and services. The growth of ATMs and debit cards, in particular, are helping to reduce the need by financial institutions to maintain expensive branch structures. Whilst home banking, based on computer technology accessible by customers in their homes, has had a mixed reception, the success of telephone banking has been spectacular and looks set to continue. Home banking, given the growth of the internet and the development of on-line banking, does, however, appear to be feasible in the long term and is likely to further revolutionise delivery channels for financial services in the United Kingdom. The point about all of these developments in electronic delivery channels is that they have reduced the entry barriers into the financial services market. UK credit unions are at the threshold and have an opportunity to benefit from these developments in the same way as their US counterparts have done. Although 'late starters', this could well prove advantageous given that the costs of these technological innovations are constantly falling. Also, since they have not borne any of the costs associated with being a first mover in technological innovation, credit unions can capitalise on the fact that such innovations cannot, in the long run, confer sustainable competitive advantage to first movers since they are so easily copied. However, the ability to provide electronic channels of distribution will prove to be essential for survival, given the likelihood of the increasing expectations and sophistication of customers towards the convenience offered by new technological innovations in running their day-to-day financial affairs.

It seems inconceivable that UK credit unions can stand aside from the opportunities afforded by the electronic revolution that is currently taking place.

The UK credit union industry is small compared with its other financial services rivals, and the size of even the largest individual credit union is still relatively insignificant when measured against other types of financial institutions. This factor combines with the 'technological imperative' for an urgent need to develop a more cohesive industry structure, especially in terms of a unified trade body that can take the lead in developing central services such as shared information technology delivery channels. Redefining the future role and function of the current UK trade associations is discussed in its own right later in this chapter. At this point, our discussion shifts to provide a detailed appraisal of the current state of play within the UK industry to draw out key features of our industry analysis. This is done as a prelude to the later discussion of our vision of the future for the UK industry and the recommendations made for its further development.

THE CURRENT STATE OF PLAY

The UK credit union industry was demonstrated to be regionally diverse, young, vibrant and high growth with much of this growth having occurred over the course of this past 10 years. Community-based credit unions were seen to be the dominating force, with only limited penetration, so far, by occupational and employer-based unions. This was viewed to be very much at odds with movements in other countries where the majority of assets are held by credit unions with employee-type bonds or those formerly of this type.

A sizeable share of growth has been in the formation of new unions and consequently a significant dichotomy was seen to exist between longer established and more recently formed credit unions. This dichotomy was most starkly manifested in terms of the viability and service on offer. With viability defined in terms of self-sufficiency, it transpired that out of the 611 registered credit unions in the United Kingdom, 122 made the grade. That is, the latter achieved a critical mass that allowed them to offer a good return on members' savings, have in place adequate reserves, and generate income to cover their operating expenditures, including salaried staff, without the necessity of recourse to outside funding sources. We viewed the fact that 20% of the UK movement is self-sufficient not as a problem but as a significant achievement, in that, as an organisational form, they simply did not exist further back than 35 years ago.

Our assessment mirrors that of the Registry of Friendly Societies. In the formative years of the movement, the registry focused heavily on the economic soundness and financial credibility of credit unions. The registry now appears to believe that credit unions have progressed considerably in the establishment of their economic worth and, consequently, it has been proactive in the introduction of legislative amendments aimed at helping credit unions enter a further stage in their development. These legislative amendments were seen to include a widening of the common bond and a raising of the maximum loan, deposit and membership ceilings.

Legislative change to enable credit unions to avail of growth opportunities was given further support by a paired difference analysis that defined the UK movement as one characterised by increasing returns to scale. There was a straight-line improvement in the operational efficiency of credit unions up to an asset level of £500,000. The break at this point was explained by the fact that credit unions, at this asset level, face a more burdensome array of input costs (they can no longer rely on donated capital and labour) than their smaller counterparts. What, however, also emerged from the analysis was that although larger credit unions found it necessary to employ more full-time and part-time staff, and this initially impacted adversely upon cost efficiency, once they achieved significant critical mass, assets in excess of £1 million, further improvements in operational efficiency were obtained.

From these findings and drawing from the history of the movement in countries such as the United States and Canada, we speculated that the idealistic view held by many credit union proponents of a movement consisting of small-scale organisations offering share savings and consumer loans to a membership forgotten by main-line financial institutions, was one very much under threat.

It was also mooted that the characterisation of the industry by increasing returns to scale was likely to dampen any potential for membership conflict. It was viewed that increasing returns to scale could be employed to provide higher returns for shareholding members and lower loan costs for borrowing members.

When the orientation of credit unions was examined it transpired that almost all exhibited borrower-dominated behaviour. Indeed, it was argued, on the basis of an examination of market rates of interest, that the UK industry was more than likely to have been characterised as pro-borrower in each of the 17 years prior to 1994. This result was, however, viewed almost as a foregone conclusion, given that the 1979 Credit Union Act requires credit unions neither to pay dividends above a stipulated maximum of 8% per annum, nor to charge loan interest rates in excess of 1% per month.

This then raised the issue of whether, in the interest of achieving a balanced treatment of their membership, credit unions should lobby for the removal of the interest and dividend rate ceilings to which they must adhere. We, however, were of the opinion that they should not. The argument put forward was that at present most are based in low-income communities where access to cheap loan funds alleviated a degree of the hardship faced by many families. Consequently, it might, in fact, be a retrograde step to create an environment where there was not an upper loan rate ceiling. In fact, we went further and stated that the UK situation of weakly borrower-orientated credit unions, while not theoretically optimal, is socially optimal.

In that a complete chapter was devoted to deposit insurance, it should be evident that we have serious misgivings about the non-existence of a protection scheme for UK credit unions. The Registry of Friendly Societies is freeing up the framework within which credit unions operate and credit unions are likely to continue to press for further freedoms. Under such a scenario it is difficult to understand the movement's reluctance to establish a protection scheme. We argued that the importance centres not just on the fact that deposit insurance protects the depositors of individual credit unions but, more crucially, that it eliminates the possibility of contagious runs. As credit unions increasingly venture into the financial marketplace, the case for comparable safeguards for their depositors, akin to those in place for depositors with other institutions, becomes more pronounced. Banks, building societies, insurance companies and friendly societies each operate protection schemes for their members. Why not credit unions?

DEVELOPMENT TYPOLOGY

In Chapter 2, a development typology was established to enable a more effective examination of the stages involved in credit union maturation. Three stages were identified—mature, transition and nascent. At that juncture, it was intimated that in all probability the UK movement fell within the bounds of the transition categorisation. From what has been described in the preceding chapters it appears that this is the case. The key attributes of an industry in transition are: large asset size; shifts in the regulatory framework; moves towards greater product diversification; emphasis on growth and efficiency; a weakening of the reliance on voluntarism; a recognition of the need for greater effectiveness and professionalism in trade organisations; and the development of central services. That is not to say that the UK movement as a whole uniformly meets these attributes, nor, for that matter, that it satisfies all the attributes. There is significant heterogeneity across the industry but overall it can be argued that despite this it is best described as in transition.

In terms of meeting the transition criteria, the most obvious shortfall rests with the fact that when the viability of credit unions was assessed, it was only possible to classify 122 as economically self-sufficient. The residual 489, in that they are small in scale, require sponsorship for their survival, emphasise voluntarism and, for the most part, are located in low-income communities, are very much in the nascent stage of development. With such a large number at this stage in their development it could be argued that the movement should more appropriately be classified under the nascent banner. Such an argument would be incorrect. Assets and membership is heavily concentrated within the top 200 credit unions and, for all intents and purposes, it is this group that will be the future of the industry. The present widening of the common bond will reduce the necessity for the establishment of significant numbers of new credit unions and, at the same time, will enable amalgamations to occur within the industry. The precedent for such amalgamations is one of larger-scale institutions taking over smaller ones. A case in point is the movement in New Zealand, which was also classified as in the transition stage (see Chapter 2). Today, there are 151 credit unions in New Zealand compared with 312 in 1985. Our expectation is that, as in New Zealand, small, and, for the most part, new credit unions, are living on borrowed time. The only exception to this would be employer-based credit unions. Therefore, the classification scheme should be based on those credit unions likely to survive the amalgamation process intact. If this is taken to be the top 200 or so credit unions, then there is significant homogeneity within the group. In general, they have the requisite asset size, they are concentrating on the achievement of growth and efficiency and they are adopting a more professional approach to the management of their organisation.

Problems for the typology do not, however, stop at this point. Some of the components of the transition typology are, at present, impossible to implement. While there have, indeed, been shifts in the regulatory environment, including a widening of the common bond, the movement as yet does not have the option of providing a wider product range. One of the main components of the transition typology was that of shifts towards greater product diversification. The movement at large is also splintered between four main trade organisations—the ILCU, NFCU, UFCU and ABCUL, with a number of smaller trade bodies such as the SLCU also competing for members. One might expect that a single trade body would be much more effective and professional in its operations relative to a series of disparate organisations. An additional consequence of a splintered membership is that the movement is less effective in the development of central services. Both the need for greater effectiveness and professionalism of trade organisations, and the development of central services, were part of the transition classification scheme.

UK credit unions occupancy in the transition categorisation is, therefore, not without its problems. Indeed, from this overview, the impression gained is that in all probability they are at the lower end of the transition spectrum, and far from entering into the mature stage of development. The next stage in this discussion, therefore, focuses not so much on how UK credit unions can move to the next development stage, but rather on how they can consolidate their position within the transition stage in preparation for the attainment of maturity at some later date.

ACTION: THE INDIVIDUAL CREDIT UNION RESPONSE

The objective for the UK movement is thus consolidation prior to moving forward into the mature setting. The response by the movement can be, and, indeed, is likely to be, at two levels—initiatives undertaken by the movement at large, primarily through its support organisations (although later in this chapter we will argue that the ideal would be if there was only one support organisation) and those undertaken by individual credit unions. Although the latter is probably less important than the former, the initial focus is on those measures that can be pursued at the individual credit union level.

As a first course of action, credit unions must have interest-competitive savings products. To grow, a credit union requires a steady stream of members' savings, which are then parcelled up and on-lent to borrowing members. Uncompetitive savings rates halts this process even before it begins. In addition to the payment of competitive rates, credit unions, within the regulatory constraints, should continually review and update savings products. As part of this, process, credit unions should survey both members and non-members to determine what savings products they require and, where possible, they should introduce new savings products that meet their express needs. Coupled with this, they should maintain marketing programmes to both sell savings products and reach new members. It is also important to use committee and general meetings to educate members regarding new savings products.

To ensure financial soundness it is necessary that the credit union has adequate financial and managerial controls and discipline. This includes the maintenance of the requisite reserve ratio and procedures to ensure the minimisation of bad debts. For example, some credit unions may allocate annually a low percentage of loans outstanding as a bad-debt provision, without considering current delinquency levels. Bad loans are not written off and hence are maintained perpetually on the balance sheet, leading to a growing excess of non-producing loans and a decline in asset quality. Action that could be undertaken would include the implementation of a risk-management programme to improve asset quality; the development of a loan collection programme; as well as implementation of an asset/liability management programme.

The quality and professionalism of management is also a key facet in the success or otherwise of the credit union. When a credit union is in its formative years there is an obligation on the trade organisation to train the leaders of that union. However, having gained a foothold, it becomes incumbent that the credit union itself sets aside a budget for training. To ensure effectiveness, part of this training process must also include identifying the skills and talents staff must have to compete successfully in the changing environment. For example, because of the shortage of skilled workers and the advances of technology, staff need technology-based training to increase productivity. Increased productivity, in turn, alleviates the need for large staff numbers. Lemmon (1995) sees the future for credit unions as one where there is increasing pressure to create unique solutions for individual members that will require a skilled, competent staff. Equally important is the retention of key personnel. In the first instance, this may take the form of gratuity payments to those members providing critical skills who perhaps previously provided their services on a volunteer basis. However, sophistication in the running of a credit union will, in the longer term, require paid career professionals. Under such circumstances, best effort is usually obtained through an emphasis on pay for performance.

It was demonstrated that credit unions are subject to increasing returns to scale, thus growth is synonymous with improved cost efficiency. The prime way to capture growth is through an expansion of the membership base. On this count, numerous policies can be adopted. One example is to target those member groups with the highest potential for credit union growth and to then set out to attract them through the provision of starter financial packages. Youth groups would be one potential target market and, from the earlier analysis of changing social and demographic trends, it is clear that pensioner groups may also prove a fertile recruitment ground for credit unions. The widening of the common bond will also make it much easier for credit unions to expand their membership. Credit unions should be aiming to expand their services to both local communities and employee groups. Delaney (1994) employs Community First credit union in Australia as an example of how to increase the membership base. Australia, through a vigorous immigration policy, has become a multi-cultural society. However, the ethnic community is one of the areas where credit unions do not have an acceptable level of presence. This, it is suggested, could be remedied by existing credit unions expanding their membership bond to incorporate specific ethnic groups; by undertaking programmes that target ethnic groups; or by assisting these communities to start their own credit unions. The extensive array of prudential requirements that must be met make the last option very difficult.

Delaney, however, argues that there are various models for starting credit unions. The one that Community First is trialling is labelled the Incubator Model. Under this approach, Community First has expanded its bond to include persons of Korean ethnic origin. Members of the Korean community in Sydney are able to join Community First as full members and have immediate access to the full range of services. Separate accounting is maintained, with the objective being for the Korean community to establish their own credit union when a viable membership level is reached.

Through this model, the potential new credit union has the benefits of its members having access to a full range of services and its staff gaining training, expertise and systems from the host credit union. It is also able to build its own capital, as the net result of its operations is reserved and transferred to the new credit union on the achievement of critical mass. The model also has a fail-safe mechanism in that if viable size is not met, the members may remain with the host credit union. Delaney emphasises the success of this initiative, stating that within the first five months of operation, $1 million had been achieved and that, shortly, the first new credit union for 20 years would be launched in Australia.

Such an approach has obvious attractions for credit unions in the United Kingdom. It offers credit unions a tactic to harness a new membership base, while, at the same time, providing a considerable incentive for the promotion of the existing credit union within the target organisation/community by that organisation/community. If the initiative is sufficiently successful, then a new credit union can be established. However, irrespective of whether or not a viable size is reached, the expectation must be that once the advantages that size bestows on a membership are recognised, the initial coming together may turn out to be permanent. The key point, in summary, is that credit unions should seek to incorporate members from diverse sections of the population who are interested in the promotion of the self-help concept. They should not, as in the past, target low-income communities almost to the exclusion of all other groups.

Finally, as the future unfolds, credit unions must recognise that they are likely to serve members that are becoming more and more demanding and increasingly they will be unable to rely on their loyalty. Consequently, to retain and increase their membership, credit unions must offer their members/ customers an attractive package. At present, this package, on the product front, consists essentially of the most basic of savings and loan products (excepting, of course, innovations such as the affinity cards provided by credit unions such as British Airways and Strathclyde Regional Council). The attractive component is introduced by pricing these products competitively and providing them within an efficient, friendly and convenient environment. The latter would include a good location for the credit union as well as customer-friendly opening hours.

ACTION: THE MOVEMENT'S RESPONSE

To maximise the movement's potential, it is imperative that the demands and needs of individual credit unions are both articulated and serviced by a strong and focused umbrella organisation. At present there are four trade organisations in operation in the United Kingdom, with periodic reports of attempts to establish further support/trade bodies. In that these organisations are competing with each other for members, they do not, and, indeed, could not be expected to, speak with a unified voice. This obviously dissipates any message that they might wish to put forward, as well as considerably weakening them as a lobby force.

The National Consumer Council (1994), as one of its 27 recommendations for change, suggested the establishment of a national liaison committee. This committee was to be made up of representatives of all the trade associations, along with members of involved and interested bodies. Once formed, this liaison committee was to have the brief of consulting with the Registry of Friendly Societies to develop appropriate sets of model rules; address ways of increasing public awareness of credit unions; take forward proposals for changes to legislation, as well as draw up a constitution to formalise its job specification and its membership. In this recommendation there is a clear recognition of a need for a single and strong voice. As the way forward, the National Consumer Council opts for a liaison committee rather than a merger of the national trade bodies. A cynic might argue that this circuitous procedure to put in place a unified action group might have something to do with the fact that the working party convened by the National Consumer Council to compile the report had formed the view that the personalities involved in the respective trade organisations would not be amenable to a merger, and the second-best alternative was that of a liaison committee.

Such a committee may be reasonably effective in the promotion of credit union awareness and as a lobby force for legislative change. However, a single trade body would have the capacity to provide a much broader range of services for its membership. The key point is that, operating on an individual basis, the various trade bodies simply do not have sufficient funds to enable them to provide an all-encompassing range of services; nor, for that matter, do they have a large enough membership to make the provision of even a subset of services cost effective. A coming together of the trade organisations would provide the unified organisation with both a significant membership and revenue pool and, consequently, much more potential in this area.

At this stage, it is perhaps useful to examine the services provided by a trade organisation in another country. The typology documented in Chapter 2 identified the movement in New Zealand as one that, like the United Kingdom is in transition. In New Zealand, there are 151 credit unions of which 107 are affiliated to the trade body, the New Zealand Association of Credit Unions (NZACU). Total membership is 120,000 with £UK equivalent assets of £200 million. The comparable figures for UK credit unions are 597 credit unions, 348,136 members and assets of £240 million. Therefore, it would appear that the achievements of the NZACU are well within the gift of the UK movement, if it were to operate as a cohesive unit. What then are the services provided by the NZACU and what is the operational structure within which they are provided?

The activities carried out by the NZACU currently fall into two categories. One is labelled trade association activities, the other is business services activities. They draw a broad distinction in that trade association activities are funded by the dues that member credit unions pay and business services are funded by the receiving credit union. The prime purpose of the trade association (dues-funded) is to influence and change the environment in which the credit union movement operates through its governance and trade activities. The NZACU views these activities as being of equal relevance to all credit unions, regardless of size. The list of trade association activities covered on a dues-funded basis is extensive. The following are but some of the services provided: marketing and public relations for the movement; support during start-up and wind-up; industry research and market information; legislation and representation at national and local government level; advice and compliance guidelines—legal, financial, operational and prudential; director training and education; credit union philosophy training; and the development and protection of standards for the movement. The NZACU views these services also being essential for the protection and well-being of all credit unions. They consider that these services are best provided on a shared-enterprise basis, being funded by all credit unions on an equitable basis. The reasoning behind the need for all credit unions to be involved is that full cost recovery by sale on an individual fee-for-service basis would not be possible.

Credit union business services are, in contrast, funded on a fee-for-service (user-pays) basis. These services are essentially commercial services provided by the trade body to its member unions. They come under three broad headings, that of a central fund, information technology services and insurance services.

The central fund is a common fund that invests on behalf of, and in the interest of, all participating credit unions. In that it is investing cumulative sums, it can generate higher returns than if credit unions were investing in an individual capacity. At present, the fund primarily invests in short-term bonds. In the near future it is anticipated that the fund will be able to offer participating credit unions such facilities as: long-term investment products; short-term development funding for purposes such as the purchase, building and renovation of premises, computer purchase, and also for liquidity during peak times; on-call investments and retirement savings.

The NZACU, in its 1993–1994 annual report, argues that at a certain point in a credit union's growth and development the number and complexity of transactions requires the assistance of a computer. Once a credit union commits to technology it then finds that its continued growth and development requires more and more sophisticated uses of that technology and this is where the NZACU's information technology services department comes into play. This department is charged with sourcing or developing, and maintaining, technology products that meet the growth and development needs of member credit unions. The technology services department is used by 40 of the 151 credit unions on a user-pays basis. One of its latest innovations, which so far is supported only by 10 member unions, is that of ACCESSCARD, which will enable ATM and EFTPOS services to be provided to members of participating credit unions.

The trade body also provides insurance services on a user-pays basis. Insurance for credit unions can, for example, cover public indemnity, fire and burglary. Pension and insurance services can be provided for the staff of both the trade body and individual credit unions. Members of participating credit unions can also avail of life savings insurance, loan protection insurance and savings protection.

While we recognise that the regulatory framework as it is currently constituted would not permit the provision of all these services, and also that one section of the UK credit union movement, ILCU affiliates in Northern Ireland, is unlikely to be part of a unified structure, the analysis nevertheless gives some indication of what could be achieved if the trade bodies were to pull together. Indeed, approaching the issue from another direction, it could be argued that the non-provision of these services gives a measure of the degree to which competition between the trade bodies has reduced the benefits on offer to member unions, as well as the overall growth potential of the movement.

NEW FREEDOMS

At present, credit unions are single-product intermediaries providing a basic savings and loan service under prespecified volume limits and interest rate ceilings. Although the volume limits, under the Deregulation (Credit Unions) Order amendment to the 1979 Act, have been somewhat eased, it is our contention that the time is approaching for credit unions to be permitted a broader role in retail financial services. It is also our view that the movement, acting as a concerted whole, should be militating for these enhanced freedoms. It is, however, also important to stress that the use of the term 'approaching' does not imply that new freedoms should be bestowed on the movement tomorrow. Rather, our vision is of a five-to-ten-year time horizon. This time horizon is chosen because by then the present easing of volume limits will, in all probability, have made the logic for new freedoms irrefutable. In short, the relaxation of volume limits will provide the catalyst for further change. Before spelling out the form these new freedoms should take, and, indeed, a justification for them, it is perhaps useful to first emphasise factors that are currently hindering the development of the movement into the wider financial services arena.

With new freedoms come new risks, and it is, therefore, imperative that the industry has in place mechanisms to safeguard the financial stability of credit unions and, in consequence, the investments held with them. At present, the Registry of Friendly Societies has this responsibility. However, it may be more appropriate to establish a credit-union-specific regulatory body to take over this function. There are, of course, many precedents. For example, the 1986 Building Societies Act established a Building Societies Commission (members are appointed by the Treasury and funded by an annual charge levied upon building societies using a fixed-percentage-of-assets scale) to take over those regulatory functions previously exercised by the Chief Registrar of Friendly Societies, as well as those additional responsibilities prescribed by the Act. The majority of the responsibilities vested with the Building Societies Commission would be equally important in the prudential management of credit unions. In particular, we would see a Credit Union Commission empowered to assess individual credit unions on the following criteria:

1. Maintenance of adequate reserves and other designated capital resources.

2. Maintenance of adequate assets in liquid form.

3. Maintenance of the requisite accounting records and systems of control of business and of inspection and report.

4. Direction of management:

    (i) By a sufficient number of persons who are fit and proper to be directors or, as the case may be, officers, in their respective positions.

    (ii) Conducted by them with prudence and integrity.

5. Conduct of the business with adequate professional skills.

The Credit Union Commission should also be given the requisite powers to carry out this supervisory role. These would include the power to: specify how liquid assets should be invested; impose limitations on the acceptance of deposits or the making of loans; require alteration in the conduct of business (namely, to ensure that requirements such as those relating to asset and liability management are met); prevent associations with other bodies; obtain information and documents; appoint persons to investigate the business of any credit union; determine whether an activity of a credit union is within the power of that credit union, and if it is not to prohibit that activity; impose conditions on, or revoke authorisation; request a credit union to renew its application for authorisation; promote mergers or enforce the winding-up of a credit union for prudential reasons subject to an appropriate right of appeal.

Many of the above powers, and, indeed, the areas in which they pertain, have been drawn directly from the framework of regulations within which the Building Societies Commission operates. Others are a reiteration of the powers currently vested in the Registrar of Friendly Societies. (In particular, the registrar has the power to: require information; appoint an inspector and call a meeting into the affairs of a credit union; suspend operations; cancel or suspend registration and petition for winding-up; and adjudicate on amalgamation and transfers of engagements.)

While the increased range of responsibilities, coupled with the burgeoning growth in the movement alone, provides justification for the establishment of a regulatory body, reasons of equal worth are that it would raise the regulatory profile of credit unions to alongside that of the banks and building societies, as well as provide a marker of the coming of age of the industry. Again, it should be emphasised that we do not envisage the establishment of a Credit Union Commission as an immediate occurrence. In fact, it is likely to come towards the end of the five-to-ten-year horizon and may require the introduction of a new Credit Union Act.

A measure of more immediate importance, and one that, in this instance, is within the gift of the credit union movement, is that of deposit insurance. It is our opinion that the introduction of such a scheme is a prerequisite to credit unions being permitted greater freedoms. Indeed, it will shortly be argued that the easing, in particular, of the upper limit on savings is unlikely to have a significant impact unless it is accompanied by the introduction of a deposit insurance mechanism. The issue of deposit insurance was the focus of attention in Chapter 9 and, without wishing to labour the point, it must be stressed that the justification for deposit insurance is that it protects the interests of credit union members and promotes the financial integrity and efficiency of credit unions. Furthermore, the introduction of a protection scheme is widely regarded as boosting the acceptance of credit unions as mainstream financial institutions and, as was seen in Chapter 2, it does not have to be a major drain on the resources of individual credit unions. In the United States the widening of the common bond to the broader concept of a field of membership has meant that amalgamations have tended to substitute for liquidations and, in consequence, since 1985, the NCUA has only once levied a premium (in 1991) for membership of the National Credit Union Insurance Fund.

Assuming that the appropriate safety nets are in place, what then are the new freedoms of which credit unions should be able to avail? A proposal set out in July 1995 under the government's deregulation initiative relaxes the limit on a member's shareholding. In addition to the fixed limit of £5000, there is the alternative that deposits can be of the order of 1.5% of the credit union's total shareholding at the last balance sheet date. A larger credit union with a total shareholding of, for example, £1 million could, therefore, have individual member shareholdings up to a maximum of £15,000. The Treasury argues that the purpose for the continued use of the restriction is that it ensures that a credit union is broadly based and is not dominated by a limited number of individuals, with the credit union also afforded protection from a withdrawal of shares by a single individual that could precipitate a financial crisis. The argument put forward for relaxing the restriction is that it is unnecessarily restrictive on large credit unions to which the withdrawal of £5000 may not be significant. Two points should be made. First, without deposit insurance this relaxation is unlikely to raise significantly the average amount saved by members. Credit union saving members, as with most investors, are risk-adverse and will be unwilling to tie up significant sums in unprotected institutions. Indirect evidence for this point can be found in Chapter 3 where it was suggested that the introduction of deposit insurance in the United States in 1970 affected the composition of credit union share accounts whereby large accounts displaced smaller accounts to the extent that the proportion of large accounts nearly doubled from 29% in 1970 to 56% by 1990. Secondly, if we assume that deposit insurance is introduced shortly, individual credit unions have in place good systems of control and competent management, a widening of the common bond occurs that in itself will ensure that credit unions are more broadly based, then it is our view that there is little justification for a shareholding limit. Such a limit reduces a credit union's efficiency and growth prospects and, in all fairness, adds little to its financial stability.

Currently, credit unions may borrow money from an authorised bank or temporarily from another credit union. The amount borrowed cannot exceed 50% of the total paid-up share capital. This is, however, unlikely to be a cheap alternative and a more preferable option to alleviate a shortage of funds is by making use of wholesale funding through, for example, the issue of certificates of deposit. Access to wholesale markets offers a particular advantage to credit unions in respect of cost because, in the retail market, they cannot differentiate between one set of shareholders and another. If new funds can only be attracted by the offer of higher dividend rates, then these higher rates will have to be paid on existing shareholdings as well as new funds. In contrast, marginal funds can be secured through the wholesale markets without paying a higher rate on funds already secured. A second advantage of the wholesale market is that it offers a degree of flexibility in terms of the amount, the timing and borrowing conditions, which, in many instances, can be greater than that available in the retail market. Consequently, credit unions could secure greater control over the volume of funds taken, as the amount can be predetermined.

Such flexibility will be of enhanced importance for credit unions as their product portfolio broadens and it becomes more important to match the term structure of their assets and liabilities. However, the dominant reason for permitting credit unions to access the wholesale market centres on the fact that, with the easing of the share limit, average savings volumes will rise (assuming the introduction of deposit insurance) and these larger savings bundles will be more likely to be interest-sensitive. Credit unions, in that they adhere to a dividend rate ceiling, may find that a sharp rise in market interest rates results in an outflow of members' savings causing difficulty for the credit union in question. Of course, another option would be the removal of the dividend rate ceiling. It is our view that permission to access the wholesale market, as well as the abolition of the deposit rate ceiling, will occur within the five-to-ten-year time horizon.

Proposals set out in July 1995 also proposed easing the loan limit. In addition to the fixed limit of £5,000 in excess of the member's share capital, there is now the alternative to on-lend 1.5% of the credit union's total share-holdings in excess of the member's share capital. A credit union with shareholdings of £10 million could, therefore, on-lend to a member £150,000 in excess of his/her share capital. (It should be noted that the MPs on the House of Commons Deregulation Committee considered that this proposal provided only limited benefit to the credit union movement as a whole. It called, in addition, for the £5000 limit to be replaced by a £10,000 limit. Fears that this could lead to smaller credit unions over-reaching themselves were to be tackled by proposals that those wishing to take advantage of the relaxation must obtain a certificate from the Registrar of Friendly Societies. The committee accepted a Treasury suggestion that the extra loans should be allowed only if the ceiling fell below 20% of the union's general reserves. The committee's suggested amendment was referred back to the Treasury for consideration. The indications are that the Treasury is likely to agree the change.) In our opinion, loan volumes on the basis of the 1.5% threshold open up the possibility for larger credit unions to step outside their traditional field of consumer credit provision and engage in, for example, mortgage lending. Such loans, in that they would be advances secured on residential property would be relatively low risk and would fit neatly within the current loan service provided by credit unions. The provision of mortgage products is likely to prove particularly attractive to those credit unions with a middle income membership and would further boost membership growth in these unions. Graham Tomlin, president of Plane Saver, the British Airways employee credit union, in a recent press release stated:

> A recent survey of our members identified mortgages as the one product which they overwhelmingly would like us to provide. Once we have demonstrated our management competence we intend to press both the Registry of Friendly Societies and the Treasury hard for the freedom to give our members what they want most.

With the increase in the loan limit, credit unions are also likely to become increasingly attractive as loan intermediaries to the small-firm sector. In Ireland, for example, credit unions are able to give commercial loans to small businesses provided that their proprietors are members of credit unions.

Opportunity for individual credit union growth also emerges in amendments to the common-bond requirement. In the first instance, members who no longer meet the test of the common bond because they have moved or changed jobs will be able to stay in their existing credit union on the same terms and conditions. Previously, such people, although they could remain in the same credit union, were offered a restricted service. Secondly, the limitation of membership to a single qualification is removed. The view was taken that it should be open to a credit union to decide whether or not it wants to adopt a qualification that allows for the membership of both residents and employees.

This widening of the common bond was accompanied by a proposal that the maximum membership limit, without need for an exemption from the registrar, would be raised from 5000 to 10,000 members.

We welcome these changes. However, even at this juncture, our feeling is that there is an argument for going a step further. That is, credit unions should not be subject to a membership ceiling. Credit unions, in that they can now avail of the broader-based common bond are likely to experience a significant increase in membership. Under such circumstances, there is little justification for having in place a ceiling that places a brake on natural membership growth. If support for this argument is required, we need look no further than Chapter 6, which revealed that UK credit unions are subject to economies of scale, thus equating growth with improved efficiency.

In summary, the position we have adopted is one that argues for new freedoms for credit unions. These new freedoms are not, however, extensive, and their purpose is more geared to the promotion of growth, broadly within the bounds to which credit unions currently adhere. The removal of the membership ceiling, the opportunity to access the wholesale markets, the option of diversifying into mortgage provision and perhaps commercial loans to small businesses, are all changes in this vein. Furthermore, it would be our contention that it would be inappropriate to grant these freedoms to all credit unions. Permission to access the wholesale markets and to provide new services should be dependent on credit unions achieving a prespecified asset size and having in place the requisite reserve requirements and prudential norms. In addition, we feel that the movement must be seen to help itself and, on this count, we refer to the introduction of a deposit insurance mechanism.

Obvious through non-mention is the subject of new freedoms in the area of money transmission. In our view, the provision of, for example, cheque book facilities, in-house credit cards and an ATM service require a membership of significant critical mass. Even allowing for the most optimistic of predictions, it is difficult to envisage credit unions, on an individual basis, achieving such a size within our five-to-ten-year time frame. That is not to say that the movement should be precluded from sharing in some of the benefits of money transmission provision. Agency agreements along the lines established by ABCUL with the US banking group MBNA for the issue of credit cards could easily be extended to most other transmission services, although, again, a trade organisation acting for all credit unions would be much better placed to negotiate percentage cuts.

CONCLUDING COMMENTS

Although this chapter was entitled, 'A Vision for the Future', our vision, in that it stretches merely over a five-to-ten-year time horizon, could arguably be viewed as not that far-reaching. Limited though it may be, we consider that this vision of future change within the UK movement will conform very much with the reality of events over the coming years. Our confidence centres on the fact that the construction of a development typology, detailed in Chapter 2, has enabled UK credit unions to be neatly ascribed within a relative framework. This relative framework was constructed at a point in time with UK credit unions firmly placed within the transition stage of development, although towards the lower end of this developmental spectrum. Having classified the UK movement, our vision was then dictated by the history of the movement in other countries, which, in their developmental journey, have passed through the stage of development that UK credit unions currently visit. Although not explicitly detailed, our vision of the future was, to some extent, shaped by the development of the New Zealand credit union movement from the late 1980s onwards, and the history of the movement in the United States from the late 1960s to 1975. Of course, country-specific occurrences may well result in deviations or, indeed, cause breaks in a straight-line progression through the development typology. However, having said this, cross-country experience suggests that significant commonality, in fact, exists. Drawing from this experience, the future for UK credit unions must, therefore, be viewed as bright, although it would be our contention that the UK credit union star will shine much brighter and, indeed, more rapidly, if the measures proposed in this chapter are adopted speedily.

11

Nascent Credit Union Industries—Ukraine, Poland and Africa

INTRODUCTION

The focus, so far, on mature and transition industries has reflected our concern to examine the evolution and operation of credit unions in the context of well-established financial services markets. Turning now to an examination of nascent credit union industries invites a somewhat different perspective, where credit unions are attempting to flourish in areas such as Central and Eastern Europe where a market economy has not existed, or in developing parts of the world where huge sections of the population have traditionally little, if any, access to formal mainstream financial services. In the introductory chapter, stress was placed on the significance of co-operatives as a major global phenomenon. The diversity of form that such co-operatives take throughout the world was emphasised. In developing countries and regions, co-operatives are seen to be fundamentally important in creating sustainable development through the mobilisation of the power of self-help programmes. Nascent credit union industries are an important instrument in helping to create conditions that support genuinely sustainable development. In this chapter, our development typology is applied to examples of nascent industries in Central and Eastern Europe and Africa. As before, these are selective case studies that aim to discuss and test the validity of the attributes identified for nascent industries. The comparative dimension in our analysis will confirm the importance of historical and culturally specific factors to the development potential of credit unions in the different countries and regions dealt with in this chapter.

In Central and Eastern Europe, the reform of centrally controlled economies has brought into sharp relief the potential role of credit unions as significant instruments of economic and social change. As indicated in Chapter 2, the development of credit union industries in Central and Eastern Europe entails a rebirth of co-operative forms of organisation as crucial components of reformed economic and social structures. The social costs of transition have been much higher than expected in many Central and Eastern European countries. For instance, the World Bank estimates that the percentage of people living in poverty has risen from 5% to 17% in the Balkans and Poland, from 3% to 21% in Russia, and from 2% to 12% in Ukraine (see ICA, 1995). Despite such difficult challenges, there can be little doubt that a significant opportunity exists for credit unions to take root in Central and Eastern Europe and to make a significant contribution to the economic and social life of the citizens in the former Soviet bloc. This chapter examines some of the major barriers and drivers to realising the potential afforded by credit unions in Central and Eastern Europe.

The opportunities for credit union growth in many parts of the world, particularly the developing economies, is equally significant. The need for credit unions and the benefits that they offer is overwhelming in the context of developing economies. Although there are real difficulties establishing credit union industries in developing economies, the potential rewards are significant. For example, after only 30 years in existence, the Republic of Korea has the largest credit union industry of any developing country with, in 1992, assets of $7.7 million and aggregate membership of 2.8 million. As stated in Chapter 1, the trend in developing countries of implementing structural adjustment programmes that aim to cut down the government's involvement in economic affairs places even greater emphasis on the need for co-operative self-help programmes as a means of helping to alleviate further poverty and social disparity in developing countries. The historic mission of credit unions of helping disadvantaged individuals and communities therefore comes into sharp focus when applied to those nascent industries found outside the context of Western industrialised nations.

In our development typology, an important aspect of nascent credit union industries is the reliance placed on support from the wider credit union movement, particularly in channelling resources and expertise from the well-developed, mature industries. As an initial start point, this chapter traces the traditions of the credit union movement in fostering the development of emerging credit union industries and examines the role and function of the World Council of Credit Unions. It is, therefore, to this issue of the credit union movement's support for nascent industries that we should turn first.

THE MOVEMENT'S SUPPORT FOR NASCENT INDUSTRIES

By definition, the concept of a 'credit union movement' implies a fraternity whereby a mission to spread the credit union word exists. In previous chapters, the significant historical role of activitists, such as Luzzati, Desjardins, Filene and Bergengren was highlighted. Both Filene and Bergengren, in particular, engaged in providing international assistance to fledgling credit union sectors throughout the world. For instance, in the 1920s, assistance was given in Novia Scotia and Canada. In the 1930s and 1940s assistance was provided in the Philippines, Jamaica and Belize. In the 1950s, support was provided to Fiji, Korea and, as discussed in Chapter 2, to Ireland.

The credit union movement's role in providing international assistance was formalised with the establishment of the World Council of Credit Unions (WOCCU) in 1971. As of 1995, WOCCU represents 87 national movements with some 90 million credit union members. The work of WOCCU places emphasis upon two major aspects; first, its trade association functions and, secondly, the provision of technical services. In terms of the former, WOCCU has an important advocacy role in the promotion of enabling legislation, and recognition of credit unions as significant players in financial markets worldwide. It also attempts to provide a forum for networking by bringing credit union leaders and executives together to share new trends and developments affecting credit unions. Similarly, through the production of regular publications, WOCCU attempts to promote information exchanges. A major component of its work also entails the facilitation of 'People-to-People Partnerships' involving exchanges between credit unions worldwide to train credit union staff, members and leaders.

The technical aspects of WOCCU's work relate to the more economic aspects of credit union activity. Here, WOCCU is concerned to develop market-orientated approaches and methods to stimulate increased savings among people of modest means. Besides this savings mobilisation, the promotion of participatory development on the basis of the democratic practices of credit unions is an important objective. Ensuring that proper financial management systems and internal controls are developed, which can assist credit unions to function efficiently and prudentially to ensure members' funds, is similarly seen as a key aspect of the technical service provided by WOCCU. Finally, the promotion of programmes that enable microentrepreneurs to access savings and credit services through, for instance, non-collateral loans, faster loan processing and market returns on deposits, are equally seen as important components of the technical services provided.

Recently, in an effort to enhance the development and growth of credit unions in developing countries, WOCCU has instigated a new strategy for credit union development known as the 'model credit union concept'. The aim of this new approach is to focus on creating financially sound and independent institutions. In the 1980s, many credit unions in Africa, Asia, Latin America and the Caribbean were inherently weak institutions that tended to encourage borrowing and discourage savings. This weakness was, in part, related to traditional credit union policies and practices that included: reliance on low-interest shares as a main source of capital and internal funding; use of external, subsidised funds for liquidity; weak credit administration policies; lack of adequate loan provisions and loan write-off procedures; and low levels of earnings and institutional capital.

Model credit union development is on the basis of the premiss that 'bottom-up', as opposed to the traditional 'top-down' approach to credit union formation in developing countries, will facilitate stronger credit union growth in areas now receiving assistance.

> Model credit unions are those which effectively meet the needs of their members while demonstrating a high degree of financial responsibility and business discipline. As the base of the movement builds, it determines its needs to provide high quality services to members. Once these needs have been identified, support components are organised as financially independent, stand alone organisations. Utilizing a market-based approach, credit unions, along with their support components, operate in an environment where pricing and satisfying needs become important aspects of survival. With high quality, financially strong credit unions at the base, the movement will thrive, and the checks and balances in the system will be the market pricing and clearing process (WOCCU, 1995a).

This approach attempts to avoid a dependency upon the establishment of a support structure that, in the past, meant too much development effort being exerted in the formation of federations, central finance facilities and regulatory regimes, at the expense of a sound credit union base. In the past there was often a tendency for higher-level support organisations to grow in proportion to funding levels, which led sometimes to a donor dependence that made the task of building a self-sufficient credit union system more difficult. The new model credit union approach is one that is, above all, needs-driven. Support organisations in this model come into existence only when there is a demonstrable need generated by the establishment of a strong base of individual credit unions. As indicated above, strong emphasis is placed upon market mechanisms. This results in a greater concern for market-based financial performance and responsibility, for instance, in pricing products and services in a way that permits developing credit unions to be sustainable in the long term. In turn, there is an equal concern in a more market-based approach to create a situation where the different organisational levels of a credit union system are capable of an independent, stand-alone viability. It can be appreciated, then, that this model credit union approach places emphasis upon strong foundations at the individual credit union level, with the superstructure of support organisations being built on needs-driven criteria and also being subjected to the financial disciplines associated with market mechanisms.

It is important to recognise that the activity of WOCCU is not the only source of international assistance given by the credit union movement. It must be borne in mind that assistance is also given directly by individual credit union industries, often in collaboration with government programmes. Australia, Canada (both English and French-speaking), France, Germany, Ireland, Korea and the United States are all active in providing international assistance. Since, in developing countries, the participation rate in credit unions is estimated to be less than 5% (WOCCU, 1995b), there is still a huge task to be done in fostering credit union growth in such countries. The aim of such programmes is, of course, not to create donor dependency but to support the establishment and growth of self-sufficient credit union industries that operate efficiently under the democratic control of their members.

CENTRAL AND EASTERN EUROPEAN REFORMS

Rekindling Voluntarism and Self-help in Ukraine

In Chapter 2, the tradition of co-operatives that existed in pre-communist countries of Central and Eastern Europe was briefly alluded to. Emerging from the shadows of the communist regime, the reforming countries of Central and Eastern Europe are rediscovering the importance of voluntary self-help organisations. Developing democratically run credit unions can, therefore, be seen as an integral component of a wider democratic transformation of society. Having endured for decades a situation where most voluntary organisations were disbanded as illegal and subversive to the communist authorities, the re-establishment of a non-profit 'third sector'—which can fill the vacuum between what the state and the market can do for citizens—is an important external indicator of democratic change. However, the development of a strong, indigenous non-profit sector, of which credit unions are a significant component, is not without difficulty, since the legacy of the communist regime has created its own unique barriers to the adoption of self-help, voluntary principles. Besides the ideological remnants of communism, there arc other practical economic and social barriers, including limited resources and inadequate legal structures, which are hindering the development of credit unions (see Davis, 1996).

In our typology of nascent credit union industries, a high commitment to self-help ideals and emphasis on voluntarism can be singled out as being especially important. That grassroots scepticism exists in Central and Eastern Europe as a direct legacy of the communist regime is, therefore, a factor of some importance. However, before considering this in more detail, the more obvious practical economic barriers affecting the emergence of voluntary, self-help credit unions in Eastern and Central Europe should be examined. To do this, two case study examples are used, the first of which looks at credit union establishment and growth in Ukraine and the second considers the situation of credit unions established in Poland. Taking the first of these case studies, the volatility of post-reform Ukraine demonstrates well the difficulties involved in the creation of a nascent credit union industry in an ex-communist society.

With independence in 1991, Ukraine immediately experienced traumatic economic conditions. As part of the Soviet centralised system, the Ukrainian economy was more closely linked than those of the other Soviet republics, which made Ukraine particularly dependent upon the Russian military–industrial complex. Post-independence trauma was evidenced by a sharp decline in output of both industrial and consumer goods, which was compounded by a sharp fall in export demand for military goods. It has been estimated that the cumulative decline in gross domestic product between 1991 and 1994 was of the order of 85%. Inflation rose from 390% in 1991 to 10,255% in 1993 as the State budget deficit mounted ever higher. Monetary controls introduced in 1994 helped control inflation, which, in 1995, fell from 21.2% in January to 4.8% in June. These difficulties associated with economic reforms are mirrored in the social predicaments endured by the citizens of Ukraine during the process of transformation.

Post-independence statistical evidence suggests a considerable increase in the rate of poverty. It is estimated, for example, that by 1993 over three-quarters of the population had official incomes below subsistence level. Even when the effects of the fairly prevalent black economy are taken into account, plus the extensive practice of home production of food on private plots of land, the overall view that the Ukrainian population has suffered impoverishment since independence can be safely maintained. The economic difficulties affecting Ukraine undoubtedly have been further compounded by the disastrous economic and social effects of the 1986 Chernobyl accident. Besides those who died, 130,000 people were resettled and nearly three million people were left with life-threatening illnesses as a consequence of events at Chernobyl. To deal with the effects of the Chernobyl disaster has necessitated state provision of free medicine, subsidised food and early retirement. One-sixth of the Ukrainian national budget is currently allocated to provide on-going support for those affected by Chernobyl. Reluctance by the Ukrainian government to cut public expenditure, particularly social expenditure, is perhaps understandable, given the combined effects of Chernobyl and the hardships created by the economic reform process.

Returning to the attitudinal scepticism towards voluntarism, which is a legacy from the previous communist regime, this is a factor obviously making the emergence of a non-profit third sector difficult. The traditional expectation amongst the citizens of Ukraine, for instance, has been that the state is a provider guaranteeing at least a subsistence level of financial security. Indeed, Ukraine inherited one of the world's most elaborate welfare systems. In 1992, half the population received cash benefits such as retirement, disability, family supplements and student benefits—although it is now clear that Ukraine does not have the economic resources to maintain this level of social expenditure.

Changing the dependency culture demonstrated by its citizens towards the state is not going to occur overnight. The difficulties experienced by the reform process itself have led to some disillusionment with it amongst segments of the Ukrainian population, since the basic security traditionally afforded to citizens has been undermined. Voluntary self-help offers a way forward, but, with no direct experience of its benefits, there is a need to appreciate that it will not automatically take root in Ukrainian society. Indeed, there are darker reasons why voluntarism will not flourish automatically.

Commentators writing of the previous communist regime highlight insidious aspects that help to mitigate against voluntarism. These include the mistrust of neighbours and lack of community relations as the product of a society where people were encouraged to gather information on their neighbours and report it to the authorities. In former Soviet bloc societies, this insipid mistrust of neighbours did much to destroy the cohesiveness of society and the community spirit that often motivates voluntary service by individuals. A further negative factor in a ready acceptance of voluntarism lies in the 'mandatory voluntarism' often associated with the communist regime. As Davis (1996) points out, there is the widespread suspicion, scepticism and distrust of non-profit organisations—particularly foundations. State-sponsored foundations introduced by communism often displaced autonomous citizen groups in Central and Eastern European societies and this helps to explain the attitude of distrust. Under mandatory voluntarism citizens 'were often expected to "volunteer" their time to official state organisations and to contribute to officially sanctioned philanthropic endeavours' (Nikolov, 1992). Often, these foundations established by the communist regime suffered from corruption, hence it is easy to understand the widespread scepticism towards such foundations by the general population of Central and Eastern Europe.

Ukraine did have, before the communist revolution, experience of credit unions. At the start of the century there had been over 3000 credit unions in Ukraine, but these did not survive the communist epoch. Efforts to establish a credit union industry in Ukraine, therefore, technically constitutes a revival of a lost co-operative tradition. The impetus for this revival owes its sponsorship to the Ukrainian Parliament, which invited a delegation from the World Council of Credit Unions, Canadian Co-operative Association and the World Council of Ukrainian Co-operatives to the Ukraine in 1992 in order to discuss the re-establishment of credit unions in Ukraine. The enactment in 1993 of Provisional Regulations on Credit Unions marks the beginning of a process of actively attempting to recreate a credit union system in Ukraine.

Tangible support for a Ukrainian credit union industry, in the form of support programmes by WOCCU funded by USAID, and the Canadian Co-operative Association, commenced in 1993. By 1994, with 20 credit unions as founding members, the Ukrainian National Association of Savings and Credit Unions (UNASCU) was established and encompassed 18 regions of the

Ukraine. Recognising the lack of financial stability in the Ukraine, the imperfections of the basic credit union legislation and the absence of any real supervisory system, the initial aim of UNASCU was to strengthen the industry infrastructure rather than to seek growth of membership. Consequently, the aims set includes the creation of more comprehensive credit union legislation and the establishment of sound business procedures and practices. UNASCU also places a high priority upon the educational development of credit union personnel and management.

The aims set by UNASCU at this time are interesting. The importance attached to the further development of legislation is easily understandable. In terms of establishing sound procedures and practices for the Ukrainian industry, emphasis has been placed on the establishment of a Stabilization Fund, which will have an audit function and which could provide financial guarantees to member credit unions. In terms of the previous discussion of 'bottom up' and 'top down' approaches to credit union industry development, the establishment in Ukraine of an institutional framework does not invalidate the approach advocated in the model credit union concept promoted by WOCCU. In the real world, separating out 'top down' and 'bottom up' approaches is not that clear-cut, and judgements have to be made about a proper balance between these two elements. The nature of this balance is, of course, likely to vary according to specific conditions found in particular locations throughout the world. In other words, there will be a contingency element to the implementation of the model credit union approach, although the philosophy and benefits that underlie it are, indeed, highly appropriate to the development needs of all nascent credit union industries.

Building Poland's Credit Union Industry

Looking briefly at Ukraine's neighbour, Poland, will provide a wider perspective on the shape of Ukraine's nascent credit union industry. Poland was the first soviet controlled society to break from the previous communist regime and the first credit union was established in Poland in 1992. In 1995, just before leaving office, the former President Lech Walesa signed legislation that allowed credit unions to expand their membership beyond the workplace to include members of associations and churches. This legislation also enabled Poland's National Association of Co-operative Savings and Credit Unions (NACSCU) to provide central credit union facilities to credit unions by taking deposits from member credit unions with surpluses and making loans to member credit unions experiencing higher loan demand. There are now some 130 credit unions in Poland with 90,000 members. In Ukraine, some 15,000 people are involved in credit unions. In both countries, development projects aimed at supporting credit unions are in operation. In Ukraine, for example, the

United Nations and WOCCU are financing the creation of a Credit Union Training Centre in Kiev. In Poland, phase two of a project funded by USAID, aimed at strengthening existing credit unions and supporting the continued development of new credit unions, commenced in late 1995.

The details of this development project in Poland give an indication of the initial progress made in Poland and the future agenda in supporting the growth of a Polish credit union industry. The aim is to expand both the employer base and the community base of Polish credit unions. Attention is being directed at strengthening the technical aspects of Polish credit unions and this encompasses a wide range of features including prudential norms, strategic planning, marketing, central finance and regulatory and supervisory issues. In terms of strengthening prudential norms, emphasis is being placed upon the further development of a stabilisation programme. Credit union profitability, reserve building and asset quality are all being emphasised in order to support good financial discipline. The role of further training is also being highlighted in support of skill transference in areas such as financial management, marketing, members' rights, accounting principles and practice and planning and policy making. It is anticipated that in the life of this project further strengthening will also occur in respect of credit union legislation.

The credit union industries in both Ukraine and Poland share in the attributes we identified for nascent credit union industries. By definition, as new industries they have a very small asset base. The need to gain statutory recognition is fundamentally important in order to create the legal framework in which to carry out their credit union activities. The main focus of these credit union industries is to provide a basic savings and loans facility, and their clientele share in a common deprivation evident in former communist societies and confront common new hardships as a result of the reform process. The traditional ideals of credit union philosophy should be seen as fundamental in helping to bring about a sea-change in attitudes towards voluntarism and democratic, self-help action. Equally, the role and function of sponsor organisations, such as WOCCU, and government agencies, such as USAID, are crucial in triggering the potential that exists for credit union development. The transference of technical skills from the wider credit union movement through the kinds of training and education programmes referred to earlier are also of paramount importance in creating more favourable conditions for nascent industries, allowing them to emerge and, hopefully, prosper.

In considering nascent industries, and the challenges and opportunities that face them, it is worthwhile to move our setting and consider the example provided by credit union development in Africa. Although nascent industries in Africa fit the characteristics laid out for such industries in our typology, there are, of course, major historical, economic and cultural factors impacting on African credit unions that are unique to them and that will influence their development. Africa is, of course, a huge continent, so that our comments are of a generalised nature and specific African credit union industries will have their own country-specific characteristics. Africa, as a location, represents a developing area of the world that has many problems yet which holds vast future potential.

PROBLEMS AND POTENTIAL OF AFRICAN CREDIT UNIONS

> Private investment on a large scale is required if African countries are to take advantage of private initiatives and realize economic growth rates that will bring about sustainable levels of economic development in the 21st century. Such a goal requires that extensive savings mobilisation be undertaken in order to provide the necessary funds for these investment opportunities, particularly in an era of greater competition for foreign investment and aid funds (ACCOSCA, 1993).

The continent of Africa has particular development challenges. Africa's gross domestic product grew by 2.4% in 1994 compared with only 0.9% in 1993. Despite this relatively modest increase in growth in 1993 and 1994, the African economy has continued to fall behind other developing regions, and GDP growth is yet to keep pace with population growth.

The role of credit unions in aiding savings mobilisation in Africa is important, therefore, in contributing to sustainable economic development. By 1990, for instance, credit unions affiliated to the African Confederation of Co-operative Savings and Credit Associations (ACCOSCA) had succeeded in mobilising US$503 million in domestically generated savings. Currently, credit unions exist in over 30 African countries and provide access to formal financial services markets for segments of the population that generally are denied access to mainstream institutions. Caisses populaires can also be found in French-speaking parts of Africa. African credit unions provide services to both consumers and producers, and are important in assisting in the mobilisation of savings and also in making funds available to private sector entrepreneurs. Credit unions are also to be found in African countries that are outside nationally developed and recognised movements. However, the vast proportion of the African population still remains outside the credit union system. Credit union savings and loans activity averages approximately 1% of commercial bank savings and loans so that the movement in Africa 'has yet to realise its full potential' (ACCOSCA, 1993).

The interdependencies of traditional African society has given rise, historically, to informal savings groups. Since the majority of the population is excluded from formal financial markets, an extensive continuum of informal financial markets has evolved. Informal credit arrangements can take a multitude of forms; for instance, the use of money-lenders, pawnbrokers, employers, rotating savings clubs, self-help groups, friends, relatives, neighbours, etc. The characteristics of informal credit usage by low-income households in developing countries has been summarised as comprising of three major features; first, the informal loans used by low-income households are small in size; secondly, loans are usually made for very short periods; and thirdly, loans are unsecured, with no use made of collateral or guarantees. The limitations of informal credit are, perhaps, obvious in that short-term savings and credit needs may be met, but access to informal credit systems often constrains longer-term investment activities. Also, since they are outside formal financial systems, informal credit systems fail to provide protection against exploitation or misuse.

Credit unions 'combine many of the attributes of the traditional savings groups, providing self-help and member controlled assistance' (ACCOSCA, 1993). Savings groups based upon villages are also prevalent and these village savings and credit associations or 'village banks' bear some resemblance to credit unions. However, their philosophy and operation reveal important differences between village banks and credit unions that are worth noting (Ouattara, Graham and Cuevas, 1993). In a credit union, a member's share contribution is crucial in determining eligibility for, and the size of, a loan. In contrast, village banks have no explicit loan-size criterion for borrowers on the basis of their shares or deposits. Again, in a credit union there is usually a formal limit on the size of a single loan, whereas this is not the case, explicitly, in a village bank, although, in reality, implicit loan thresholds are used. The single major difference between credit unions and village banks relates to interest rate policy. Village bank loan and deposit rates are much higher than those normally found in credit unions. In the case of village banks, annualised short-term loan rates of 40% to 60% are to be found. Credit unions, however, generally charge a 12% annual interest rate on loans and usually require instalment payments of principal plus 1% interest each month. It is common for village banks to expect payment only at the end of the loan term. A final difference between these institutions relates to the 'democratic' decision-making process found in each of them. Village banks, through the use of open village assemblies, allow a broad role for non-member villagers to influence interest rates and other loan and deposit terms and conditions. Decision-making in credit unions is restricted to members only.

Growth in African credit unions has slowed in recent years. In a study of the African credit union movement, ACCOSCA has identified its major strengths and weaknesses (ACCOSCA, 1993). In keeping with the role of credit unions in nascent industries, African credit unions are servicing the needs of members drawn from disadvantaged positions in society who are not generally favoured by formal financial institutions. ACCOSCA believes that credit unions have a comparative advantage and experience over other non-governmental organisations in providing financial services. As grass-roots community-based organisations, they provide an opportunity for members to engage in democratic decision-making in a forum that empowers them with an ability to better control their economic future. The African credit union movement also has a regional/national network in place, where, for instance, village banks do not. Credit union membership provides not only reasonably priced financial services and products, but offers ownership of an asset that can aid in wealth-creation and long-term savings.

The African credit union movement also faces a number of particular weaknesses. Credit unions tend to be used as borrowing, not savings, institutions. Savings and loans interest rates are not market-based. Savings yields are, therefore, below market rates and generally negative in real terms, thus penalising member savers and discouraging savings. Low interest rates on loans, conversely, favour borrowers when below market rates and are generally negative in real terms. This weakness, in turn, means that the savings base is insufficient to meet members' borrowing needs, which leads to reliance on external funds to finance loans to members. ACCOSCA openly identifies outdated operating policies and procedures, plus inadequate financial policies and procedures and inadequate external supervision of credit unions as major weaknesses. Inadequately trained and qualified staff, plus poorly trained leadership within the African movement, further contribute to weakness. A high loan delinquency rate and a lack of financial self-sufficiency within the credit union system offers further evidence of weakness. Finally, ACCOSCA also highlights the restrictive and archaic legislation that governs the activities of credit unions.

WOCCU, with financial assistance from USAID, is undertaking a credit union development programme based on the African continent that commenced in 1994 and is planned to run until 1999. The broad aim of this project is 'to develop a package of policies, products and services for individual African credit unions that will render them more competitive in the financial market-place, and thus [enable] them to enjoy rapid growth' (WOCCU, 1994). The technical assistance in this programme is highly focused and aims to transform individual credit unions into 'prototype, market based models of financial services providers'. This project is utilising the model credit union approach to help overcome some of the weaknesses identified for African credit unions and to base the further growth of the African credit union movement on a more solid foundation of financially viable credit unions. The stronger credit union base aimed for will, in turn, result in a greater contribution by credit unions through dues and fees towards the cost of national association operations. WOCCU anticipate that this project will lead to at least half of ACCOSCA's affiliated national associations being financially self-sufficient and able to cover their costs from within the African movement.

CONCLUDING COMMENTS

Speaking in 1993 at the International Credit Union Leadership Institute in Cork, Ireland, The Chief Executive Officer of WOCCU articulated the optimism of the credit union movement concerning the potential for credit union growth in a global context:

> The last few years have created unprecedented opportunities to start, restore and strengthen credit unions around the world. Clearly, it is our duty to respond. Our success will depend on reaffirming our traditional credit union values, exploiting new methods of spreading the credit union message, creating in each national movement a demonstrated commitment to international credit union development, and, finally, cooperating as we rarely have before (Charbonneau, 1993).

This chapter has attempted to highlight, through the use of some selective examples, that opportunities exist to establish nascent credit union industries, particularly in countries within the reform economies of Central and Eastern Europe and throughout the developing world. Indeed, a perspective was used that tried to show that the unmet potential demand for the services of credit unions in these areas of the world is huge, and that future economic and social conditions are likely to further increase this demand. Consequently, it can be argued that the establishment and development of nascent industries is, in fact, of major significance in the credit union movement's agenda for the strategic development of credit unions, and that credit unions will play an increasingly important global role in the twenty-first century.

Whilst our development typology aimed to describe the common attributes of nascent industries, examination of particular case study examples, such as the Ukraine, immediately revealed the importance of any given historical and cultural context. In the case of the Ukraine, the historical and cultural realities of the previous communist regime are not proving entirely conducive to supporting the ready take up of credit union philosophy. As has been argued previously, credit unions do have a distinctive ideology based on the ideals of democratically controlled member-owned organisations. The role of credit unions in providing a demonstration of the benefits of such an ideology is particularly important, given the transformation process within the reform economies. Despite the barriers to credit union development that we outlined, the kind of progress beginning to be made in Poland indicates that credit unions do have a future in reform societies.

Historical and cultural factors are equally important when considering Africa. Although our consideration of the African credit union movement focused upon the continent and the broad parameters of credit union development, country-specific factors will also play an important part in the take up and acceptance of credit unions. The African credit union movement through ACCOSCA has identified its own particular weakness, and this case study helped to locate the need for the more market-orientated approach to credit union development promoted by WOCCU in its model credit union approach. The reported African development project is based on this approach and aims to overcome past weaknesses in credit union development, where a dependency on donor funds has tended to occur.

The emphasis placed by the Chief Executive Officer on 'reaffirming traditional credit union values' as an important determinant in successful credit union development leaves no room for doubt that the strategic development of credit unions will be heavily influenced not only by technical and resource issues, but also by ideological ones. In the next chapter, we revisit our development typology and draw out some of the insights it has provided. This evaluation is undertaken against the backdrop of credit union values and their relevance to the rapidly changing world that credit unions will confront in the twenty-first century.

12
Conclusion

INTRODUCTION

Debating any overall strategic development for the credit union movement needs to take account of both the diversity and the commonality within various credit union industries. The preceding chapters, therefore, have attempted to demonstrate the need to appreciate different credit union industries in the context of particular economic, social and political environments. The interlinkages between credit union industries has been stressed, particularly with regard to the development support given by the mature industries—through a variety of agencies—in helping to foster nascent industries around the world. What happens in the mature, larger credit union industries also has, we believe, a demonstration effect for the probable development path of transition industries, especially where these industries are experiencing the kinds of pressures and opportunities created by a deregulated, competitive financial services marketplace. Nothing is static in any sphere of life and credit unions are no exception. In the case of credit unions, it is not only a question of considering the process of change but also of looking at continuity, particularly in respect of credit union ideals. Do the core values of the credit union movement provide constant and enduring guiding principles? To determine strategic direction the start point is to define and rank governing values. Most commentators agree that it is common for approaches to rational strategy formulation to begin from this point. Nowadays, it is fashionable to also describe this initial start point for strategy formulation in terms of a 'vision' for the future. At the International Credit Union Leadership Institute in 1995, one of the contributors defined the components of a strategic 'vision' in the following terms:

> ...an organisation's preferred future, its preferred long-range outcome, its desired end-state. A vision can be simple or complex, concise or elaborate, but it must be engaging, compelling, sincere and stretching (Joseph, 1995).

The traditional vision of credit unions has been a simple one and it has been engaging, compelling and sincere. The power of this vision led to the establishment of a worldwide movement that, as acknowledged at the outset of this book, has been a co-operative success story. The guiding principles and core values of the credit union movement, as stressed in earlier chapters, define the organis- ational distinctiveness of credit unions and their fundamental ways of operating. 'Vision' is not a value-free concept. On the contrary, it implicitly contains a set of governing values that determine the acceptability or otherwise of possible future strategies. Visions are unacceptable if they offend an organisation's governing value set; for example, transforming credit unions into for-profit organisations would offend the dominant value set governing credit unions, which therefore makes it unlikely as a consciously desired future vision for the movement.

This chapter re-evaluates the distinctiveness of credit unions and their fundamental ways of operating in the light of the material presented for the different industry types described previously. There is, for instance, an ongoing debate about values and purpose within the US mature industry. In an earlier chapter, the question was asked whether the core values of the US mature industry could change to the extent that a transformation might occur whereby, as with UK mutual building societies in the late 1980s and early 1990s, the industry gravitates towards the status of a multi-product, mainstream, for-profit financial services provider. Is it possible, through a more business-orientated approach, that the distinctiveness of member-owned US credit unions could be eroded to the extent that they lose their uniqueness? In this chapter, the evidence obtained from transition and nascent industries is also reconsidered in the evaluation of the condition of credit union core values. As a prelude to this evaluation of credit union values in the context of different industry types, a brief overview is initially given of changing co-operative values at the broadest level given the dynamic and unstable environment of the late twentieth century.

CHANGING CO-OPERATIVE VALUES?

The significance of a changing, turbulent global environment to the interpreta- tion of co-operative values has been highlighted by a number of writers (Book, 1992; Volkers, 1994; Srinivas, 1995). In a recent study of co-operative management, Davis (1995) identifies the key environmental changes impacting upon co-operatives in the late 20th century. The major net effect of global environmental change, according to Davis, is an increasing polarisation of wealth and poverty in the world's economies brought about by a number of interrelated factors.

1. There has been an intensification of competition and a growth in size and concentration of capital-based businesses.
2. It is possible to point to widespread labour market deregulation in OECD countries and in the former communist states.

3. Throughout the world many states are experiencing a crisis in terms of the continued funding of state welfare provisions.

4. The lower labour costs of the newly industrialising nations, particularly the Pacific Rim, pose a competitive threat to the industrialised economies.

5. There is an increasingly ageing population in the world's key economies.

6. There is a breakdown of traditional social patterns as evidenced in a decline in rural employment and community and an attendant rise in homelessness, poverty, alienation and crime in urban areas.

The implication drawn from the audit of these kinds of forces operating in the turbulent global environment is that the need for co-operative organisations has never been greater. If the adverse effects of this harsh environment are to be mitigated or reversed, co-operative philosophy and organisation has a significant role to play. In other words, the continuing polarisation of economic power within the global economy makes the overarching purpose of co-operatives that of redressing an increasing imbalance in market power. It can, indeed, be argued that the need for co-operatives is greater in the late twentieth century than at any time in their history. However, agreement about the scale of the economic and social need that exists, and unanimity about the role of co-operative organisation in addressing these needs, does not automatically mean that the question of governing values takes care of itself or that values within the co-operative movement are unproblematic.

For instance, as we approach the end of the twentieth century, debate about the purpose and values of co-operatives often centres upon the perceived tensions between professionalisation of management in co-operatives and the need to guarantee proper membership involvement and control of co-operative organisations. The increasing scale and complexity of co-operative organis- ations has added to this tension. A recent study sponsored by the ICA on the corporate governance and management control systems in European co- operatives highlights the low participation of members within formal democratic structures, especially in large-scale co-operatives (Volkers, 1994). Such weakness in membership involvement in corporate governance adversely affects the functioning of co-operatives and, in instances where mismanage- ment or financial irregularity occurs, represents a failure that undermines the credibility of all co-operatives. Whilst corporate identity and the message of co- operatives is often held to be a straightforward and clear one, sometimes, in the eyes of members and the public, there is a danger that it has, in reality, become blurred and interchangeable with that of private competitors. For instance, with a rising trend towards business transacted with non-member customers in some co-operatives, the benefits of membership can be put in danger of being somewhat diluted. The recommendations of the ICA study strongly reinforce the primacy of democratic control by the member-owners of co-operatives, and the study's recommendations offer detailed guidance on strengthening the formal mechanisms of corporate governance within co-operatives to better facilitate membership participation in the management process.

MATURITY OR TRANSFORMATION?

We found that the credit union industries in the United States, Canada and Australia shared similar characteristics, and all these industries matched the criteria by which we judge maturity. The same general speculation might be made of all of these industries; that is, will the process of maturity inevitably lead to a transformation in these industries, where credit union distinctiveness is lost through a desire to become more and more like their market-driven financial competitors? For such a fundamental transformation to occur it would, of course, imply a huge shift in the governing values of these industries; nevertheless, these industries operate in environments that have required constant adaptation, and the changes they have experienced were worthy of detailed scrutiny. We chose the US industry as the platform for an in-depth examination of the meaning of 'industry maturity'.

The dynamics involved in the US credit union industry provided, we believe, an interesting case study that revealed tensions associated with the continuing adaptation of credit unions to a deregulated competitive environment. The concept of common bond proved to be a fluid one, where its liberalisation reflected environmental pressures to make credit unions more responsive to changing economic and social conditions. Equally, there appears to be an inexorable trend towards an increasing concentration in the US industry which, coupled with an aggressive approach to membership growth, is making the industry's profile stronger in the broader financial services marketplace. Competitors, particularly those in the banking sector, complain that the special status afforded to credit unions is unfair and that the competitive advantage accruing to them because of their tax-exempt status should be reformed. As we highlighted, the focus of attacks from the banking sector relates to the liberalisation of the common bond where, at its most cynical, complaints are made that if the industry keeps loosening its common-bond and fields-of-membership framework, then eventually an acceptable common bond might be simply that 'members breath the same air'. The banking industry, certainly, on the grounds (it claims) of establishing a competitive level playing field, would prefer that US credit unions be subjected to a stricter regulatory regime, not only in terms of tax matters but also, for instance, in relation to issues such as capital adequacy, risk-based assets and so on. From the banking sector's perspective it would be better if credit unions were treated like banks.

As expected, the US industry is resisting the efforts of the banking sector to undermine its tax-exempt status. The issue of tax exemption brings into focus the recurring debate about the distinctiveness of credit unions. And it is not merely a pragmatic matter that credit unions retain their tax-exempt status. Tax exemption is an external indicator that there is official recognition that credit unions are different from for-profit organisations because they pursue a legitimate social purpose based on mutual principles of organisation. The distinctive social purpose of US credit unions, as we saw in Chapter 3, is clearly expressed in the governing federal legislation, namely '...to make more available to people of small means credit for provident purposes...'. Maintaining a balance between the needs of a mass membership credit union industry and serving the needs of disadvantaged individuals and communities is a fundamental issue that is high on the industry's policy agenda. Striking a proper balance on this issue is a matter that raises important value questions. In finding answers to such questions the industry is forced to define and rank its governing values. Other issues equally make the determination of its core values by the industry an important matter.

The scale and complexity of the US industry in itself creates particular tensions, especially with respect to the balance between increased professionalisation of the management of credit unions and the role and function of the membership in member-owned organisations. With product diversification, and the involvement of credit unions in new financial areas, an increased emphasis is also being placed upon the role of technical specialists. This can be seen, for example, in the increasing involvement of credit unions in the electronic banking channels that are becoming so prevalent in the provision of financial services. Also, recent concerns surrounding the activities of some corporate central credit unions demonstrate not only increased complexity, but also the potential for new risks where credit union activity encompasses new areas such as foreign investments. Interestingly, through the encouragement of the regulator, the industry is revisiting its core values in a renewal debate. Supporting the democratic traditions and fundamental purpose of credit unions in the context of a large, complex industry that has to live in the competitive jungle of the US financial services marketplace is the challenge facing the US industry. Without a concern for credit union values, there may be a danger that encouragement could be given to the seeds of transformation whereby credit unions progressively become more like their rival mainstream financial institutions. Despite these kinds of tensions, which make ideal credit union values sometimes difficult to achieve in practice, the overwhelming evidence still remains that US credit unions are wholly committed to their traditional credit union values. The fact that these are constantly scrutinised in the light of changing economic and social circumstances does not detract from the overall health of the core credit union values governing the US industry. The fact is that there is no evidence that the US industry wishes to transform itself; the changes we described in this mature industry are indeed a process of evolution necessary in adapting to a deregulated, competitive marketplace.

Our interest in the mature US credit union industry also centred upon the question of a potential demonstration effect for transition industries. This is not to imply that transition industries will simply be clones and replicate in every detail the US experience. However, we feel that the US industry does provide important lessons about the evolution of a sophisticated 'credit union system' and the operation of credit unions in a deregulated, competitive financial services market. As pointed out on numerous occasions, much of the empirical research on credit unions—particularly empirical economic research—originates from work carried out in the United States. Given the development lag between transition and mature industries, this US research is valuable in pointing up issues that are of concern to transition industries. By re-examining through original empirical research some key economic issues affecting credit unions in the UK industry, a major aim has been to complement earlier US credit union research and test its broad validity.

THE UK TRANSITION INDUSTRY—GROWTH AND DEVELOPMENT

In the previous chapter, the vision for the UK credit union industry was that it might occupy, in the long term, a significant position in the provision of financial services in the United Kingdom. The view taken was that this industry stands at a defining moment in its historical development. It has already enjoyed high growth to achieve a degree of critical mass that has taken it to a stage where it now has a potential to take off in a significant way. It was suggested that, given the favourable conditions that now exist in the United Kingdom, credit unions could rise to fill important gaps left by the demutualisation of building societies. Already, credit unions in Northern Ireland enjoy status as important providers of financial services, and, given time, it is, we believe, the case that the rest of the UK industry should be able to emulate the success of these longer-established Northern Ireland credit unions. In keeping with the comments made earlier about the centrality of values to strategic development, it is certain that the future development of the UK industry will be affected by the values implicit in any particular vision held out for it. This being the case, it is perhaps incumbent upon us to revisit our own vision for the UK industry and again re-examine it in the light of broader co-operative values.

Our economic analysis of the structure and performance of the UK industry lends support to further building the industry upon the foundations of credit unions that are economically viable in terms of asset size, membership level and cost efficiency. At this critical stage of development it should also be clear, for the reasons previously stated, that the establishment of a statutory deposit insurance scheme is imperative. Additionally, the prospect of future development is less assured without the development of central credit union services to support future industry growth. There is also the question of the best way to proceed in terms of attracting future growth in the industry, and this will, no doubt, entail adjustments to the common bond. How these future changes actually affect the boundaries of membership will, of course, have important implications for changing the contours of the future UK industry. In the short term, it will also be an important matter of policy as to which segments of society are targeted to join credit unions; the traditional credit union purpose of serving disadvantaged communities is not likely to diminish, but this may increasingly be accompanied by a drive to increase membership across a much wider membership base, including, for instance, better-off salaried employees.

A major lesson from the US industry concerned the importance of occupational credit unions in terms of their contribution to growth in overall membership. In the United Kingdom, employer-based credit unions are very much underdeveloped, with most membership deriving from community-based credit unions. The take-off potential of the UK industry is perhaps contingent upon mobilising increased support for employer-based credit unions. Although there are credit unions sponsored by public sector employers, the development of credit unions amongst private sector employers is still negligible. As an examination of the US research showed, there are risks attached to employer-based credit unions, but at this stage of industry development in the United Kingdom greater involvement by private and public sector organisations would ensure that membership expansion reached volumes that approach the critical mass necessary for the vision of UK credit unions as 'significant providers of financial services'.

Promoting credit unions to the public, to employers or promoting the cause of future legislative changes to politicians are all contingent upon a coherent vision from within the industry itself. Although UK trade organisations subscribe enthusiastically to credit union values, it is still the case that with four of them, plus differences in membership policy, diverse value positions exist towards membership growth and how this might be achieved. The distinction between ABCUL and the NFCU in terms of their views on optimum credit union size illustrates this point. Without suggesting the eradication of pluralism within the UK industry (given the heterogeneity created by different credit union types, pluralism is, to an extent, inevitable) it is perhaps an obvious point to make that the industry could be better served in the longer term by a more rational, unified trade organisation structure. The level of support services required by the fast-growing UK industry will eventually demand similar sophistication to that found in the US mature industry. The existence of four separate trade organisations is not, therefore, an ideal approach to achieving appropriate professional support mechanisms for this industry or for promoting the general credit union cause.

The tensions created by increasing scale and complexity are likely to be exacerbated as the UK transition industry continues to grow. Equally, evolving technological innovations in the financial services marketplace will place technical expertise at a premium in the management of credit unions. The tension, therefore, between increasing professionalisation and member involvement in the management process is as much an issue in the context of a transition industry as it is in a mature one. Achieving a proper balance between increased professionalisation and democratic processes will, consequently, be an important challenge for the growing UK industry. Equipping sufficient members in such an expanding industry with the knowledge and skills to enable them to become active, participating members of their credit unions seems to be a fundamental prerequisite for the further development of the industry. Again, a more unified trade organisation would seem to place the industry in a better position to provide the kinds of training and development support required. Similarly, the marketing of credit unions to an expanded membership base would seem to be more feasible on the basis of a unified trade structure, rather than through the possible duplication of effort associated with a number of separate trade bodies.

Both Ireland and New Zealand were held, in our classification, to be transition industries, although in terms of their industry operation they are further along the development path towards maturity than the UK industry. Significantly, both of these transition industries have active, single trade organisations able to speak with a single voice for their respective industries. The legislation governing the activities of credit unions in both Ireland and New Zealand permits greater product diversification and more scope for a larger individual credit union membership base than permitted to credit unions in the United Kingdom. It can, in fact, be argued that the operation of existing credit union legislation in the United Kingdom is actually hindering the industry's long-term growth and development. With ceilings placed upon the membership size of individual credit unions and on the volume of lending, plus the limits placed on the interest charged on loans and interest paid on dividends, these have become real constraints that are hindering the expansion of the industry. In contrast to the United Kingdom, the situation both in Ireland and New Zealand is more progressive in terms of the scope for credit union growth, since both of these industries operate in a less constrained regulatory environment, where the rigorous loans and dividend ceilings to be found in the United Kingdom are absent.

The interest rate ceilings that apply to the operation of the UK industry lead—as discussed in Chapter 7—to a borrower-orientated membership bias. This was seen as perfectly justifiable in that access to cheap loans provides a social benefit to borrowers from disadvantaged or low-income communities. From another perspective, the existence of such interest rate ceilings can be viewed as a mechanism that protects the UK industry from the vagaries of the market. Whilst relaxation of the maximum membership ceiling and the ceiling on maximum lending will facilitate a push towards increased membership growth, moves towards interest rates based on market rates will necessarily increase the exposure of the industry to the volatilities of a market-rate system.

It should be recalled that UK inflation and UK interest rates are currently at an historically low point, which makes the interest rate paid by UK credit unions very competitive. However, in the long term, development to the status of a mature industry—given the position of market-based interest rates in our typology of a mature industry—would require the UK industry, sometime in the future, to base its interest rates on market rates.

Windows of opportunity are exactly that and the vision of the future of the UK industry is dependent upon an agreed strategic focus emerging to capitalise on the favourable conditions that exist for expansion. It is in the interests of the industry to maximise the common benefits that will accrue from an expanded industry, and the first step in this is perhaps to adopt the perspective that credit unions in the United Kingdom in fact, constitute 'an industry'. It should be recalled that the more successful a credit industry becomes, rivals, such as the banks, will increasingly attempt to throw up barriers to credit unions' entry as significant players in the provision of financial services. No doubt we will see a replication of the battles played out in the United States concerning the special status of credit unions. The major challenge for the UK industry is to maximise its appeal to as wide a membership as possible without losing its unique identity. In other transition industries, such as Ireland and New Zealand, this challenge is being successfully met, and, equally, it is our contention that the same is true in mature credit union industries. The future, therefore, although not without difficulty, should be exciting for the UK transition industry as it maximises the opportunity that now exists to achieve a prominence in the UK financial services scene.

NASCENT INDUSTRIES—SELF-HELP FOR THE TWENTY-FIRST CENTURY

Stressing the democratic ideals and social purpose of credit unions is nowhere more important than with respect to nascent credit union industries. In the context of developing and reform economies, the value system of the credit union movement stresses empowerment through self-help, and member-owned credit unions are regarded as a means of enabling more people to have access to a formal credit system. The economic need for credit unions throughout the developing world is an overwhelming one, but with an estimated membership penetration of some 5% of the population in the developing world, there is still much to be achieved. The significance of credit unions in the developing world might be regarded better if cognisance is also taken of their role as schools for democracy. Credit unions provide at a grass-roots level direct experience of formal democratic processes, often in situations, as in Eastern Europe, where such processes have been suppressed or usurped in the past. In stressing the values associated with self-help and democratic ideals, nascent credit union industries demonstrate that the importance of credit union industries does not lie simply in their asset or membership size or in their financial sophistication. Given this fundamental democratic ideal, nascent industries are very important in demonstrating the attractions and benefits of democratic institutions within the fabric of civil society. Credit unions aim to alleviate not only economic disadvantages but also to provide positive experience of self-help in the context of democratic, autonomous institutions owned by their members.

Our case study evaluations of the nascent industries in the Ukraine and Poland stressed this democratic and self-help dimension of credit union activity and debated the difficulties of overcoming the legacy of the previous communist regime. The volatile economic conditions in these countries also present particular challenges to the establishment of credit unions over and above the barriers created by a previous cultural dependency upon the State. Equally, the economic conditions in Africa provided a difficult context for the nascent industries we examined. In considering nascent industries in Africa and Eastern Europe, recognition was given to the power of indigenous factors that make the simple transplanting of credit unions difficult. The historically specific factors associated with different nascent industries nevertheless do not prevent examination of the common issues affecting all nascent industries. Here, the message to emerge was one of credibility and that credit unions have to be built upon a sound basis, which, in effect, means taking a 'bottom-up' approach. Building an extensive superstructure of central support facilities should be contingent upon a solid base of credit unions existing where there is a need for such institutions—not as has occurred sometimes where it was believed that the supply of such facilities would, in itself, help generate the growth of credit unions at ground level.

The international assistance provided by the movement to nascent industries is an expression of a solidarity built on the role and function of credit unions as instruments of economic and social betterment. The emphasis placed on model credit union development by WOCCU represents a new focus in the approach taken to international assistance. The logic behind this approach is one that can be supported given that it aims to reduce the past failure rate of some credit union initiatives in the developing world. The importance of credit union activity to improving the lives of people throughout all areas of the world in the twenty-first century has been stressed. The assistance given by the credit union movement to the developing world and the reformed economies is a tangible expression of ideals relating to international co-operation which again strongly marks out the value set governing the credit union movement.

CONCLUDING COMMENTS

Credit unions are unique financial institutions that offer wide benefits to their members, and they are distinctive, democratically controlled organisations that have important social, as well as economic, functions. Their importance is likely to increase rather than diminish in the future. The strategic development of credit unions will be different depending upon particular historical, economic, social and political contexts. Thinking in terms of different credit union industry types allows us to consider in a more focused way the issues affecting the strategic development of credit unions in particular parts of the world. The evaluation of credit unions we have offered is a positive one, and although our selection of credit union industries has been limited, it nevertheless represents the spectrum of strategic development within the credit union movement. Credit unions are not perfect and they will inevitably suffer setbacks. The recent scandals, for instance, at the Kizu Shinyo Kumai and Tokyo Kyowa credit unions in Japan illustrate that they can be the subject of corruption and fail to live up to their high ideals and values. Despite such rogue exceptions, our view is that the role of credit unions has been an honourable one. It cannot be doubted that they have demonstrated the efficacy of co-operative ideals to improving the lives of millions of people. In time to come, future commentators may look back to the twenty-first century as the watershed period for credit unions. The vision of credit unions is a simple one, but a changing, complex world means that it has to be kept relevant to new times. Credit unions have proved themselves to be adaptive, yet true to their core values. We predict that credit unions will not only endure into the future but will continue to evolve as important institutions in many societies throughout the world.

References

ACCOSCA. (1993) *Service and Market Development, the Case of ACCOSCA.* Cork, Ireland, International Credit Union Leadership Institute, July 1993.

Amburgey, T. L. and Dacin, M. T. (1993) *Evolutionary Development of Credit Unions.* Madison, Wisconsin, Filene Research Institute, Centre for Credit Union Research.

Berger, A. N., Hunter, W. C. and Timme, S. G. (1993) 'The efficiency of financial institutions.' *Journal of Banking and Finance*, **17**, 221–249.

Berthoud, R. and Hinton, T. (1989) *Credit Unions in the UK*, Research Report 693, Policy Studies Institute.

Black, H. and Duggar, R. H. (1981) 'Credit union structure, growth and regulatory problems.' *Journal of Finance*, **36**, 529–556.

Book, S. A. (1992) *Co-operative Values in a Changing World.* Report to the ICA Congress, ICA, Geneva.

Boreham, G. F. and Bodkin, R. G. (1988) *Money, Banking and Finance, the Canadian Context.* Holt, Rinehart and Winston, Canada.

Brockschmidt, P. (1977) *Credit Union Growth in Perspective.* Federal Reserve Bank of Kansas City, Spring, 3–13.

Burger, A. E. and Dacin, T. (1991) *Field of Membership: An Evolving Concept.* Madison, Wisconsin, Filene Research Institute, Centre for Credit Union Research.

Burger, A. E. and Zellmer, M. (1995) *Strategic Opportunities in Serving Low to Moderate Income Members.* Madison, Wisconsin, Filene Research Institute, Centre for Credit Union Research.

Calomiris, C. W. (1989) 'Deposit insurance: Lessons from the record, Federal Reserve Bank of Chicago.' *Economic Perspectives*, **13**, 10–30.

Canadian Co-operative Association (1991) *Taking Responsibility for the Future; Co-operatives in the year 2004.* Report to the Triennial Congress, Calgary, Alberta.

Cargill, T. F. and Vincell D. C. (1969) *Costs and Profits of California Credit Unions.* Presented at the Western Economic Association, Long Beach, California.

Cargill, T. F. (1975) 'Performance of limited-income credit unions: 1969–1970.' *National Commission on Consumer Finance Technical Studies: Volume II*, Washington D.C., National Commission on Consumer Finance, 1975.

——. (1976) 'Recent research on credit unions: A survey.' *Journal of Economics and Business*, **29**, 155–162.

Charbonneau, G. A. (1993) *The Future of This Great Movement.* Cork, Ireland, International Credit Union Leadership Institute.

Christensen, C., Jorgensen, D. and Lau, L. J. (1971) 'Conjugate duality and the translog production function.' *Econometrica*, July, 255–256.

Clair, R. T. (1984) *Deposit Insurance, Moral Hazard, and Credit Unions.* Federal Reserve Bank of Dallas, July, 1–12.

Copson, N., (1992) *Economic Viability of Credit Unions.* Neil Copson Limited.

Cox, W. N. and Whigham, P. V. (1984) 'What distinguishes larger and more efficient credit unions?' *Economic Review, Federal Reserve Bank of Atlanta*, **69**, 34–40.

Crecelius, A. M. and Comrie, S. A. (1994) *Strategic Management Creating your Credit Union's Future.* Credit Union Executives Society.

Credit Unions Services Corporation (Australia) Ltd (1996) *The Inside Story, 1995.*

Croteau, J. T. (1963) *The Economics of the Credit Union.* Detroit, Wayne State University Press.

Crow, I., Howells, G. and Pick, K. (1993) *Credit Unions.* Joseph Rowntree Foundation.

Crowther Committee (1971) *Report of the Committee on Consumer Credit*, London, HMSO.

CUNA (1994) *Field of Membership Task Force Report.* Credit Union National Association, Inc., Government Affairs Division, Washington, DC, 21pp.

D'Amours, N. (1994) 'Delegates debate interlocks', *Credit Union Newswatch.* Wisconsin, Madison, 8pp.

Davis, P. (1995) *Co-operative Purpose, Values and Management into the 21st Century.* Geneva, ICA, 1–10.

Davis, R. J. (1996) *The Re-birth of the Nonprofit Sector in Post Communist Eastern Europe.* Centre for Civil Society International.

Delaney, K. (1994) *Service and Market Development.* Paper presented to the International Credit Union Forum, Cork, Ireland.

Department of Trade and Industry (1994) *Deregulation: Cutting Red Tape.* London, HMSO.

Digby, M. (1960) *The World Co-operative Movement*, London, Hutchinson University Library.

Dunn, M. (1995) 'Compliance issues still a factor.' *Credit Union Executive*, **35**, no. 2, 16–20.

Flannery, M. J. (1974) *An Economic Evaluation of Credit Unions in the United States*. Federal Reserve Bank of Boston Research Report No. 54.

——. (1981) 'Credit Unions: An Economic Theory of a Credit Union'. by Smith D. J., Cargill T. F. and Meyer R. A. (1981) *Journal of Finance*, **36**, no. 2, 554–556.

Flood, M. D. (1993) *Deposit Insurance: Problems and Solutions*, Federal Reserve Bank of St. Louis, January/February, 28–34.

Garrett A. (1993) 'Credit unions move upmarket.' *The Observer*, 25 July, 8.

Glass, J. C. and McKillop, D. G. (1992) 'An empirical analysis of scale and scope economies and technical change in an Irish multiproduct banking firm.' *Journal of Banking and Finance*, **16**, 423–437.

Gosling, P. (1995) 'Unions vie with big lenders.' *Independent on Sunday*. 31 December, p. 8.

Goudzwaard, M. B. (1968) 'Price ceilings and credit rationing.' *Journal of Finance*, **23**, 177–185.

Griffiths, G. and Howells, G. (1991) 'Slumbering giant or white elephant: Do credit unions have a role to play in the United Kingdom credit market.' **42**, NILQ, 199–211.

——. (1993) 'Credit unions in the United Kingdom and possible legislative reforms to the Credit Unions Act 1979.' in G. Howells, I. Crow and M. Moroney (eds.) *Aspects of Credit and Debt*. London, Sweet and Maxwell.

Harvey, V. (1995) *Planning and Growth in a Regulated Environment*. Australia, AIC Conference, May 1995.

International Co-operative Alliance (1995) 'Co-operatives and sustainable human development.' *Regional Perspective, Europe*.

Joseph, B. (1995) *Creating a Vision of Greatness for your Credit Union: Why and How*. Honolulu, International Credit Union Leadership Institute, 1–14.

Kaushik, S. K. and Lopez, R. H. (1994) 'The structure and growth of the credit union industry in the United States.' *American Journal of Economics and Sociology*, **53**, no. 2, 219–243.

Kim, H. Y. (1986) 'Economies of scale and economies of scope in multiproduct financial institutions: Further evidence from credit unions.' *Journal of Money Credit and Banking*, **18**, no. 2, 220–226.

Kohers, T. and Mullis, D. (1988) 'An update on economies of scale in credit unions.' *Applied Economics*, **20**, 1653–1659.

Koot, R. (1978) 'On economies of scale in credit unions.' *Journal of Finance*, **33**, 1087–1094.

Lemmon, N. (1995) 'Credit unions—The Next Generation.' *Credit Union Executive*, January/February, 14–17.

Long, M. S. (1976) 'Effect of lending rate ceilings and money costs on extensions of consumer credit.' *Journal of Bank Research*, Autumn, 206–212.

Manrell, T. (1995) *Global Credit Union Development Explosion*. Honolulu, International Credit Union Leadership Institute, July 1995.

Mason, B. J. and Lollar, J. L. (1986) 'Developing market driven strategies for credit union growth and survival.' *Journal of Professional Services Marketing*, 2(1/2) Winter, 91–107.

McArthur, A., McGregor, A. and Stewart R. (1993) 'Credit unions and low-income communities.' *Urban Studies*, 30, no. 2, 399–416.

McKillop, D. G. and Ferguson, C. (1993) *Building Societies: Structure, Performance and Change*, Graham & Trotman, Member of the Wolkers Kluwer Publishing Group.

McKillop, D. G., Ferguson, C. and Nesbitt, D. (1995a) 'Paired difference analysis of size economies in UK credit unions.' *Applied Economics*, 27, 529–537.

———. (1995b) 'The competitive position of credit unions in the United Kingdom: A sectoral analysis.' *Local Economy*, 10, no. 1, 48–64.

Mester, L. J. (1990) 'Curing our ailing deposit-insurance system.' *Business Review, Federal Reserve Bank of Philadelphia*, September/October, 13–24.

Mladentaz, G. 1933 'Histoire des Doctrines Cooperatives' in Digby, M. (1960) *The World Co-operative Movement*, London, Hutchinson University Library.

Moody, J. C. and Fite, G. C. (1971) *The Credit Union Movement Origins and Development, 1850–1970*. University of Nebraska Press.

Murray, J. D. and White, R. W. (1983) 'Economies of scale and economies of scope in multiproduct financial institutions: A study of British Columbia credit unions.' *Journal of Finance*, 38, 887–902.

Nakamura, L. (1990) 'Closing troubled financial institutions: What are the issues?' *Business Review, Federal Reserve Bank of Philadelphia*, May/June, 15–24.

National Consumer Council (1994) *Saving for Credit: The Future for Credit Unions in Britain*. UK, National Consumer Council.

National Credit Union Administration (1982) *Annual Report, 1982*. Madison, Wisconsin.

Navratil, F. (1981) 'An aggregate model of the credit union industry.' *Journal of Finance*, 36, 539–549.

New Zealand Association of Credit Unions (1995) 'Choices and challenges.' *Annual Report, 1993–1994*.

Nikolov, S. (1992), 'The emerging nonprofit sector in Bulgaria: Its historical dimensions.' in K. McCarthy, V. Hodgkinson and R. Sumariwalla (eds.) *The Nonprofit Sector in the Global Community*, San Francisco, Jossey-Bass.

Ouattara, K., Graham, D. H. and Cuevas, C. E. (1993) 'Alternative financial networks: The village savings and credit associations in the Gambia.' in *Financial Markets in the Gambia, 1981–1991*, A Report to the USAID Mission Banjul, The Gambia.

Patin, R. P. and McNeil, D. W. (1991a) 'Benefit imbalances among credit union members.' *Applied Economics*, 23, 769–780.

———. (1991b) 'Member group orientation of credit unions and total member benefits.' *Review of Social Economy*, December, 37–61.

Pearce, D. K. (1984) *Recent Developments in the Credit Union Industry*, Federal Reserve Bank of Kansas, June, 3–19.

Pickersgill, M. (1995) *What is the Future of NBFI's*, AIC Conference, Australia, May 1995.

Quinn, A. P. (1994) *Credit Unions in Ireland*. Dublin, Oak Tree Press.

Registry of Friendly Societies, *Annual Reports*, Various Issues (1989/90—1992/93), London, HMSO.

Smith, D. J., Cargill, T. F. and Meyer, R. A. (1981) 'Credit unions: An economic theory of a credit union.' *The Journal of Finance*, **36**, no. 2, 519–528.

Smith, D. J. (1984) 'A theoretic framework for the analysis of credit union decision making.' *The Journal of Finance*, **39**, no. 4, 1155–1168.

———. (1986) 'A test for variant objective functions in credit unions.' *Applied Economics*, **18**, 959–970.

Spencer J. E. (1996) An Extension to Taylor's Model of Credit Unions, *Review of Social Economy*, **54**, no. 1, 89–98.

Srinivas, H. (1995) 'People-centred credit systems in developing countries: The need for regional networks.' *Cornell Journal of Planning and Urban Issues*, 10th Anniversary edition.

Taylor, R. A. (1971) 'The credit union as a cooperative institution' *Review of Social Economy*, **24**, 207–217.

———. (1979) 'Optimal reserve levels for credit unions.' *Rivista Internationale di Scienze Economiche e Commerciali*, **26**, 971–983.

Thomas, I. C. and Balloch, S. (1994) 'Local authorities and the expansion of credit unions.' *Local Economy*, **9**, no. 2, 166–184.

Thordarson, B. V. (1990) *North–South Institute Briefing Paper*. Community Support Organisation Atlantic, 1–4.

Treasury (1995) *Draft Regulations to amend the Credit Unions Act 1979*, Treasury, April.

Tripp, J. D. and Cole, C. S. (1994) 'Credit union growth: When bigger is better.' *Credit Union Executive*, CUNA and affiliates management journal, **34**, no. 1, 14–17.

Volkers, R. (1994) 'Report on management systems and co-operative governance.' *Review of International Co-operation, Geneva*, **87**, no. 3, 1–45.

Walker, M. C. and Chandler, G. G. (1977) 'On the allocation of the net monetary benefits of credit union membership.' *Review of Social Economy*, October, 159–168.

———. (1978) 'Equitable allocation of credit union net revenues: a goal programming approach.' *Journal of Economics and Business*, **31**, no. 1, 63–69.

Wolken J. D. and Navratil, F. J., (1980a) 'Economies of scale in credit unions: Further evidence.' *Journal of Finance*, **35**, no. 3, 769–777.

——. (1980b) 'The economic impact of the federal credit union usury ceiling.' *Journal of Finance*, **36**, 1157–1168.

World Council of Credit Unions, (1994) Africa regional, Project Profile. Madison, Wisconsin, WOCCU.

——. (1995a) *Model Credit Union Development.* Madison, Wisconsin, WOCCU.

——. (1995b) *Statistical Report.* Madison, Wisconsin, WOCCU.

Zinger, J. T. (1994) *Credit Unions and Caisses Populaires: Background, Market Characteristics and Future Developments*, Centre for the Study of Co-operatives, University of Saskatchewan.

Index